Home Bodies

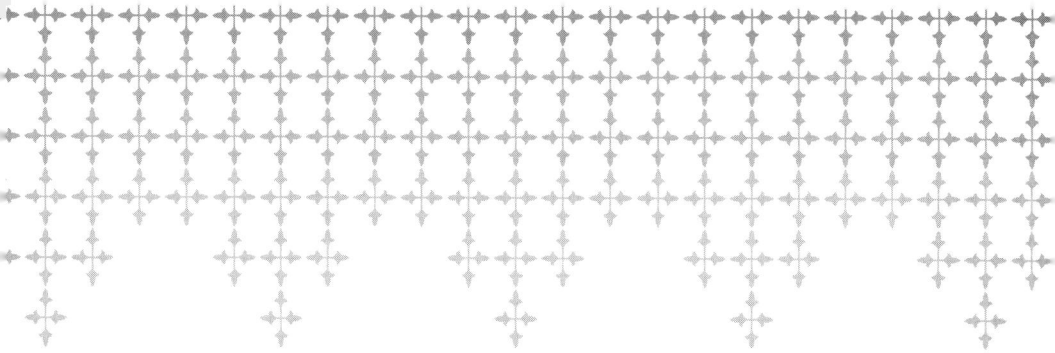

HOME BODIES

Tactile Experience in Domestic Space

JAMES KRASNER

THE OHIO STATE UNIVERSITY PRESS • COLUMBUS

Library of Congress Cataloging-in-Publication Data
Krasner, James.
  Home bodies : tactile experience in domestic space / James Krasner.
    p. cm.
  Includes bibliographical references and index.
  ISBN 978-0-8142-1134-2 (cloth : alk. paper)—ISBN 978-0-8142-9233-4 (cd-rom)
  1. Human body in literature. 2. Touch in literature. 3. Touch. 4. Home in literature.
  5. Home—Psychological aspects. 6. Domestic space in literature. I. Title.
  PN56.B62K73 2010
  809'.933561—dc22
                                    2010013528

This book is available in the following editions:
Cloth (ISBN 978-0-8142-1134-2)
CD-ROM (ISBN 978-0-8142-9233-4)

Cover design by Mia Risberg.
Text design by Jennifer Shoffey Forsythe.
Type set in Adobe Palatino.
Printed by Thomson-Shore, Inc.

9 8 7 6 5 4 3 2 1

For my wife Laura and my sons Gray and Cole, who are my home

Contents

Acknowledgments

Arnold Arluke and Peter Gollub were both very generous with their time and expertise on animal hoarding; they continue to do valuable work helping hoarders and their animal victims. A version of chapter 1 appeared previously as "Doubtful Arms and Phantom Limbs: The Tangible Experience of Mourning," *PMLA* 119.2 (2004): 218–32. It is reprinted by permission of the copyright owner, The Modern Language Association of America. A version of chapter 2 appeared previously as "Accumulated Lives: Metaphor, Materiality and the Homes of the Elderly," *Literature and Medicine* 24.2 (2005): 209–30. It is reprinted by permission of the copyright holder, The Johns Hopkins University Press.

My colleagues at the University of New Hampshire, especially Janet Aikins Yount and Michael Ferber, have given me all kinds of support—professional, emotional, moral, and occasionally immoral—as I have followed the winding path toward this publication. Like all teachers, I owe my students a great debt for keeping my mind engaged, attentive, and continually off-balance. The students in my graduate "Architecture and Victorian Literature" class, who pushed me to think in even more painfully interdisciplinary ways, deserve a special thanks: Holly Allaire, Meredith Cartmill, Courtney Condo, Courtney Dziuba, Melanie Goss, Elizabeth Montville, Vilija Pauliukonis, Kathleen Rinaldi Boisvert, and Julie Samara. Heather Froehlich, from my "Bible as Literature" class, offered useful insights into the Hebrew translations of the book of Job.

The editors at The Ohio State University Press, especially Sandy Crooms and Maggie Diehl, are notorious for their astonishing good-heartedness and hard work; no one has yet been able to fully explain the phenomenon. My friends Allyson Booth, Susan Greenfield, Jules Law, Wendy Wall, and Matt Weissman remind me how to interweave the irregular strands of everyday life and literary study. Finally, I would like to thank my family: my wife, Laura Tanner, who is always right beside me, completing every space I occupy, and my sons, Gray and Cole, who have brought me fully in touch with the world; some day, I hope, they will read this book and say, "Okay, ..."

Introduction

This study argues for the centrality of the sense of touch to our experience of life at home. Highlighting the significance of tactility as a critical and experiential framework through which contemporary cultural constructions of intimacy, domesticity, and embodied subjectivity can be understood, my argument explores representations of tactile experience to unveil the complex operation of the sense of touch in the domestic realm. This work contributes to theoretical dialogues about the body that attempt to redress our cultural neglect of embodied experience and cultural analyses of domesticity that highlight the spatial dynamics of daily life. While these critical approaches focus our attention on the practical dynamics of bodily experience, they nevertheless tend to neglect the prominence of tactile sensation in our lives, particularly our lives at home.

My analysis draws on two critical traditions: body theory and the study of domestic space. Body theorists, whose analyses of somatic boundary and orifice seek to counter an optical model of embodiment, nevertheless tend to implicitly favor ocular over tactile metaphors for enunciating bodily identity and lived experience in society. The operation of domestic space has been analyzed most extensively by cultural theorists, who have addressed the home primarily as a material staging ground for economic forces or gender relations; while they base their arguments on the materiality of the home, they give little attention to the material experience of the body within that home. *Home Bodies* establishes a new dialogue among these various approaches to material domesticity

1

and embodied identity by situating embodiment in its particular postural relationship to the emotionally resonant spaces of the home. I hope
to enrich this dialogue by including voices from a variety of humanis-
tic disciplines such as architectural theory and media studies, and most
extensively from the medical and social sciences, including gerontology,
neurology, sociology, and geography, which tend to address the practical
and habitual operations of the body at home. Such an analysis of domestic embodiment will foreground tactile perception and unveil how the
tangible dynamics of our everyday lives create our identities and come
under stress when those identities are called into question.

Critics of art, literature, and culture who wish to emphasize embodiment typically frame the relationship between visual and tactile experience in social and political terms; tactility has been suppressed by a
dominant Cartesian perceptual culture that favors spectacle and visual
surface. Building primarily on Maurice Merleau-Ponty's work, this argument, which is enunciated in a variety of ways by Michel Foucault, Luce
Irigaray, and Roland Barthes, traces the "ocularcentrism" of the Western tradition, which becomes crystallized in a modernist aesthetic that
attempts to establish a hegemonic bodily observer. The body's materiality becomes subsumed within a visual panorama that can be controlled,
objectified, and ordered; a return to tactility would thus require a radical
repossession of the embodied self through what Martin Jay calls a "hos-
tility to visual primacy" (15). While the centrality of vision in Western
culture cannot be doubted, I would like to point out how complicit this
wide-ranging critical critique has itself been in promoting an essentially
ocular model of embodiment. In this formulation the body lurks, like the
Furies, below the surface, struggling to break out through cuts and orifices in the body's boundary. Ocular power establishes and maintains this
boundary, a culturally constructed envelope or membrane useful in polic-
ing social identity. Mary Douglas, in her discussion of biblical leprosy as
a "breach of the body's containing walls" (190), constructs a gendered
boundary discourse, which Julia Kristeva applies psychoanalytically,
contrasting the patriarchal formulation of the "clean and proper" closed
or "phallic" body with the open, porous, and thus apparently monstrous,
female body (102). Elizabeth Harvey and Claudia Benthien, following
Mikhail Bakhtin's discussion of the "grotesque" medieval body, identify
a historical moment when the body's margin begins to be imagined as a
net, garment, or enclosed "vessel" (Harvey 85, Benthien 41). In all versions of this argument, the body's material essence is accessed by breaching or distorting its enveloping margin.

Despite their critique of ocularcentrism, analyses focused on the skin envelope tend to reassert the dominance of visual perception by relying upon a figure/ground apprehension of bodily form. Bakhtin conceives of the grotesque as a visual aesthetic in which "the stress is laid on those parts of the body that are open to the outside world, that is, the parts through which the world enters the body or emerges from it. [. . .] This especially strikes the eye in archaic grotesque" (26). Lacan and Bakhtin both establish a fundamental distinction between surface and orifice which assumes the eye's tendency to complete forms or to be attracted to their points of incompletion. As such, they aren't comparing closed and open bodies so much as closed and not-completely-closed bodies, the orifice being the specific, limited site where the formal boundary of the body is breached. When Benthien describes the pre-eighteenth-century conception of the skin surface "less as a wall in which closable windows and doors were embedded and more as a kind of porous tissue that could potentially have an opening anywhere" (40), she is commenting on the size and location of the orifices, not on the visibility of the boundary. Kristeva's analysis of the maternal "trace" also depends on figure/ground distinctions, although in this case it is the mark or wound rather than the orifice. Kristeva points to the visual discourse, inherent in Mosaic Law itself, that defines admixture through the "sore on the visible, presentable surface" (101). Even Luce Irigaray, who explicitly argues for the dissolution of the body's "envelope" into a "fluid" (60) relation between self and other, reverts to figure/ground language, describing such fluid relations as "[s]ense mirrors where the outline of the other is profiled through touch" (77).

Didier Anzieu is the body theorist who comes closest to arguing for the tactile indeterminacy of the body's edge. Anzieu describes the ego forming within the womb through a physically contiguous integument shared by mother and child. "[T]he common skin ensures direct communication between the two partners, reciprocal empathy and an adhesive identification" (62). Anzieu argues that as the child develops, this contiguous, translucent membrane becomes the psychic foundation for the child's ego, becoming a shield or carapace to protect it from the pain of the world. By touching and holding her child, a mother "maximizes the function of the maintaining, containing skin so that the child may introject his skin sufficiently as a background object, reestablish its Skin-Ego, re-enforce its protective shield, tolerate pain" (201). Anzieu's argument thus begins with tactility but moves toward visibly definable boundary. In pressing together, mother and child reenact the blended boundary of the womb, but the purpose of their embrace is to reestablish a linear, containing boundary.

Architectural theorists such as Juhani Pallasmaa, or Kent Bloomer and Charles W. Moore, have been most successful at avoiding this anti-ocular ocularcentrism by insisting on the importance of the posture and location of the body. They thus represent it as a collection of tactile interactions and mobile engagements rather than a visualizable outlined form. Pallasmaa, for example, suggests that "[a]s we open a door, the body weight meets the weight of the door; the legs measure the steps as we ascend a stairway, the hand strokes the handrail and the entire body moves diagonally and dramatically through space" (63). The body in this passage emerges as vectors of force among spaces and surfaces; it is not an open or closed unit but a sequence of actions (pushing, stroking, climbing) upon and among specific architectural forms. Kent Bloomer describes such movements in architectural space as a form of dance (107–8). By contrast, Bakhtin's architectural parallel for the grotesque body equates its orifices and protuberances with "towers and subterranean passages" (318), making the body itself a building with openings rather than investigating the body's motion through architectural space.

Pallasmaa's attention to the body in motion emerges from Merleau-Ponty's analysis of movement as a fundamental aspect of the "working, actual body": "[N]ot the body as a chunk of space or a bundle of functions but that body which is an intertwining of vision and movement. [. . .] Because it moves itself and sees, it holds things in a circle around itself. Things are an annex or prolongation of itself" ("Eye" 162). The body's movement undercuts any possibility of static perspectival perception that would "set up before the mind a picture or a representation of the world" (162). While the body "holds things in a circle around itself," it does not do so standing still; the body extends out into the world by perpetually moving through it, thus setting up a dynamic network of postural relations. Pioneering haptic theorist David Katz notes that the "touch organ, when kept motionless relative to the object, is beset with a partial anaesthesia. Movement is as indispensable to touch as light is to vision" (qtd. in Krueger 17). To feel the world, one must move a part of one's body against it. To move a door or walk up a stairway is to hold the architecture of that building in a circle around oneself as a group of haptic movements and sensations (pressure, solidity, empty space), rather than to consider it a visual background against which one's body appears. This contiguity can operate only through dynamic perception in which the body, especially the hand, actively engages with material phenomena, thus creating an ever-changing sequence of extensions and reorientations of bodily form. It is virtually impossible to visualize such a mobile, always changing, constantly prolonging and interweaving body as a visual figure. The prolongation of the hand's tactile perception through a stick, for example, involves for Merleau-Ponty the "incorporation" of the stick into the body (*Phenomenology* 143). While we are all familiar with this sort of perception—we feel the paper through the pen or the road through the bicycle's handlebars—it does not lend itself to visual representation. Such a sensory prolongation is distinct from Bakhtin's "bulge" of the body outward, which easily corresponds to, even calls for, a visual image.

Because our physical experience of home life is intimate and habitual, and our tactile sensations of the home's spaces and surfaces are so familiar, they serve as the most recognizable example of the sort of located tactility I will investigate. My focus is the relationship among our perception of the body's edge, the space that surrounds it, and the material forms (including people, objects, animals, and architectural features) that make up domestic space. I argue that the emotional power of domesticity is fully located in the relations between these phenomena as much as it is in the home's geometrical space or ideological formulation. While the home is both a cultural formulation and a building, it is, more than either of these, a cluster of tactile sensations and bodily positions that form the somatic groundwork through which we experience its emotional sustenance. If we focus more on motion and location in domestic space rather than on geometric or spectacular function, domesticity ultimately becomes contiguous with the body's sensorium. Embodied identity at home cannot be defined by a clear edge or reduced to figure/ ground distinctions; rather, it must take into account the body's intimate and dynamic engagement with the home's resonantly familiar materiality. The home, in the analysis that follows, emerges as a bodily operation rather than an architectural structure.

I have tried to avoid the slippage between material space and text that tends to characterize literary criticism focused on architecture. Richard Wittman argues that beginning in early-eighteenth-century Europe, as print culture became pervasive and the body ceased to serve as the central location of identity, architectural meaning ceased to be conveyed by "the allusive, poetic language of stones and mortar" and was communicated instead by written description of buildings, thereby "offering the word as a *substitute* for architectural expression" (3). Wittman's historical analysis helps explain the enduring critical tradition whereby architectural space is analyzed not in relation to an "embodied community" of critics but as a textual discourse interchangeable with other cultural texts. In *Housing Problems,* Susan Bernstein's analysis of the houses of Goethe, Walpole, and Freud in relation to their aesthetic and psychoanalytic theories, for example, she seems at first to call for an embodied approach: "the habit of the literal is housed in the house, our usual dwelling, the unaccountable spaces and rooms through which even the most philosophical bodies pass" (13). Bernstein proceeds to dismiss her attention to the home's materiality as an argumentative "feint" (154), however, asserting that "the experience of place is actually an opportunity to connect texts, images recollections, and representations[,] [. . .] a dense layering of texts that rhetorically produce certain effects of authenticity and connectedness" (15). This elision of the architectural and the textual is sufficiently conventional as to be assumed by some architectural critics as well. Writing in the *Chronicle of Higher Education* in 2008, Norman Weinstein bemoans recent architectural students' inability to move gracefully between design and text through the creation of "complex, multidimensional, written descriptions that, nevertheless, can be put into commercially compelling narratives for the general public" (B21). While such an approach offers valuable insights into the semiotic power of architecture, it applies largely to philosophical bodies rather than literal ones.

My approach to domesticity, which defines the home as at once material and apprehended, resides somewhere between that of philosophers such as Gaston Bachelard and Michel de Certeau and cultural theorists such as Michael McKeon and Victoria Rosner. Bachelard's *Poetics of Space* establishes the home as an imaginary or mnemonic realm in which architectural structures are synecdoches for the emotional states defining selfhood. While Bachelard gestures toward the reality of attics and basements, the material structures of the home loom largest as imaginary forms through which "the sheltered being gives perceptible limits to his shelter. He experiences the house in its reality and its virtuality, by means of thought and dreams" (5). Similarly, de Certeau, in his distinction between the "map" and the "tour" of lived space, argues for an understanding of the home as a "chain of spatializing operations" (120) that establishes identity through mobile engagement between body and space. Yet de Certeau's is largely a semantic space, in which walking is a "space of enunciation" (98), and rooms serve to define narrative, rather than bodily, limits. Rosner and McKeon, on the other hand, address the actual material surfaces and structures of the built environment in order to understand the home as a (primarily visual) "grid of social relations" with "spatial hierarchies demarcating" economic and gender politics (Rosner 2). Their work has demonstrated the home's ability to amplify the social symbolism of the material distinctions it creates, particularly those between interior and exterior spaces. I hope to combine Bachelard's awareness of the emotional resonance of familiar space with McKeon's belief in the determinative power of material surfaces in order to address the emotional impact of the material aspects of the home in relation to the materiality of the body.

Throughout I concentrate on those moments when body or home or both are at risk, and their tactile relation thus becomes most apparent. Our perceptions of our own bodies, and of the spaces in our homes, are fraught with anxieties that emerge most vividly when the tactile practices of embodiment become misaligned with the material structures of domesticity. Grief, memory loss, psychological disorders, and disease all reveal the tactile aspects of our intimate, embodied relations with our loved ones, caregivers, pets, and prized objects. Physical and psychological dysfunction threatens the graceful motion of the body through the home, reorganizing the boundaries and valuations of its spaces, to threaten both body and domestic order. As Laura U. Marks has argued in her discussion of cinematic tactility, embodiment should not be reduced to numinous universal repleteness but rather placed in the context of particularized bodily distress. "[P]erception is not an infinite return to the buffet table of lived experiences but a walk through the minefield of embodied memory" (152). These crises, by forcing us to negotiate memory and identity somatically, reveal how grounded in tactile sensation our home lives are and make us aware of how the experience of embodied domesticity always returns us to tactile apprehension.

By focusing on the body's edge in illness and grief, my discussion often broaches theories of the abject. Both Douglas and Kristeva argue that the spatial dynamics of purity and impurity follow a "logic of distribution" (Kristeva 91) in which the impure is defined by its exclusion from the Temple's sacred space. To accurately locate the abject, then, one must define both the body's and the building's walls, and their crucial relation to one another. The corporeal dysfunctions of one's bodily boundary "correspond to one's being allowed to have access or not to a place—the holy place of the Temple" (93). Kristeva goes on to discuss the interiorization and metaphorization of holy space in the New Testament, so that the abject becomes fully internalized as sin through "the building of that archaic space, the topological demarcation of the preconditions of a subjectivity" (117). This inversion of Levitical pollution, by which it is the body's interior that opens to pour forth its corruption, is borne out in many of the scenarios of domestic pollution I address. For health care workers, elderly homeowners, and animal hoarders, the body, alone or in combination with other bodies, is the disorderly center that spreads contamination outward through the home. I would argue, however, with Kristeva's use of the term "archaic space" to define an interiorized self; identity becomes spatial only when it has become contiguous with or located in relation to the body as a material form. Contagion involves opening and spreading of the body outward, but that same process is always at work in the home, as our domestic lives tend to materialize and externalize our subjectivity in tangible self-representations and material engagements, located in specific architectural spaces or postural relations to other bodies. In the home, we are always in a sort of Temple, in which the embodied self, no matter how profane, is tangibly present.

Consequently, a tactile definition of the body's edge invariably complicates the process of locating purity. The distinction between the body's inside and outside articulated as the skin envelope largely depends, as I have suggested above, upon visual distinctions that can't be fully translated to tactile experience. The abject is located "at the border of my condition as a living being. My body extricates itself, as being alive, from that border" (3). But such extrication cannot be perceived tangibly without a reinfection; the abject is the "in between, the ambiguous, the composite" (4), but the sense of touch operates only in between. In her famous example of the skin on the surface of milk, Kristeva elides touch and vision: "When the eyes see or the lips touch that skin on the surface of milk [. . .] I experience a gagging sensation" (2–3). Seeing and touching are not comparable in this case, however, since once the lips have touched the milk, the body's boundary is already blended with it. Moreover, the pharyngeal, or gag, reflex is most often incited by touch, a neural response to something touching the pharynx, or the soft palate. This sort of sensation registers when something has already invaded the body or has already begun to emerge from it; it is a bodily behavior that highlights the ambiguity of the body's boundary. Kristeva's equation of vision and touch points to the inapplicability of this sort of abjection to tactile experience, since the self-reflexive quality of touch consistently eludes the desire for the precise location of the self.

My attention to the suffering body, and my application of literary studies to health concerns, position this book within the growing field of Medical Humanities. This field has emerged from medical ethics, motivated primarily by doctors seeking to employ the disciplinary tools of literary and cultural theory, philosophy, sociology, and anthropology to improve the empathetic communication between doctor and patient. In a 2001 "Editor's Preface" to the journal *Literature and Medicine*, Rita Charon and her co-editor Maura Spiegel offer the following useful formulation of the goals of the field:

> Narrative medicine has developed in tandem with literature and medicine, weaving together theoretical perspectives, literary texts, and

creative methods for the benefit of the practicing doctor and the ailing patient. We should all take heart that the scholarship of literature and medicine, over the years, has contributed to these fundamental changes in how medicine is practiced, taught, evaluated and experienced. (viii)

Like Arthur Kleinman, William F. May, and Arthur W. Frank, Charon and Spiegel establish the practical goal of improving medical practice as central to their intellectual endeavor. Literary studies operates in "tandem" with or is "woven" into the analysis of medical practice, both metaphors suggesting a cooperative, hands-on approach to complex intellectual materials. There is also a strong pedagogical impulse underlying Medical Humanities, no doubt in part because of its common association with medical schools. Most significantly, Charon and Spiegel identify a specific set of beneficiaries for their scholarly endeavor—"the practicing doctor and the ailing patient." While it is common for scholars in the humanities to identify an audience (typically other scholars in their field or general readers), it is quite unusual for them to identify beneficiaries. Undertaking the theoretical analysis of texts with the stated goal of benefiting ailing patients is a distinguishing feature of the Medical Humanities. Charon purposefully rejects the impulse to establish a clear boundary around the field, calling it "not so much a new specialty as a new frame for clinical work" (*Narrative* 13). To be successful, scholarship must resonate outward to doctors, patients, and society at large, as Kleinman enunciates in *The Illness Narratives.*

> My clinical work [. . .] has been described for a fairly narrow professional readership. My aim in this book is altogether different. I write here to explain to patients, their families, and their practitioners what I have learned from a career passionately devoted to this interest. I write because I wish to popularize a technical literature that would be of great practical value for those who must live with, make sense of, and care for chronic illness. Indeed, I will argue that the study of the experience of illness has something fundamental to teach each of us about the human condition, with its universal suffering and death. (xiii)

Beginning with the specialists in his professional field, Kleinman moves to doctors and patients, then to families and caregivers, and finally to "each of us" who will inevitably experience physical suffering and medical care. Kleinman's phrase "the study of the experience of illness" is particularly telling, as it nudges "experience," often used as an affective term, into the realm of thoughtful and meticulous analysis. Medical Humanities thus demonstrates a fundamental faith in the ability of literary analysis to improve the lives of suffering human beings in the most tangible way: by helping doctors diminish that suffering. As Charon writes in her foundational work *Narrative Medicine:*

> What literary studies give medicine is the realization that our intimated medical relationships occur in words. [. . .] They are based on the complex texts that are shared between doctor and patient, texts that encompass words, silences, physical findings, pictures, measurements of substances in the body, and appearances. (53–54)

The primary texts of this sort of literary study are these doctor-patient interchanges, rather than literary representations of illness. While works such as May's *The Physician's Covenant* do use passages from works by Faulkner, Dostoyevsky, Sophocles, and other major authors to illustrate the archetypal images through which patients tend to relate to their doctors, Charon argues that "[m]ore fundamental by far than the content of *Bleak House* or *King Lear* is the modeling, by literary acts, of deeply transformative intersubjective connections among relative strangers fused and nourished by words" (54). While Bernstein's analysis of architecture redefines physical engagements with the home as texts, Charon attempts to understand verbal engagements between doctors and patients in embodied terms; as Frank puts it, Medical Humanities uses literary analysis to help doctors "make sense of illness stories as being told *through* the diseased body" (*Wounded* 3).

The interdisciplinary methodology of scholars in the Medical Humanities resembles the work of what Julie Thompson Klein calls "academic intellectuals" who are willing to "follow problems across disciplinary boundaries" because they are "[a]ccountable to a wider audience" (*Interdisciplinarity* 183). Interdisciplinary scholarship, as Klein points out, has expanded significantly in the twentieth and twenty-first centuries, largely as a result of disciplinary fragmentation.

> Over the course of the twentieth century, the fracturing and refracturing of disciplines into new specialties has been the dominant pattern of knowledge growth. This phenomenon has resulted in both greater fragmentation and greater convergence. A significant number of new specialties have a hybrid character, and their variety is as striking as their number. (44)

Klein's wide-ranging and comprehensive analysis of academic inter-disciplinarity offers various models of how disciplinary boundaries are crossed and re-formed, models that fall roughly into the categories of territorial and reproductive engagement. Klein tends to be most critical of territorial interdisciplinary models, such as migration. She rejects Stanley Fish's geopolitical formulation in which disciplines "expand imperialistically into other territories" in favor of Araballa Lyon's riverine metaphor, in which they move with "currents and flows, tributaries, eddies, and confluences" (qtd. in Klein, *Humanities* 98). The metaphor that Klein ultimately finds most useful is that of reproduction, or "hybridity" (*Crossing* 45), which reconciles boundary and permeability, while accounting for the quirky yet cooperative disorder of field development. Like Charon's metaphor of weaving and Lyon's of fluid dynamics, hybridity necessitates the intertwining of different realms of knowledge to produce a new one; it also evokes tactile, rather than visual, perception. Constance Classen, in her introduction to *The Book of Touch,* notes that ocular metaphors for thought imply that scholarship should cultivate an elegant detachment, while the tension and amalgamation essential to interdisciplinary thinking might be better understood haptically. "Touch is better served by a rough and ready approach that acknowledges and grapples with the tangled, bumpy and sticky nature of the topic" (5). Combining fields often leads to an intellectual scrum, along with its ensuing bumps and scrapes, but such grappling can have great practical value. Klein notes that "mission-oriented projects" have been instrumental in generating interdisciplinary scholarship throughout the twentieth-century (*Interdisciplinarity* 33). Having a practical purpose, a set of specific beneficiaries, and a sense of accountability to a wider audience makes a field such as Medical Humanities more mission-oriented than self-reflexive. As a literary scholar rather than a practicing physician, I don't have quite the same set of beneficiaries as Charon or Kleinman, but I do share their faith that the analysis of literature, and its interweaving with other fields, can help address human suffering in practical ways.

✣ ✣ ✣

This book is divided into three parts and seven chapters, each chapter addressing the way a particular form of physical or psychic stress reveals the tactile dynamics of domestic embodiment. The first three chapters (Part One) establish the centrality of tactility to our domestic relations with the people and objects in our homes; and they trace mechanisms of domestic dissolution, whereby the psychological rewards of tactile engagement interfere with the smooth motion through and the clear limitation of domestic space. The distortions of domestic life caused by grief, the hoarding of objects, and the hoarding of animals all involve an intensification of habitual somatic engagements with the home. These three chapters address the way the homeowner's sense of self relies upon the habitual touch of familiar people and objects in the home, as well as movements through and interactions with its tangible surfaces. This reliance becomes more intense, but also less reliable, in times of crisis and can endanger the homeowner's psychic and physical health, even as it causes the home to degenerate. Chapters 4 and 5 (Part Two) show how the overwhelming importance of tactility to our perception of home can, in some cases, allow domestic experience to operate irrespective of architectural structures. The home can become in a sense portable, operating through our somatic attachment to other bodies; this is the case among homeless pet owners and medical caregivers, for whom the bond with a familiar, caring body can take the place of the familiar structures and spaces of the home environment. The final two chapters (Part Three) discuss how the collapse of domesticity to the body's edge operates individually rather than between bodies and results from boundary anxiety caused by neurological disorders or skin diseases. People with Autism Spectrum Disorder perceive their body's boundary as under assault, so that the comfort available by pressure upon that margin becomes their only approximation of domestic sustenance. The opposite response to boundary fragility is apparent in the works of artists suffering from skin disorders; these artists propose a material model for somatic boundary that is at once dynamic and fragmentary. My argument thus gradually spirals inward, beginning with the way we come to understand ourselves through touching people and things at home, and eventually focusing upon touch itself as a nonarchitectural medium of domestic experience. In the process I hope to challenge vision-based conceptions of bodily identity and domesticity, while also investigating the unique sensations that domestic tactility offers.

Chapter 1 argues that domestic intimacy can be understood as a series of physical habits that create tangible contiguity between ourselves and the people we live with. It investigates the literary portrayal of grief in the context of phantom limb pain, a neurological response to loss that is quite literally embodied. Neurologists Ronald Melzack and Joel Katz have documented that the enduring and painful apprehension of a lost limb does not follow the process of gradual detachment which Freud describes. Losing a loved one means losing not just that one body but also one's own bodily engagements with it in familiar domestic spaces. Our grief becomes a series of slight physical adjustments based on the fact that a body that was always here, in a certain spatial and postural relation to our own, is now gone. Expanding on arguments about the impact of habit upon the internal perception of the body by neurologist V. S. Ramachandran, philosopher Maurice Merleau-Ponty, and feminist theorist Elizabeth Grosz, I argue that the body image can extend beyond our skin, across intervening space, and to our loved ones. By comparing Jacques Derrida's image-based discussion of mourning ("By Force of Mourning") with theories of embodied habit by Maurice Merleau-Ponty and of disability by Lennard Davis and Rosemarie Garland Thompson, chapter 1 investigates the physical apprehension of loss in literary representations by Donald Hall, Virginia Woolf, Mark Doty, and Alfred Lord Tennyson.

Chapter 2 also addresses the operation of materialized memory in the home by focusing on our habitual tactile engagement with objects and spaces. Studies of place attachment among the elderly by qualitative gerontologists such as Robert Rubinstein, Graham Rowles, and M. Powell Lawton employ the contradictory metaphors of navigation and amalgamation to describe the complex relationship among self, space, and habit when elders identify with their homes. Familiar objects and domestic routines reinforce the failing memory, while those same objects endanger the frail body. Drawing on Jean Baudrillard's distinction between accumulating and collecting, Gaston Bachelard's discussion of domestic nostalgia, and Malcolm Quantrill's analysis of the memorial power of architecture, as well as novels by Charles Dickens, Pat Barker, Doris Lessing, and Barbara Pym, this chapter investigates the way personal history becomes carried by, hidden in, and materially experienced through disorderly accumulations.

Companion animals stand somewhere between human bodies and objects as somatic repositories of emotional identification. Like the physiological engagements with people and objects addressed in chapters 1 and 2, our embodied interactions with pets serve to support the strategies of identification and self-integration in the home, offering a reciprocally tactile engagement that intensifies the home's safety, peace, and emotional richness. Focusing on animal hoarding, chapter 3 tracks how domestic space is ruined and made public when the bond between humans and animals overwhelms normal domestic boundaries. Animal hoarding is distinct from other obsessive-compulsive collecting because it deracinates the hoarder from his personal history and redefines private domestic spaces as public, spectacular ones. Unlike the accumulation of memorabilia investigated in chapter 2, animal hoarding tends to efface memory and identity, allowing physical connections with animals to crowd out human relationships. Literary works by Doris Lessing and Susan Cheever; the 1974 documentary film *Grey Gardens;* and journalistic accounts, veterinary studies, and sociological analyses of animal companionship all center on how the home is redefined as public space, and the hoarder as a type of degenerate celebrity.

While obsessive animal attachment can undercut the home's boundaries, chapter 4 investigates how tangible connection to a companion animal can also establish an apprehension of home in the absence of any architectural structure. This chapter elaborates upon the previous chapter's analysis of animal attachment, while also beginning a new section of the book's argument, in which domesticity is unhoused, relocated to the body's edge. The close relationship between the legal and cultural operation of disability and homelessness is apparent in the autobiographical writings of homeless and disabled dog owners, for whom bodily motion through the landscape challenges typical definitions of the body's domestic identity. Disability theorist Rod Michalko's theoretical analysis of his relationship with his service dog Smokie, and Lars Eighner's autobiographical writings about his homeless travels with his dog Lizbeth, relocate domesticity into the tactile dynamics of human/canine companionship. Where hoarding renders private homes into public space, tactile contiguity between dog and owner can create a sense of privacy and self-determination in the public realm. Engaging with the legal and cultural discourses of homelessness and disability, as well as sociological studies of anthropomorphism, this chapter demonstrates how animal attachment offers an alternative corporeal model of domesticity.

Home health care workers also engage in a redefinition of domestic space through their physical interactions with the abject bodies of the elderly and afflicted. Since illness disrupts and disorders domestic space, calling into question its power to support the homeowner's identity, the tactile intimacy between caregivers and patients may replace tactile engagement with the home. Acts of nursing that involve touching patients' bodies tend to intensify the confusion of identity brought on by illness, however, so that the identities of both the healer and the healed become blended and enigmatic. Chapter 5 demonstrates the centrality of tactility to the ethical enactment of compassion by analyzing first-person accounts of caregiving by Nesta Rovina, Rebecca Brown, and Thomas Edward Gass in the context of theories of the abject by Mary Douglas and Julia Kristeva. Portrayals of the polluted body in biblical and classical literature, as well as the current medical debate over the nursing practice called "Therapeutic Touch," expose the heroic, yet perilous, operation of the healing touch.

The final two chapters of the book focus upon the body's edge, showing how domesticity can be redefined in both the intensification and the dissolution of its boundary. Chapter 6 investigates the perception of home at the body's edge, not through bonding with other bodies as in the previous two chapters, but through the sensation of pressure on the body's surface. For both Sylvia Plath and Temple Grandin, the sensory key to domestic comfort is tactile pressure, which defines and reinforces bodily coherence. The normal spaces of the home fail to provide this pressure, and both authors respond to their boundary anxiety through the somatic identification with animals' bodies in confining architectural spaces. Grandin's designs for meat-processing facilities and Plath's poetic and fictional representations of domestic life place bodies in tunnels, chutes, crevices, and passageways that exert pressure on them while limiting other sensory stimuli. The works of both writers, read in the context of writings on Autism Spectrum Disorder and deep pressure therapy, present a version of domesticity that is located, immediate, and embodied.

While Plath and Grandin respond to boundary anxiety by intensifying pressure and tactility, Paul Gauguin and John Updike, both sufferers from psoriatic skin disorders, take the opposite approach. In their artworks and personal writings, they create imaginary domestic spaces in which the home is emptied and purified, offering a sublime, purely visual environment, and the body's surface becomes similarly clean and hard-edged. This yearning for domestic emptiness is associated with the creative process, but both artists ultimately reject this disembodied aesthetic for one that reflects the dynamic fragmentation and dissolution of their own body's boundary. This chapter investigates the association between creative power and fragmentation of the body's surface in Gauguin's and Updike's artworks and personal writings, in the work of tactual perception theorists such as S. J. Lederman, and in the book of Job. In doing so, it links a nonlinear, textural definition of the body's boundary to the somatic experience of the creative body working in the home.

Mark Paterson notes that "[i]f, ostensibly, vision affirms and reproduces boundaries, exaggerating the atomistic and the individual, then it is arguably *touch* and *tactility* that can explore relations *between* subjects, between bodies" (158). Throughout this work I focus upon the tactile sensations, which involve contact between the body and other bodies or objects and which are registered primarily through pressure on the skin. To a lesser degree, I also address the kinesthetic, vestibular, and proprioceptive sensations, which track the body's motion through and position in space and which are sensed through the muscles, joints, and inner ear. My emphasis on tactility reflects my interest in contiguity between the body and the home; I want to investigate those moments when the body is woven into its domestic environment rather than isolated in space. In arguing for a tactile rather than a kinesthetic home, one we push and rub up against rather than moving through gracefully, I implicitly assume that intimacy, rather than individuation, is the home's central function.

Central to my argument throughout is the concept of "body schema" or "body image," which V. S. Ramachandran defines as "the internal image and memory of one's body in space and time. To create and maintain this body image at any given instant, your parietal lobes combine information from many sources: the muscles, joints, eyes and motor command centers" (44). Within neurological science there is a technical distinction between "body image" and "body schema." "Body image" refers to the neural self-representation of one's body in relation to surrounding space, based in part on memory and habit, while "body schema" describes the continual, sensorimotor mapping of the body in relation to its immediate surroundings (Paillard 209). While I address both of these at different points throughout this study, my emphasis on the role of memory and familiar bodily activity in domestic space directs the preponderance of my discussion to body image, so I will use that term throughout. Nevertheless, I want to emphasize the distinction between the sort of somatic self-representation I am addressing and the term's more popular usage.

While the concept was first described by Sir Henry Head in 1911, Paul Schilder is generally credited with applying the term "body image" to psychological and sociological definitions of self in *Das Körperschema* (1923). It has since been adopted by psychologists and cultural theorists to refer to a broad variety of perceptions about oneself in society, including size, beauty, strength, and social power. Feminist theorists in particular have employed the term in order to analyze the social construction of an ideal female body. Susan Bordo critiques the medical approach to anorexia (Body Image Distortion Syndrome), arguing for a more complex understanding of the cultural construction of ideal female shape (55). Cultural critics (e.g., Sander Gilman) who are interested in the body as a cultural staging ground for the politics of race and ethnicity have made good use of the concept of body image; they also emphasize the visual apprehension of somatic identity. "Body image" is now such a pervasive and useful term for describing such cultural constructions of the body that its neurological meaning tends to be deemphasized. Because this book involves foregrounding the somatosensory aspects of domestic experience, however, I will employ the term in its original denotation.

The literary works I analyze are all by Anglo-American writers from the mid-nineteenth to the late twentieth centuries, a 150-year period when the middle-class home is established as a culturally central space. I am not making a historical argument about the home during this period; there are significant differences between the size, use, and social function of the homes portrayed by Charles Dickens, John Updike, and Marilynne Robinson. Nevertheless, all of these authors, I would argue, consider domestic space, and our bodily dynamics in it, central to their investigations of family life, memory, and identity. The only literary texts outside this period are the biblical and classical works through which I address abjection or abomination. In doing so, I follow the lead of critics such as Julia Kristeva and Mary Douglas, who identify these texts as foundational to modern cultural definitions of sacredness and profanity at the body's edge.

Ultimately, my interdisciplinary approach is like that of the patient who, when asked why he wanted a priest, a rabbi, a Muslim cleric, and a Buddhist monk to visit him in the hospital, responded that he would take whatever help he could get. My hope is that my analysis may combine with those of scholars from other disciplines to further our common practical concerns, regardless of whether our disciplinary projects are the same. While I do not expect my discussion of mess and memory in chapter 2 to break new ground in the field of gerontology, my hope is that I may join gerontologists and home health aides in helping elderly homeowners and their families understand why they are so strongly attached to their messy homes, and reluctant to leave them. My discussion of animal hoarding in chapter 3 will, I hope, contribute to the interdisciplinary understanding of animal attachment generated by the sociologists, psychologists, and veterinarians who cooperate in groups such as the Hoarding of Animals Research Consortium. By addressing the tactile aspects of caregiving and grief, in chapters 5 and 1, respectively, my goal is to participate with grief counselors, psychologists, and grieving families in finding richer and more trenchant ways to express the lineaments of these common forms of suffering.

Through analysis of a range of literary and cultural texts from various historical periods, these chapters open up theoretical and experiential dialogues about the role of touch in domestic experience. In allowing diverse texts to speak to one another, my intent is not to ignore the historical specificity of cultural constructions of somatic and domestic identity, but to highlight the radical ways in which the introduction of a tactile epistemology might unsettle existing critical and theoretical paradigms often applied un-self-consciously to cultural analyses. Recent scholarship addressing touch, such as Mark Paterson's phenomenological study of haptics, David Howes's anthropological analysis of sensation, and Laura U. Marks's studies of tactility and the gaze in contemporary film, have demonstrated the value of touch for interrogating such paradigms. The theoretical and thematic structure of the book will, I hope, continue to invite additional analyses focused on representations of tactile experience in the home. Arthur W. Frank compares the interdisciplinary interchanges created by Medical Humanities to a "clinical reflecting team" (*Renewal* 7) of medical experts working on a patient's treatment. He notes that such a team "is, literally, a crowded room full of voices that speak from different perspectives but share commitments about how human life works and what's good for humans" (8). My hope is to invite in such a boisterous crowd and, through the resulting dialogue, generate insight into our experience as home bodies.

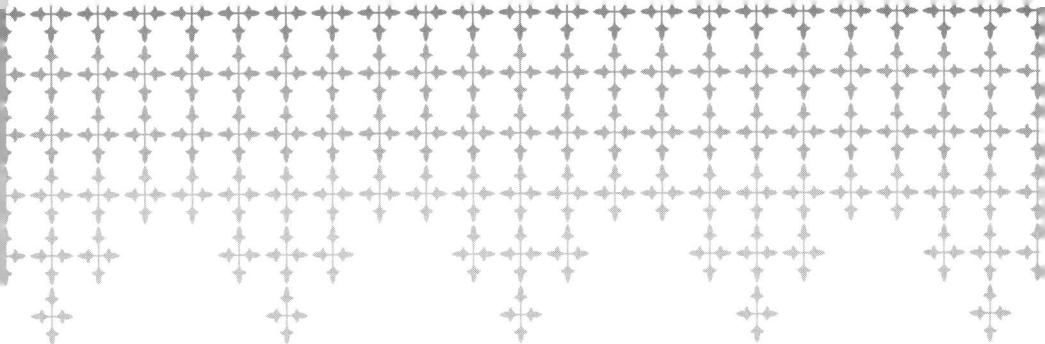

PART ONE

BROKEN HOMES

Intimacy, Tactility, and the Dissolution of
Domestic Space

Chapter 1

Tangible Grief

> Mr. Ramsay, stumbling along a passage one dark morning, stretched his arms out, but Mrs. Ramsay having died rather suddenly the night before, his arms, though stretched out, remained empty.
>
> —Virginia Woolf, *To the Lighthouse,* 128

In this passage from *To the Lighthouse,* Virginia Woolf lets us experience some of the desperate confusion that Mr. Ramsay feels in the brief moment when he still expects his wife's body to fill the space between his outstretched arms. Reading this passage for the first time, we are shocked, then incredulous, then bereft. Mr. Ramsay's forlorn grasping at the air is the only grieving we see him perform in the novel, and its particular pathos comes from its embodiment of the physicality of his loss. He stretches out his arms, and they remain stretched out for a long clause and two phrases before he, and we, discover his mistake. This passage places the reader in the midst of grief—grief not simply as an emotional state but as an embodied condition that involves posture and location. Grief occurs *here,* in this hallway, when Mr. Ramsay is in this posture; it emerges as an emotion not just incited but defined by physical circumstance.

In this chapter I will demonstrate the significance of tactility to domestic life by focusing on the painful and disorienting bodily postures that grief compels us to enact in domestic space. We feel the loss of our loved ones not just as a psychological or an emotional absence, but in our bodies, and this somatic grieving is perhaps the most vivid example of how domestic affection depends upon and operates through the sense of touch. Literary critics who attend to the portrayal of grief have placed emphasis on particular, intensely painful moments like Mr. Ramsay's in order to critique Freud's portrayal of the mourning process. In her discussion of the "psychic pain" of grief, Kathleen Woodward attempts to define a "middle position" ("Freud" 100) between mourning, in which the mourner detaches himself from his lost beloved through a methodical sequence of "reality-testing," and melancholia, in which the mourner clings to his lost love in a "wishful psychosis" (Freud 243). Woodward objects that "Freud defined mourning as a way of divesting ourselves of pain, of getting it over and done with. [. . .] In 'Mourning and Melancholia' Freud leaves us no theoretical room for another place, one between a crippling melancholia and the end of mourning" ("Grief-Work" 116).

I would like to consider Woodward's negative use of the word "crippling." In her attempt to foreground the "affective dimensions of the experience of mourning" ("Freud" 94), Woodward wants to portray it as non-melancholic. She wants to clear those who continue to grieve from the charge that they are engaging in pathological behavior and attend to the strength and insight grief can bring. We are not crippled if we will not be comforted, she suggests; Freud's overly schematic portrait of the grieving psyche is contradicted by our common experience of a grief that, without ruining us, remains painfully immediate. Rather than taking place in "the private mise-en-scène of the psyche" (99), Woodward suggests, grief occurs in a rich affective environment of lived emotion. By invoking bodily disability, however, Woodward indulges in the same sort of rarefying distortion with which she charges Freud. As Laura E. Tanner has argued, any comprehensive discussion of grief's affects must revisit Freud's model of mourning within a framework of embodied subjectivity. Drawing on the work of Maurice Merleau-Ponty and Elizabeth Grosz, Tanner calls for the development of a theory of embodied grief. "By failing to acknowledge the extent to which we experience loss as a bodily phenomenon," Tanner argues, "we doom ourselves to a 'failed' mourning that returns us again and again to the unspoken absence of the body" (87).

Any theory of embodied grief, I would add, must situate the survivor's body in a particular place and position. A child, expecting his mother to be standing beside him, reaches a hand toward where hers should be. A father leans over to steady a missing car seat. A woman thinks she feels the heavy collapse of her dog beside her chair, and she shifts slightly to accommodate its now-missing head on her feet. Our grief becomes a series of slight physical adjustments based on the fact that a body that was always here, in a certain relation to our own, is now gone. Mise-en-scène does matter in Mr. Ramsay's sad grasping for his wife's missing body, but it is the mise-en-scène of Mr. Ramsay standing and leaning in a particular hallway in a particular house, where physical disorientation becomes concomitant with emotional pain. Mr. Ramsay "stumbles" trying to touch his lost wife. What Freud would call his "reality testing" results in the disabling of his body's easy motion through familiar space. While Woodward argues that Freud's "bit by bit" detachment glosses over the affective and productive aspects of grief, I would add that Woodward's model can be further grounded by focusing on how intense moments of grief are manifested as a sort of "crippling," as a disabling of our bodies in specific postures and in particular physical relations to our environment.

Disability theorist Lennard Davis argues for a "continuum" between the disabled and abled body that, like Woodward's "middle ground" between mourning and melancholia, critiques a discourse of normalcy that disallows variegated—or in Davis's words "ragged"—bodily experience (5). The essentially "fragmented body [. . .] that precedes the ruse of identity and wholeness" (141) is repressed, Davis claims, in order to construct a smoothly functioning cultural body. The culturally normative body depends, as Rosemarie Garland Thompson suggests, on its spatial location.

> As the norm becomes neutral in an environment created to accommodate it, disability becomes intense, extravagant and problematic. [. . .] The cripple before the stairs, [. . .] the amputee before the typewriter, and the dwarf before the counter are all proof that the myriad structures and practices of material, daily life enforce the cultural standard of a universal subject with a narrow range of corporeal variation. (24)

I would argue that grieving people also find themselves in an unaccommodating physical environment, in which the absence of the beloved's body changes their habitual motions through space. Thompson claims that the staircase itself serves to define the "crippled" body; similarly, the practices of material daily life experienced by the grieving as they move through newly empty domestic spaces enact their grief. Mr. Ramsay's stumbling is nothing if not "intense, extravagant and problematic." Laurence Rickels notes a metaphorical dissonance between Freud's comparison of grief to an open wound in "Mourning and Melancholia" and the "etymological association with falling" in the German "trauer" (Rickels 13). If perpetual mourning means excessive chronic bleeding, then we must understand it in terms of Freud's favored metaphor of fluid dynamics, the ego bleeding out through its pierced margin. But if mourning is more like chronic falling or stumbling, then we should understand it as the dynamic relation of bodies in space. To put it another way, mourning as chronic bleeding represents a medical crisis; mourning as chronic stumbling represents a physical disability.

I would like to address embodied grief by looking at the experience of people with a certain sort of "disability"—phantom limb pain. Those who have lost limbs through accident or amputation frequently retain a perception of that limb as physically present. These phantoms, caused by enduring neurological patterns, are rarely quiet ghosts, often causing prickling or burning pains and sometimes seeming to protrude at strange, inconvenient angles. Even when they are not painful, phantom limbs can cause their owners to misjudge distance and lose their balance. Amputees experience their losses as physical sensation and are quite literally disabled by them; like Mr. Ramsay they stumble around and against their ghosts. While their "real" disability is the missing limb, the perceived presence of that limb, a perception which can't be detached, can often be even more crippling.

Phantom limb pain is a response to loss that is quite literally embodied. We can most fully ground grief in embodied life by trying to understand our pain for our lost loved ones in neurological terms, as a bodily phenomenon, as well as psychological and affective ones. By applying this neurological model to literary portrayals of people overcome by loss, we may explore representations of grief through a framework of tactility. Freud's model, which involves holding up memories in order to put them aside, relies implicitly on defining the lost beloved as an image that can be placed at a distance from the mourner. Literature, with its great facility for establishing experience in enduring images, would seem well-suited to the task of putting our grief to rest by telling stories designed to solidify our lost loved ones in pleasing, distant images. Yet, I will argue, literary portrayals of localized, embodied loss often evoke the insistence and immediacy of touch rather than sight and frustrate the Freudian impulse to isolate and withdraw from the beloved. In *Prosthesis*, David Wills describes how one particular literary image must, for him, be translated through a childhood memory of his father's phantom limb pain. Wills remembers standing beside his father who winces in pain and shifts his wooden leg about, trying to find a comfortable position while washing dishes at the sink. His father's jerky motions as he rocks back and forth are matched by the line he recites from Virgil, which describes, with rhythmic perfection, horses galloping across a plain.

> He quotes it at the kitchen sink bent over with discomfort, shifting from one side to the other [. . .] until on the sixth foot he achieves a harmoni-

ous resolution, the equilibrium of perfect self-division, and outruns the spasm that lurks behind every single uttered syllable. Or doesn't, and jerks himself up suddenly out of joint, the body off beat. (4)

While literature should allow his father to memorialize the absent foot through a classical poetic image, the poetic rhythm is disrupted by his own bodily rhythms through which his loss lurches back into motion. Wills's own grief can't come to rest in the image of his father washing dishes either. Wills's memory of his father, his apprehension of his father's absence, works through an apprehension of his own body's location relative to his father's, which is itself defined by its relation to a missing limb that can't be quieted. By focusing on his father's prosthesis, Wills is able to unveil the literary image's inability to settle the lost body at a safe, monumental distance. It keeps returning him to "an amputee father's discomfort" (10). I am concerned with the way literature may bring about a similar discomfort by allowing us to participate in the illusions of physical presence to which the grieving are prone, placing us in the midst of an irritatingly and cripplingly present grief.

Let us begin by thinking of grief as a series of physical acts, using theories of embodiment, habit, and disability in order to define embodied grief. I will compare Jacques Derrida's discussion of mourning, which emphasizes the image, with theories of habit by Maurice Merleau-Ponty and Gaston Bachelard and of disability by Lennard Davis and Rosemarie Garland Thompson, which emphasize embodied identity. Placing these discussions in the context of phantom limb theory allows us to think of grief as a somatic response. Because the neurological phenomenon known as "body image" suggests that we experience our loved ones' bodies as contiguous with our own, grief can be understood as bodily dismemberment, and the pain of grief as phantom pain. I will then discuss literary portrayals of grief that focus on the location and disabling of the griever's body. Such passages, which portray either the collapse into a space left vacant by the lost body or the contortion around a phantom loved one who seems to endure, move uneasily between the comic and the tragic. Ultimately, they present the physical confusions and discomforts of grief not as mere byproducts of loss but as emotionally profound and psychically redemptive acts that validate the significance of the lost beloved's physical being. Yet they derive their literary power from the way they force the reader into an uncomfortable awareness not of the lost body but of the grieving body.

✣ ✣ ✣

The aching desire to touch the departed, so often stated in expressions of grief, is generally explained by the fact that while memory may conjure a visual impression of a face or hand, the palpation of corporeal bodies is now impossible. The apostle Thomas offers perhaps the most memorable statement of this assumption: "Except I shall . . . put my finger into the print of the nails, and thrust my hand into his side, I will not believe" (John 20:25). Seeing the dead is easy, Thomas claims; exchanging a touch would be miraculous. Peggy Phelan, discussing Caravaggio's *The Incredulity of St. Thomas,* describes Thomas's desire to touch the unreachable, formless body of the dead as the central point of the resurrection story.

> The failure of the body to remain a solid set of remains is underscored by Caravaggio's painting. [. . .] It is the lack of form, the lack of anything to hold onto in death, that inspires the drama of love that can offer us only bodies with holes in them. The radical formlessness of the beloved's body (its utter failure to remain static) creates the wild terror of Caravaggio's painting. (41)

This "wild terror" grips Jesus's apostles, Phelan argues, because death so absolutely severs our tangible links to love. Imagistic memories linger in the mind, but touch can't linger. Grief centers on the contrast between lingering images and nonlingering bodies.

Derrida also emphasizes the staying power of the image and the complete loss of tactile apprehension of the lost body. Mourning, he argues, works through "a geometry of gazes, an orientation of perspectives," which transcend or replace a body that can't be located. "[Images] which might be memories or monuments, but which are reducible in any case to a memory that consists of *visible* scenes that are no longer anything but images. [. . .] [H]e whom we see in images or in recollection [. . .] is no longer here, no longer there" ("By Force" 188). When someone can't be located "here" or "there," he can still be envisioned in a scene—in imaginary space partaking of none of the material specificity of the object world. Following Louis Marin, Derrida further argues that memory through images cancels out or overwhelms our knowledge of the physical body. When the angel at the tomb declares Christ's absence with the words "he is not here, he is elsewhere" (179), he establishes an image of Christ that, in effect, creates Him. This image has more historical power than the body ever did. "[T]he body is not first founding and then, once dead or absent, confirmed in its founding power. No, this power comes to it from the imaginal transfiguration. [. . .] [T]his founding power of the image or of the portrait (of the king, for example), [. . .] did not exist before death" (180). Derrida not only asserts the power of the image to last beyond the body; he also suggests its dominance over the body itself. The desire to establish a clear, usually romanticized, image of the lost loved one is, in part, what funerals are for; wakes and memorial services often consist of little more than outpourings of anecdotal images in which the dead beloved's identity can come to rest. "Do you remember how she used to hold the umbrella over the cat?" "He always wore that red shirt and those baggy black pants." Such images have the power to endure and have a greater "effect" or "visibility" (181) than any one memory. If the dead person is a king, Derrida points out, then the whole country engages in the creation of such a lasting image, the image becoming the thing we love.

But unlike kings or messiahs, our family members engage with us physically on a daily basis. Our love for them exists in an embodied environment, and our memories of that love will always be associated with memories of that lost embodied world: for losing a loved one means losing not just that one body but also one's own bodily engagements with it. It means losing a whole set of postural habits that exist in the rooms, halls, beds, sofas, and cars those bodies share. The question "Do you love me?" "is fundamentally a question of perspective," says Phelan, "of where one is in relation to the other" (31). But "where one is" may define not only optical perspective but also physical position and bodily posture in relation to other bodies, even absent ones.

Such illusions of presence derive from enduring physical habits rather than failures of memory or attention. They are what Merleau-Ponty calls "knowledge in the hands" (144). Just as we still reach for a light switch that now, after house renovations, is somewhere else, we expect a physical presence and are confused and disappointed when we don't feel it. Bachelard has described the way a house can impose corporeal mannerisms upon us.

> But over and beyond our memories, the house we were born in is physically inscribed in us. It is a group of organic habits. [. . .] We would push the door that creaks with the same gesture, we would find our way in the dark to the distant attic. The feel of the tiniest latch has remained in our hands. (14–15)

The tangible presence of our loved ones, whom we must also push past with a certain gesture and for whom we also reach in the dark, would also be experienced as a group of organic habits. Our bodily habits place us in the physical world where we have lived with other bodies. We shuffle and push in bed, reach for a hand that is always just down and to the left when we sit *here* on the sofa and lean against a shoulder. And we feel the emptiness when that body can no longer be pushed against, or held, that is, when our body's posture and motion recall a similar posture and motion adopted to interact with the lost one's body.

Davis argues that "the construction of a disability is based on the deconstruction of a continuum" (11) between the healthy and the impaired body. Such deconstruction is artificial, an attempt to repress the fundamental fragmentation of the body (145). Habitual engagements with our environment create a somatic continuum, or perhaps it is better to say contiguum, between ourselves and our lost loved ones that manifests itself as bodily impairment. Merleau-Ponty uses the phantom limb as an example of habitual somatic experience, as a bodily "refusal" to let go of its past.

> What it is in us which refuses mutilation and disablement is an *I* committed to a certain physical and inter-human world, who continues to tend towards his world despite handicaps and amputations and who, to this extent, does not recognize them *de jure.* [. . .] The body is the vehicle of being in the world, and having a body is, for a living creature, to be intervolved in a definite environment, to identify oneself with certain projects and be continually committed to them. In the self-evidence of this complete world in which manipulatable objects still figure, in the force of their movement which still flows towards him, and in which is still present the project of writing or playing the piano, the cripple still finds the guarantee of his wholeness. (*Phenomenology* 81–82)

Our habitual experience of living among objects that we can physically manipulate, objects that take a "definite" position in the "practical field" (82) around us, remains with us out of habit. Our "habit-body" continues to behave as it always has, ignoring the limitation of the "body at this moment" (82). Merleau-Ponty's emphasis on "commitment" to physical engagements with a particular world can be elegantly applied to one's commitments to a spouse or a child whose body has been part of that world and similarly engaged with it. In both cases physical proximity and emotional engagement are entwined. The person is, in Derrida's words, "no longer here, no longer there," but the places he was still are, as is our habitual physical relation to him—our bodily memories of the spaces through which he moved. Because these are physical habits, which we perform repeatedly, they make the loss continually renew itself. Again and again we make the mistake of positioning ourselves to touch the lost body, and these erroneous physical acts amount to our body's grief.

This cyclical reliving of loss bears a strong resemblance to the experience of phantom limb pain. Amputees continue to feel their limbs, or other body parts, after amputation and are shocked when, upon turning their eyes toward the limb, they see that it is gone. Their bodies feel as they have always felt: they reach for a telephone with a missing hand; they try to push open a door with a lost shoulder; they swing out of bed, step on both feet, and fall to the floor because one leg is gone. Ronald Melzack emphasizes that we shouldn't designate such experience as a failure or malfunction. "[T]he phantom represents the normal experience of the body. It is not a pathological entity due to a psychological aberration, or due to an abnormal functioning of the brain. It is the body we always feel. [. . .] It is evident that our experience of the body can occur without a body at all. We don't need a body to feel a body" (4). The neural matrix in the brain that defines the body image continues to recognize the missing limb despite sensory inputs showing that no limb exists. These people suffer because the way they feel their body in the world has survived the loss of the limb. "For the amputee, perceptual organization of bodily integrity is so stable that it resists change even though visual and proprioceptive information necessitate perceptual reorganization" (Chapman 170). While the phantom limb is an illusion, it is one based on stability; the way we have always felt our bodies stubbornly endures. Such phantoms are by no means a rare phenomenon. Occurring in over 80% of cases, the phantom is "so common that it is considered a 'normal' sequel to amputation" (Katz, "Individual Differences" 51).

Such a "normal" response to limb loss bears little resemblance to Freud's portrayal of "normal mourning."

> Each single one of the memories and situations of expectancy which demonstrate the libido's attachment to the lost object is met by the verdict of reality that the object no longer exists. [. . .] [F]irst one and then another memory is activated, and [. . .] the laments which always sound the same and are wearisome in their monotony nevertheless take their rise each time in some different unconscious source. (Freud 245, 255)

At the end of this process of "detaching the libido bit by bit" (256), the ego is "persuaded by the sum of the narcissistic satisfactions it derives from being alive to sever its attachment to the object that has been abolished" (255), and the individual emerges from the long mourning process suitably separated from the dead beloved.

But for sufferers of phantom limb pain, the repeated dissonance between perception and reality makes the pain worse rather than dissipating it. Phantom limbs often progress from feeling normal, to feeling clumsy, to feeling intensely painful, thus becoming "an overwhelming presence in the patient's awareness" (2). Melzack theorizes that such pain results from the repetitive neurological processes that continually attempt to define the limb's presence.

> I believe that the active neuromatrix, in the absence of modulating inputs from the limbs or body, produces a signature pattern that is transduced in the sentient neural hub into a hot or burning quality. The cramping pain [. . .] may be due to messages from the action-neuromodule to move muscles in order to produce movement. In the absence of feedback from the limbs, the messages to move the muscles become more frequent and "stronger" in the attempt to move the limb. (Melzack 13)

The similarity between Freud's and Melzack's descriptions of the process is striking: in both cases the mind cycles, continually returning to "the object that has been abolished"; in both cases the expectation is repeatedly met by the "verdict of reality." But with opposite results: In the neurological version, nothing takes the judicious role of the ego, weighing love of life against loss and choosing the first. The repetitive "laments" of Freud's mourners may be "wearisome in their monotony," but each one bespeaks another "bit" of the process being gradually accomplished. No such progress characterizes the increasingly insistent "messages" from the action-neuromodule; rather, their iteration becomes more purposeless and thus more grueling. Neurological memory, continually frustrated by the lack of exterior reassurance, creates a "signature pattern" that cycles with intensifying insistence. The brain, if you will, shrieks and beats the ground, tears its clothes, and pours ashes on its head, but it doesn't sever its attachments.

The hard distinction Freud draws between normal and pathological mourning has been revised over time. Melanie Klein, while still considering mourning an "illness" that the mourner must "overcome" (354), questions the systematic progression of Freud's model by suggesting that the mourner, like a developing child, "goes through a modified and transitory manic-depressive state" (354). John Bowlby attempts to disentangle the study of grief from that of depression, arguing that the emotional conflicts of mourning arise less from identification than from "a persistent, though disguised, striving to recover the lost person" (30).

Widows often manifest this desire by feeling the persistent, located presence of their lost husband; "the spouse is experienced as located somewhere specific and appropriate. Common examples are a particular chair or room which he occupied" (98). Bowlby thus rejects Freud's claim that detachment is necessary for normal mourning, arguing for "a continuing sense of the presence of the dead" (100), although he does continue to claim that mourning progresses in a "succession" or "sequence" of phases: numbing, yearning, disorganization, and reorganization (85). As John Archer has noted, the concept of "phases" or "stages" to grief, which emerges from Freud's positivistic presentation of grief work in "Mourning and Melancholia," continues to be the dominant metaphor for understanding bereavement, and the basic structure of amelioration through cyclic repetition remains in place (26).

Phantom limb sensations do diminish with time, but the process is rarely "monotonous," often generating more awkward and fantastic bodily experience than the original phantom. When a limb "fades," sections of the limb seem to dissolve, so that "the phantom hand or foot feels as if it were hanging, unattached, in empty space" (Katz, "Individual Differences" 52). Some phantoms "telescope," gradually pulling inward.

> The phantom is perceived gradually to approach the stump so that the hand is located in phenomenal space on a level with the elbow of the arm. As the process continues, [. . .] the amputee may find that the hand is protruding from, or attached to, the end of the stump. Later, the phantom hand may retract into the stump so that only the tips of the fingers jut out. (53)

Though gradual, this process is not entirely predictable; telescoping limbs can temporarily lengthen or shorten without warning. In the case of "shrinking" phantom limbs, "[a]dult amputees have reported the phantom to be the size of a doll's hand or a baby's hand[,] [. . .] a silver dollar[,] [. . .] and even as small as a postage stamp" (55). The shock experienced when one expects a limb and then perceives its absence is bad enough, but the healing process seems even more subject to bodily shocks as arms swell, shrink, and hang in mid-air. Indeed, such illusions would intensify the feelings of disorientation and disempowerment associated with the loss of a limb, rather than allowing them to gradually dissipate. The healing process of phantom limbs suggests that unexpected, even grotesque, assaults of somatic memory are more typical of the extended experience of loss than the slow, smooth disconnection Freud describes. According to Katz, the odd perceptual experiences that accompany fading, telescoping, and shrinking result not from a slow numbing of the nerves, a metaphor we often use to describe the mourning process, but from their intense activity. "The gradual fading of the phantom is thought to represent a perceptual correlate of the re-establishment of control over hyperactive or spontaneously active cells which subserve the phantom" ("Individual Differences" 55). It is the insistence of these cells, their constant recreation of first the full limb, then distorted or partial versions of it, that will not leave the sufferer in peace.

In order to apply the structure of neurological phantoms to the experience of grief, we must make the leap of considering another person's body an element of our own body image. Merleau-Ponty describes habitual engagement as a form of material incorporation.

> To get used to a hat, a car or a stick is to be transplanted into them, or conversely, to incorporate them into the bulk of our own body. Habit expresses our power of dilating our being-in-the-world, or changing our existence by appropriating fresh instruments. (*Phenomenology* 143)

Whereas Nicolas Abraham and Maria Torok use the term "incorporation" to describe a pathological fantasy of consuming the lost beloved (126), Merleau-Ponty and Grosz apply it to a dilation or extension of the *body's* edges to form a new silhouette that then engages with the spaces and structures of the surrounding world. V. S. Ramachandran, who emphasizes the "malleability" of the body image, makes the striking claim that "*Your own body* is a phantom, one that your brain has temporarily constructed purely for convenience" (58), one which can be easily reshaped by context. He describes an amputee with a "telescoped phantom hand" that could "reach" for an object placed a few feet away: it "felt as if it were zooming out to grab the cup" (42). This experiment suggests the existence of what Grosz calls a "zone of sensitivity outside the body, occupying its surrounding space, which is incorporated into the body" (79). Grosz, in her discussion of Paul Schilder's theories, explicitly includes other bodies among the objects we incorporate into our own. Something that "comes in contact with the surface of the body and remains there long enough will be incorporated into the body image—clothing, jewelry, other bodies, objects" (80). Grosz's use of the term "surface" seems odd here because her description supposes the dissipation of bodily surface. Rather than just the surface of the skin, our body image includes the overlain surfaces of clothing or jewelry, as well as the adjacent surfaces of objects and other bodies. The body image thus extends beyond our skin, across intervening space, and to our loved ones, who are physically attached to the surface of our bodies at various times throughout the day but who are more often annexed to us by a thin band of intervening space. Their bodies become incorporated into our body image by the repetitive and enduring interplay of reciprocal gestures across and through this intermediate bridge of space. The knowledge of another body on the other side lets us understand our bodies as companioned, accompanied, beloved.

When we lose the ones we love, we mourn them, in part, by continuing to feel the vitality of this intervening space as the dilation of our body image, and we know terrible confusion when the space turns out not to be *between* two bodies but only *around* the edges of ours. Why do the grief-stricken yearn for the beloved's touch? It is not so much, Phelan argues, that they recognize the impossibility of ever touching as that they continually expect that touch, and even fleetingly feel it. The physical imbalances and disturbances, the repeated, irritating confusion over that expected-but-then-absent body, are expressed as the desire to touch. Abraham and Torok's notion of incorporation serves as a useful contrast here. Normal introjection, they argue, allows for the loss to be discarded, but abnormal mourning involves the incorporation of a spatial construct, or crypt, "complete with its own topography' (130). Abraham and Torok thus make explicit Freud's imagistic equation of normalcy with motion and detachment, and of pathology with location in a particular space. Yet the actual "topography" of the life we lived with our lost loved ones, the halls and rooms and beds, remains with us, and so the lost bodies seem also to remain, not encrypted within us but pressing against and moving past our body's edges.

Gabriel Josipovici, discussing our reliance on familiar objects, offers a useful description of such tactile expectation.

> It has something to do with trusting things, with taking them for granted as allies and companions rather than enemies and obstructions. If the garden wall were not there, reassuringly under my hand, I would feel that something was wrong. [. . .] [L]ike the mother's hand which the child instinctively takes as he sets out for a walk. He does not take the hand to confirm anything or to test anything; he merely takes it because that is what one does at the start of a walk. Yet if the hand is withdrawn the world collapses. (29)

As his hand moves past where the other hand, or the garden wall, should be, the character of the space that is being felt undergoes changes. Like a sudden shift in density or temperature, we feel the shift from intervening to exterior space as a "collapse" of the body image back to the surface of our skin. Such a collapse also occurs when we realize that our dead loved one is not beside us—we suddenly know that we are physically alone. Josipovici describes the garden wall under his hand as "reassuring," even though taken for granted. Each time he touches it, he feels assured again. Similarly, each time we misperceive the bodily presence, we feel dispossessed again—rebereaved.

✣ ✣ ✣

The suffering caused by phantom limbs derives not from the loss itself but from the sufferer's belief in the limb's enduring presence. This belief manifests itself physically either as collapse or as contortion. When an amputee feels his "normal" body and steps on the phantom leg, he collapses or stumbles. Like Mr. Ramsay, he moves his body in the old way even though his world has changed. Phantom limb pain occurs when the limb feels abnormally present but it is actually abnormally absent. His body registers the dissonance between these two abnormalities as pain, or the contortions necessary to avoid pain. Literary portrayals of grief that emphasize embodiment present the bereaved with compromised bodies, stumbling or contorting as they fail to adjust to the physical postures and environments their losses have left to them. Those which portray collapse gesture toward comedy, presenting the bereaved as somewhat ridiculous. Falling through a void is risky, after all; you're liable to hurt yourself or at least look foolish. Benighted and drowsy, stretching and leaning toward the wife who is not there, Mr. Ramsay must fall, try to right himself, swerve, stub a toe. Portrayals that emphasize continued contiguity with the lost body present a more heroic sufferer whose physical maladjustments, like those of Wills's father at the sink, still retain an air of pathetic absurdity. Whether comic or tragic, such portrayals make us uncomfortable. Whether grief emerges as torture or mercifully resolves itself into slapstick, we are mostly irritated and embarrassed by the indecorousness of the scene and are made to feel somewhat complicit in the griever's vulnerability.

In "In Memoriam A.H.H.," Tennyson compares his mourning for Hallam to that of a widower who believes that his wife lies beside him and then "moves his doubtful arms, and feels / Her place is empty" (13.3–4). Like Mr. Ramsay, Tennyson's widower experiences a moment of misapprehension, of reaching expectantly toward an absent body and feeling instead the "place" where that body belongs. His own arm, so habitually contiguous with his wife's back as they lie in bed, has over time developed its own somatic intelligence, which has now become confused and "doubtful." The widower "weeps a loss forever new / A void where heart on heart reposed; / And where warm hands have prest and closed, / Silence, till I be silent too" (13.6–8). The full space between "warm hands" just before they "pressed and closed" becomes a "void" as the body image retreats to the surface of the skin. Tennyson's repetition of "where" points again to the physical location of such experience. When he describes visiting Hallam's house, Tennyson focuses on the awkward moment when, standing outside the door, he again experiences the expectation of Hallam's touch.

> Dark house, by which once more I stand
> >Here in the long unlovely street,
> >Doors, where my heart was used to beat
> So quickly, waiting for a hand,
> A hand that can be clasped no more—
> >Behold me, for I cannot sleep,
> >And like a guilty thing I creep
> At earliest morning to the door. (7.1–8)

He stands in the same place, with the same physical posture, experiencing the apprehension of a nearby body. He portrays this cycle of expectation and realization in the alternation of "once more" and "no more." The hand should be there; he waits for it, reaches for it, and continually returns to the same spot to try again, making the loss "forever new."

Tennyson must "creep" "like a guilty thing" to Hallam's door because he knows he looks a fool, taking up, once again, his remembered posture to await his friend's touch. No doubt he is a familiar sight to the neighbors. "Behold me," he invites the reader, encouraging a sort of indelicate voyeurism. Donald Hall also portrays the experience of phantom presence as a foolish, indelicate accident. He concludes "Letter at Christmas" from his book *Without* with the following passage, which also allows us access to an intimate, physical act of grieving.

> [I] wash my hands at the sink
> as I look at Mount Kearsarge
> through the kitchen window
> where you stood to watch the birds.
> Often I came up behind you
> and pushed against your bottom.
> This year, home from unwrapping

presents with grandchildren
and children, sick with longing,
I press my penis
into zinc and butcherblock. (67)

Like Tennyson, Hall portrays his expectation of the missing body as debilitating—the accident of being in that position relative to the sink and the window renders him "sick with longing," just as it rendered Tennyson sleepless. But Hall's mildly bawdy memory, and his explicit description of his penis colliding with hard kitchen surfaces, make even more explicit the ludicrousness, the pathetic clumsiness, of the grieving body. Whenever we reach for the hand that is not there, we stumble and fall. Such misplaced physical confidence amounts to a pratfall; the slap-stick comedian always imagines a world of friendly supports and always finds a void. Mr. Ramsay seems rather laughable stumbling about in his dressing gown—a befuddled Scrooge, nightcap askew. Woolf extends the phrase "his arms, though stretched out, remained empty" so that we see him lurching forward, like Karloff's monster, in an endless second of pained confusion.

This is humiliating, of course, especially for Mr. Ramsay who of all people doesn't want to appear infantile and ridiculous. The mourner becomes a child again, learning to walk, reaching for a hand he doesn't find, stumbling through unexpected emptiness, and (if anyone is watch-ing) embarrassing himself. Grief always has the power to make people lurch under its great weight to a nearly laughable degree. The power of *King Lear* in performance derives in part from the way old men do become babes again; Lear and Gloucester trip and fall about the stage, at the perilous edge of slapstick. When, in his most intense expression of grief, Lear staggers onto the stage carrying Cordelia, the ungainly physi-cality of his pain is realized—absence of life becomes something so heav-ily present that it makes knees buckle—and actors must struggle to keep the distracting bodily logistics of the scene from undercutting its emo-tional depth. Funny anecdotes of dropped Cordelias and herniated Lears abound. But when that heavy weight of grief is invisible, the absurdity of the bereaved's clumsiness seems all the more pronounced.

Many people with phantom limbs do not simply feel the missing part as present, but as recalcitrant and ungainly—causing the whole body to become clumsy or contorted.

In some people, the arm is continually felt in an abnormal position and cannot voluntarily be moved into a more comfortable one. In one person, the phantom arm was felt to extend straight out at the shoulder and at a right angle to the body; the phantom was so vivid that he turned sideways to walk through a doorway so that the phantom would not hit the wall. (Melzack 3)

The sufferer twists and turns his way through rooms, dodging to the side to make way for an arm that, in its absence, becomes more physically present. When asked, they say, "My arm is cast in cement, doctor," or "It's immobilized in a block of ice" (Ramachandran 43). Because he contorts to avoid an arm that is not there, his behavior appears ludicrous, a Monty Python funny walk, a Dickensian tick, but also deeply disturbing to watch. A grieving body compromised by its enduring contiguity with a lost loved one becomes similarly contorted. In his memoir *Heaven's Coast*, Mark Doty describes how, after losing his partner to AIDS, he suffers terrible back problems. Having repeatedly carried his beloved's body while he still lived, Doty's still bends under a heavy weight. "I'd hobble, face to the earth, hunched and clenched, unable to even straighten up enough to look at the sky. I feel more profoundly misaligned than I ever have, literally bent out of shape, my parts in a jumble of unhappy connections" (118). While Mr. Ramsay's and Donald Hall's bodies instinctively re-create habitual moments of affection, Doty's body can't give up even the most grueling, strenuous postures of caregiving. His body adopts the shape it held caring for his partner's form, even though this shape bends and painfully misaligns his own. Joel Katz describes how for amputees "the phantom limb may assume the same painful posture as that of the real limb prior to amputation, especially if the arm or leg had been immobilized for a prolonged period" ("The Reality" 159). What remains is not simply the presence of an ungainly appendage, but the pain that was (or could have been) experienced when the living limb was twisted, cramped, or controlled, even for its own sake. In Doty's case this twisting of his own limbs was a necessary part of caregiving. "[H]ow hard I worked, how long, to hold Wally in a space of relative safety, a zone in which it was possible for him to live as long and well as he could. My arms feel so tired, weary of controlling, protecting, lifting" (123). Here the postures of love are neither graceful nor pain-free; caregiving seems to involve bending and reaching as Aeneas did, twisting his body to foster both the old and the young. The body image dilates, absorbing the beloved's body into a "space of relative safety" composed of both bodies in combination. According to Merleau-Ponty, our sense of being depends on an understanding of our bodies as "the pivot of the world" (82). How much more difficult it must be to make the world pivot on two bodies;

once such a precarious balance is achieved, what happens when one is taken away? Parents, nurses, and spouses lean and twist painfully to create this zone of protection, often hurting their own arms, necks, and backs. When the cared-for body disappears, but the "zone" remains as part of one's own body image, the precarious poses of love, and their pain, remain also.

Such portrayals return us to the bereaved body, focusing upon the body that still lives and loves. Both the humor and the painfulness of reading these passages come from the reader's apprehending the writhing and contorting of the griever. This inappropriate intimacy in which Hall, Tennyson, or Doty place us has to do not simply with their opening their hearts, or their bedrooms, to us, but with their allowing us to understand them as physically compromised mortals. To celebrate and demand the return of the lost beloved's body, they must let us perceive their own compromised embodiment. Davis's discussion of the uncanny is relevant here. He argues that while Freud labels the dismembered body *unheimlich*, it is the familiarity of the repressed, fragmented body that we must acknowledge. "Dominant culture has an investment in seeing the disabled, therefore, as uncanny, as something outside the home, unfamiliar, while in fact where is the disabled body found if not at home?" (142). By inviting us into their homes to experience the intimate bodily aspects of their grief, these writers show how thoroughly the lost body remains with them and how fundamentally fragmented their own bodies are.

These literary representations undercut the reader's power to perceive these grieving figures as smoothly symbolic literary images. Early in *To the Lighthouse,* Mr. Ramsay strides up and down the lawn reciting "Someone had blundered." He wields the quotation in order to place his identity, imagining himself in the literary image of a military hero and, later, as a dying explorer. But in the middle of the book, as he stumbles about in the hallways grasping for his wife, we perceive his blunder, his error, through his blundering body. David Mitchell and Sharon Snyder have described how writers traditionally use the disabled body as a material ground for bearing meaning that will not adhere to its smoothly functioning counterpart (64). By adapting this strategy, writers portraying grief make the body that has been impaired by grieving capable of bearing the dead.

The sort of grieving I am describing does not operate through the construction of the stable, monumental images that we come to expect of literature. Phelan and Derrida demonstrate how naturally we favor visual language when discussing the dead; they also suggest that only visual models can serve a memorializing function. Pictures can be looked at, pondered, physically or mentally held up for inspection. Can the sort of fleeting perceptual illusion I have been discussing here do the same? How do we hold up or hold on to lasting perceptions of touch? Ramachandran's recent experiments with neural remapping show that the apprehension of phantom limbs can be incited by the habitual acts of other parts of the body. Because of the interpenetration of cortical regions, "every time Tom smiles or moves his face and lips, the impulses activate the 'hand' area of his cortex, creating the illusion that his hand is still there" (33). Tom need not see something worth reaching for to feel his phantom; he needs only to smile, and his lost body is given to him.

Unlike visual memorializing—dwelling on pictures, reimagining scenes from the past—bodily memorializing emerges spontaneously from habitual bodily acts. Rather than Thomas, or the angel at the tomb, we can think of this sort of memorializing through the story of the apostles on the road to Emmaus, who, subtly and without seeing, apprehend the physical presence of their lost loved one.

> And, behold, two of them went that same day to a village called Emmaus, which was from Jerusalem about threescore furlongs. And they talked together of all these things which had happened. And it came to pass, that, while they communed together and reasoned, Jesus himself drew near, and went with them. But their eyes were holden that they should not know him. [. . .] And it came to pass, as he sat at meat with them, he took bread, and blessed it, and brake, and gave to them. And their eyes were opened, and they knew him; and he vanished out of their sight. (Luke 24:13–31)

In contrast to Thomas's dramatic confrontation, this seems like the stuff of comedy. The two men walk ahead, eyes forward, arguing and holding forth about the death of their beloved leader, farcically unaware as they walk, talk, and sit down to dinner that he is with them. The ease with which they accept him into their company, keeping stride, shoulder to shoulder or falling back, swaying and jostling as the conversation flows, suggests how easily we take up habitual bodily engagements with the dead. Christ remains as the familiar body beside them on the road or at the table; his presence seems the most natural thing in the world. They walked and talked this way as Christ's apostles. Their habit of doing so even after his death represents a living physical memorial.

We shape our movement through, or stillness in, the space around that other body, which, like the apostles, we're used to feeling just beside us. But when we turn our heads or our attention, when the apostles actually *look* at Jesus, when the amputee looks at the place his arm should be, the body is gone and we are "terrified and affrighted" at that sudden disjunction between presence and absence. The world collapses. Grief leaves one compromised, exposed, a stumbling, ridiculous child. And yet that childish stumbling offers a physically enacted proof of love. We're never sure that Mr. Ramsay does love his wife until we see his lonely grasping in that hall. We love others with our bodies until their bodies are suddenly gone. Then we continue to love them by expecting their presence, by seeming to feel it, or just by walking, eating, moving through the world with physical gestures designed to accommodate them. The apostles on the road to Emmaus are obeying Christ's command at the Last Supper without even knowing it; they sit, they eat and drink, and suddenly he is with them. Our bodies can't help remembering other bodies—even when we don't know it, even when we don't want to. This physical awareness of loss serves as both grief and memorial.

Chapter 2

Mess and Memory

When my parents passed away and my brothers and I were left to clean out the house, we expected the worst. My father was wheelchair-bound and hadn't been upstairs in decades, and my mother's vascular dementia had led to peculiar housekeeping practices, so we were prepared for heavy cleaning. But it wasn't the size or dirtiness of the task that defeated us; it was the power of our own memories. Each grubby, broken toy, each battered box of school art projects or tacky souvenirs, stopped us in our tracks. I would turn a corner to find one of my brothers standing, staring abstractedly at a grimy action figure or a bent cufflink, sometimes smiling, always stalled and entranced. After two days we fled, overwhelmed by the number and intensity of unexpected ghosts raised by these soiled and useless items. We hired a cleaning company: people to whom such speaking objects were mute, people who could disinterestedly claw through and dispose of them without being touched by the memories they carried. The challenge we all face cleaning out basements and attics is primarily one of being disarmed by materialized memory. Objects become repositories of memory, making touch itself a mnemonic, as well as a haptic, act, and the longer one has lived in a home, the more extensive this materialization becomes.

Gerontologists who study place attachment among the elderly address the complex relationship among self, space, and habit when elders identify with their homes. M. Powell Lawton, Robert L. Rubinstein, and Graham D. Rowles are among those who have pioneered the field of qualitative gerontology, which promotes the gathering of contextualized data about the emotional and psychological experience of aging through personal interaction with elders. These researchers have found that long-time home residence represents a crucial imaginative structure through which elders define themselves and their life stories. In this chapter I will investigate the role of tactility in domestic memory by focusing on the process of material self-representation in the homes of the elderly. The interchange between memory and environment is always at work in the home, but it is particularly apparent, and particularly critical, in the homes of the elderly. Because elderly people tend to lean more heavily on their home environment, and because they are often forced to choose between leaving this memory-laden space behind or becoming debilitated by caring for it, this process of material self-representation assumes even more crucial, and often painful, significance for them. Novelists such as Doris Lessing, Pat Barker, Muriel Spark, and Barbara Pym, all of whom portray the daily lives of the elderly, dwell on the operation of self-defining metaphor in domestic space, demonstrating the perils associated with environmental self-representation. Domestic fiction that dwells on the investigation of personal history, like Charles Dickens's *Bleak House* or Arthur Conan Doyle's *Sherlock Holmes* stories, demonstrate the power of space to place material limitations on memory and thus on the representation of life stories.

Scholars who study the home life of the elderly typically argue for the value of remaining in the home because of the comfort and support that familiar surroundings and objects provide. "It is a self that is embodied in the home. And this appears to be especially the case for those who live alone" (Rubinstein et al. 82). How do we interpret the phrase "embodied in": has the home has become a physical correlate to the self, or is the elderly person only a fully embodied self in the familiar environment of the home? This ambiguity is apparent in the two, somewhat contradictory, metaphors of navigation and amalgamation employed by gerontologists when describing how life history is represented in the home. Leon Pastalan and Janice Barnes, for example, argue that elders find great comfort in "smooth routines": habitual physical behaviors resulting in effortless navigation through the home (83). Pastalan and Barnes point to David Seamon's studies of "at-homeness" in which "a person who is at home can move fluidly through the dwelling because the body-subject knows that space intimately" (Seamon 79). Seamon gives the example of an elderly woman finding string by going to a bureau and opening a drawer without even thinking about it. Scholars who emphasize habits that create a sense of safety through ritualized behaviors tend to portray elders' relation to the home in terms of movement. Describing the environmental behaviors of the rural elderly, Rowles dwells on the importance of routine motion.

> Over time the establishment of a regular set of paths results in these
> routes becoming ingrained in the individual's subconscious. A "body
> awareness" of the setting, functioning much like an automatic pilot,
> may facilitate ongoing participation in an environment that otherwise
> might be beyond the physiological and cognitive capabilities of the
> individual. (142)

Yet intimately entwined with this habitual engagement with the spaces
of the home is an apprehension of having no boundaries between the
self and home—of the blending of oneself with the home. Amalgamation with one's environment, which Rowles calls "insideness," is the
other main metaphor employed in these studies. "[A] sense of physical insideness, of being almost physiologically melded into the environment, results from an intimacy with its physical configuration stemming
from the rhythm and routine of using the space over many years" (146).
The bodily awareness of the home's spatial dynamics results in a loss
of boundary between self and environment; the words "intimacy" and
"insideness" suggest a nearly physiological union.

In her novel *Union Street*, Barker portrays the last few days spent by

Robert Rubinstein and Patricia Parmalee also argue that elderly people who remain in their homes but become spatially limited by physical
frailty experience a bodily identification with their environment.

> [S]ubjectively, the boundaries between self and object are blurred.
> [. . .] [T]he home itself "becomes" the person, and she believes herself
> unable to live without the home. In effect place takes on a role that
> supplements the self, becoming a tangible embodiment of the personal
> identity that is itself, at least in its corporeal form, under duress. (152)

The relationship between home and occupant involves a supportive
interdependence in which boundaries become soft and overlap.

In her novel *Union Street*, Barker portrays the last few days spent by
Alice Bell in the home she can no longer manage. Despite the extreme
discomfort of her life, Alice takes pleasure in her sense of amalgamation
with her home.

> Whenever she moved newspapers stirred and rustled all around her.
> The bed was full of them. [. . .] A stranger coming into the room would
> hardly have noticed, at first, that there was a body in the bed, for Alice's
> emaciated frame scarcely raised the covers, and her skin, over the

years, had yellowed to the same shade as the pillowcases and the wall: smoke-cured. [. . .] The smoke formed layers of soot on all the furniture. You could dust it one minute, and it would be there again the next.

Still she loved the house. Over the years it had become a refuge. Finally almost an extension of her own body. (212–14)

Barker uses smoke and soot as an image of the pervasive dissolution of the self into the surfaces of the house. The comparisons of Alice's body to wallpaper and a "smoke-cured" ham offer a mildly comedic demonstration of her physical amalgamation with her environment. The grotesque potential of the scene is subverted by Barker's emphasis on the comfort Alice feels; the "body in the bed" may be cadaverous and dirty, but "she loved the house."

The home of an elderly person brings together two models of embodied memory that have traditionally been separate; we can describe them as the memory palace and the memory mirror. The memory palace is a familiar mnemonic strategy first proposed by Cicero in *De Oratore* and described at length in Quintilian's *Institutio Oratoria* as the "Method of Loci." The orator is encouraged to support his memory with the specific features of a house.

> Some place is chosen of the largest possible extent and characterised by the utmost possible variety, such as a spacious house divided into a number of rooms. [. . .] The first thought is placed, as it were, in the forecourt; the second, let us say, in the living-room; the remainder are placed in due order all round the *impluvium* and entrusted not merely to bedrooms and parlours, but even to the care of statues and the like. This done, as soon as the memory of the facts requires to be revived, all these places are visited in turn and the various deposits are demanded from their custodians, as the sight of each recalls the respective details. (221–23)

Implicit in this approach is that orderly surroundings make memory possible, allowing us to find stored memories as easily as we can find the solid and definable features of a building. Memory depends upon the yoking of vision and movement; mental images linked to actually seen objects can be recalled by moving through the remembered spaces of the house. Our ability to "place" mental images in parts of a building corresponds to our placement of our bodies within its rooms by opening up a series of well-proportioned mental spaces in which to deposit memory.

Dena Shenk, Kazumi Kuwahara, and Diane Zablotsky, who study

elderly widows' attachment to their homes, adopt the "lifecourse per-spective" in which "[e]ach person's journey through life can be viewed as a road map, offering many alternative routes to many alternative des-tinations" (158). This topographical model for life can be mapped onto the home. "These assumptions led us to believe that the home, and its contents, would represent anchors in various ways to the woman's past role as wife (and mother) and provide representations and guideposts to her future life as a widow" (158). The physical organization of the home thus becomes a representation not only of the owner's identity but also of her life story. For an elderly homeowner, as for Quintilian's orator, space has a narrative function; the home, with its various familiar routes and smooth routines, offers a spatial representation of the life narrative.

When Alice is forced to leave her home, she establishes her connec-tion to it one last time through navigation. "She began to wander about the house, opening and shutting drawers, caressing each battered object that had accompanied her through life. Everything was steeped in mem-ory" (237). Alice moves through the space, her smooth routes allowing her easy access to familiar objects that support her identity. Her motion through the house becomes identified with her motion "through life," and the objects become the sort of "guideposts" or "anchors" described by Shen, Kuwahara, and Zablotsky.

While the memory palace focuses on habit, the symbolic power of possessions is central to other theories of memory. Jean Beaudrillard, in *The System of Objects*, attends to the way objects mirror one's identity.

> Collections invite us to come through the door and see how their own-ers are mirrored in them. [The object's] absolute singularity [. . .] arises from the fact of being possessed by me—and this allows me, in turn, to recognize myself in the object as an absolutely singular being[,] [. . .] thereby contributing to the creation of a total environment, to that total-ization of images of the self. (89–90)

The memory mirror emphasizes identification with rather than navi-gation of the environment. In a "total environment," memory can be accessed by any and all visible objects. Robert Rubinstein, Janet Kilbride, and Sharon Nagy point out that to elderly homeowners, "personal pos-sessions and objects" are "more than just shrines to the past, since their efficacy is often in the present, in that they help to bring the past into the present when the past may have been forgotten or overwhelmed" (83). The self as present body and as past history exist side by side, with pos-sessions yoking them together.

> [W]alls of personal photographs, scrapbooks, collections, furniture, and
> all the myriad of objects and objectifications embodied in the home
> may at times serve to direct and stiffen consciousness of self and act in
> a sense ritually to reinforce or remind the person of who he or she was
> and still is lest the self be forgotten or misplaced with the difficulties of
> everyday life. (82)

Transcending time, these objects unite the past and present self—the
"was and still is." The memory mirror functions not through narrative
but through symbol; objects allow a quick, instantaneous access to a
significant experience. The atemporality of this operation is apparent in
Rubinstein and Parmalee's description of objects as "lightning rods for
memory" (153). We see our past suddenly illuminated as a dazzlingly
bright image rather than an extended story. Indeed, photographs—particularly of weddings or vacations—are often among the objects collected
and displayed, along with china, trophies, and souvenirs; the home thus
becomes a "total environment" of self-mirroring surfaces in which virtually every object serves to "stiffen" identity (Rubenstein 82).

Both of these approaches to memory are important to the functioning of seniors in their environments, yet both are susceptible to physical frailty. The materiality of the self-embodying environment is, so to
speak, the rub. A smooth routine is not an abstract arc across a map but
actual motion of a physical body through doors and rooms, past dress-
ers and chairs, and among touchable, self-mirroring objects. Tangibility
is a central aspect of mnemonic mirroring, as Russell W. Belk points out.
"[T]he sacralizing mechanism [for treasured objects] is contagion from
the proximity of the object to a special time, place, event, or person in
our lives. [. . .] We seek to tangibly memorialize these parts of our lives
with various souvenirs and mementos" (40). By touching the object that
was touched by an important event, one can be reinfected with the past;
memory becomes like dust or the molecules of Caesar's air that we are all
supposed to be breathing. Alice Bell moves through her home "caressing
each battered object." Rubinstein and Parmalee agree that "one key role
of objects is merely to be at hand, to function as reminders" (153). In her
discussion of souvenirs, Susan Stewart also emphasizes the mnemonic
power of touch while noting its corollary powerlessness.

> From the child's original metonymic displacement to the love object,
> the sensual rules souvenirs of this type. The acute sensation of the
> object—its perception by hand taking precedence over its perception
> by eye—promises, and yet does not keep the promise of, *reunion*. (139)

It is the unreliability of this material link to the past, its power to invoke rather than re-create, that makes tactility both seductive and frustrating. Rubinstein and Parmalee point out that physical frailty tends to shift the balance from visually based memory to tangibly based memory. "With decreased spatial functioning the role of cherished personal objects as such facilitators may increase" (154).

The cruel irony, however, is that with decreased spatial functioning, one's ability to handle those cherished personal objects will also decrease. For the infirm elderly, the relationship to space is frequently character-ized by "environmental centralization." Elders often establish a central location, the kitchen table or living room sofa, and cease to utilize more peripheral rooms of the house. "In the case of Mrs. Quinn, centraliza-tion means giving up the use of areas of her home, such as the second bedroom, most of the basement, and the backyard, and restricting most of her living to a central corridor in her home" (Rubinstein 144). In order to preserve her present identity, Mrs. Quinn becomes distanced from whatever objectifications of herself are stored in the abandoned parts of her house. Even the immediate space around her becomes crowded with "important functional items" (Rubinstein et al. 85) such as medications, vacuum cleaners, and clothing that prevent her free movement. While environmental centralization brings crucial functional objects to hand, it distances one from souvenirs and mementos, and thus also from the ability to touch and be "infected by" the memories they carry.

For obvious reasons, environmental centralization also places signifi-cant limitations on the smooth navigation associated with the memory palace. Mrs. Quinn has a very different relationship to space than Quin-tilian's orator. Inhabiting her central corridor, she can't place mnemonic signals upon spacious and elaborate architectural features; she has aban-doned her "smooth routines" and the support they offer. Her inability to move through and see her house enacts her inability to marshal the sort of narrative memory that depends upon such motion.

Doris Lessing, writing under the pseudonym Jane Somers, in *The Diary of a Good Neighbour* portrays environmental centralization as the progression from motion to stasis and enclosure, with domestic space collapsing inward on its inhabitant. Janna, a stylish, successful magazine editor, begins helping an impoverished elderly woman named Maudie Fowler and, painfully, gains imaginative access to her life.

> I am thinking of how Maudie Fowler one day could not trouble herself
> to clean out her front room, because there was so much junk in it, and
> then she left it and left it; going in sometimes, thinking, well, it's not so

bad. Meanwhile she was keeping the back room and the kitchen spotless. [. . .] She wasn't feeling well, and didn't bother, once, twice—and
then her room was not really cleaned, only the floor in the middle of the
room sometimes, and she learned not to look around the edges under
the bed. Her kitchen was last. She scrubbed it and washed shelves,
but then things began to slide. [. . .] And at last, she was upright in
her thick shell of black, her knickers not entirely clean, but not so bad.
[. . .] But she, Maudie Fowler, was still there [. . .] and everything has
collapsed around her, it's too difficult, too much. (55)

The repetitive motions of cleaning, and the cycles of motion through the
rooms of the house necessary to complete them, occur in smaller arcs.
Rather than navigating the front room, Maudie only goes in and out; the
circle of cleaning in the back room closes to a small space on the floor
and then disappears. Finally, the environment presses so closely upon
her that it becomes a sort of carapace, and the only distinction is between
her "upright" form and the "collapse" of everything else. Maudie hopes
to stand rather than fall, like the last column of a ruin, but any hope of
movement has ceased to exist. Navigation has been completely displaced
by amalgamation.

In his discussion of Quintilian's memory palace, architectural theorist
Malcolm Quantrill points out that "[o]rder is the essential prerequisite of
architectural space. [. . .] As the orator moves around the remembered
building in his imagination, he will find all the points of his speech in
the correct order, since the order is fixed in the sequence of spaces in the
building" (12). But order is not always a characteristic of the home, especially the elderly home, as Lawton's studies demonstrate. Baudrillard
distinguishes between collection and accumulation on the grounds that
the collector has a "door open onto culture" because he collects objects of
"preservation, trade, social ritual exhibition." Collecting thus "involves
the social world outside, and embraces human relationships" (103). The
accumulator, on the other hand, has "regress[ed] to the ultimate abstraction of a delusional state" (106) and withdrawn from the world. Maudie
must literally regress from the front room because there is "so much junk
in it." Accumulations block our way through the door while also blocking the messages they may contain about their owners' lives.

We often identify senility as the moment when the self-identifying
passion of collecting gets applied to accumulation. We become wary
whenever we find motion impeded as living space becomes storage
space; when we have to step around piles of books and old clothes;
when broken appliances remain in the room. Tacky souvenirs or piled

magazines cease to be quaint when they begin to block hallways. In such circumstances the value of objects to access the past is overshadowed by disruption of the narrative motion through the house that would attest to its owner's agency. In *Elders Living Alone,* Rubinstein, Kilbride, and Nagy offer the case of Mr. January, whose living space is no longer navigable.

> Mr. January's own apartment was incredibly filthy and messy. He did not clean because he was unable to do much physical work and, in addition, was too depressed. He had to muster his limited energy for projects that were more vital, such as shopping or washing his clothes. [. . .] Most of the living room furniture was covered with a thick coat of dust and was used by Mr. January primarily for storage. Beside the broken and dusty furniture, major features of the room were several hundred books (he was an avid reader) and a large, nonfunctioning refrigerator (he had damaged this beyond repair when he tried to defrost the freezer using an awl and had punctured the freezer lining). (138)

This passage offers various examples of how Mr. January's life is robbed of its narrative elements. Quantrill describes the memory palace as a "storage system" which allows its viewer to "recall the salient" memory instantly (12). Mr. January's living room is used for "storage" in a different sense; things are stored here which impede motion and thus memory. The refrigerator disaster, which ought by now to have dematerialized into a story told parenthetically and with some humor, remains an object blocking his path. His books, which served to help mirror his identity ("he was an avid reader"), now only place physical limits on their reader. Rather than objects containing stories through and in which he could represent himself, they have become blocks impeding his motion. "Memories are motionless," writes Gaston Bachelard, "and the more securely they are fixed in space, the sounder they are" (8). For Mr. January, however, motionlessness locks memory into the immediate past of physical frailty rather than a life course.

While elderly people use both motion and mirroring to access memory, these strategies have an uneasy alliance, and their mutually competitive qualities become apparent when elders lose their ability to move freely through their houses and interact with their possessions. The practical perils implicit in this competition have been characterized by Lawton's scale of "environmental press." Lawton portrays this precarious dance of the frail body through a familiar, though increasingly treacherous, domestic landscape. While their homes abound in "poorly lit work areas or pathways, furniture blocking access to frequently used areas, rugs or other surfaces with uncertain footing," elderly homeowners have adapted to these hazards and don't want to leave because "a change would require both divesting themselves of some of these possessions and learning a whole new repertory of traffic patterns" (61–62). Lawton insightfully combines the metaphors of navigation and amalgamation, showing us smooth routes littered with hazards that overlap with or impinge upon the body. The home becomes a busy street, and "the myriad of objects and objectifications" (Rubinstein et al. 82) in it becomes encroaching traffic. The irony confronted by the elderly is that their self-representations in the home increase in importance as their ability to engage in this self-representation (through either motion or mirroring) becomes increasingly limited. Furthermore, the process of representation is undercut by the very materials that bring it about—the physical layout of house and the treasured objects in it.

✛ ✛ ✛

Literary works that focus on the way memory operates in domestic space attend closely to the sort of metaphorical engagements we see in quantitative gerontology. The elderly home is more like a fictional world than most spaces, because every path and every object is likely to be "storied." As we have seen, the power of mementos to bring the past into the present operates symbolically; it could also be said that literary images operate like mementos in that they serve as vivid signifiers, linking characters to their past selves or crucial parts of their histories. Just as smooth routes allow the elision between physical motion and life story, physical motion often becomes entwined with the motion of the narrative in literary works that focus on the management of memory. For the remainder of this chapter, I will address literary works by Barbara Pym, Pat Barker, Muriel Spark, Charles Dickens, and Arthur Conan Doyle that either explicitly portray the self-representation of the elderly or address the material limitations placed on identity by the operation of memory.

In *Quartet in Autumn*, Barbara Pym portrays the gradual decline of Marcia Ivory, a retired single woman who begins hoarding clothes, food, and milk bottles even as she starves herself to death. Marcia's ability to engage in the sort of physical rituals that reinforce memory becomes disrupted by the increasing squalor of her environment.

Marcia still missed the old cat, Snowy, and one evening she found herself particularly reminded of him when she came across one of his dishes in the cupboard under the sink. She was surprised and a little upset to notice that it still had some dried-up fragments of Kittikat adhering to it. [. . .] The finding of the dish gave her a desire to visit the cat's grave which was somewhere at the bottom of the garden. When Snowy had died, Mr. Smith, who had lived next door before Nigel and Priscilla came, had dug a grave and Marcia had laid Snowy in it, his body wrapped in a piece of old blue ripple-cloth dressing gown which he used to sleep on. [. . .] She had not marked the grave in any way, but she remembered where it was, for when she walked down the path she would think Snowy's grave; but as time went on she forgot the exact spot and now, in the season of high summer with the weeds flourishing, she could not find it at all. [. . .] Then it occurred to her that if she were to dig in that bit of the garden, she would surely come upon the grave, perhaps uncover a fragment of the blue-ripple-cloth and even find the bones. She went to the shed and fetched a spade, but it was very heavy and if she had ever wielded it in the past, she was certainly unable now. (139–40)

Pym acknowledges the power of an object (the dish) to reignite a personal story and also to be related to a particular physical motion, which in turn creates a sensory memory of another cherished object (the cat's body). Both senses of the "contagious" quality of memory are apparent in Pym's delicate balancing of disgusting images—such as old cat food on a dish, weeds, and old bones—with Marcia's nostalgia for a friendly neighbor, a well-tended garden, and her lost pet. The very dirtiness of the dish allows her to remember her pet more vividly, while the weediness of the garden prevents her from reenacting the motion that served as a physical tribute to it. Her inability to "dig in that bit of the garden," something any gardener would recognize as a self-defining act, cuts her off both from the cat itself and from her past self as a gardener. Marcia's odd desire to dig up the cat's body, something she never wanted to do when she could just walk by it on the path, seems more accurately a desire to exhume a memory that became unmoored when her smooth route through the garden was lost. As long as she could navigate her garden, she could accept the absence of the cat's actual body, but once memory is attached to neither object nor motion, she becomes desperate to lay her hands on even the decayed fragments, literally the rags and bones, of the past.

Similarly, in Pat Barker's *Union Street*, Alice finds comfort in the squalor that surrounds her.

> Everything was steeped in memory. The smell of mothballs from the drawers where she stored her bedlinen. The crack in the fireplace where she had dropped the iron. [. . .] Her home. They were taking it away from her. The dirt and disorder, the signs of malnutrition and neglect which to them were reasons for putting her away were, to her, independence. (237)

Barker could perhaps have written a more appealing scene by describing in detail the particular objects that Alice caresses, allowing us to appreciate their significance to her. Instead, the novelist emphasizes their cracked, battered, and dirty appearance. Memory is dispersed and saturated, or "steeped," in the whole space, like the pervasive smell of mothballs or the smoke and soot Barker mentions earlier. Alice does not see through the dirt and disorder to some clean and happy memory, as we would hope. Rather, she identifies the home's squalor as an inevitable and perhaps necessary result of her relationship to her own past. The rooms are worn and soiled by the life that she has lived in them, and she cannot reject their squalor without rejecting herself.

Marcia Ivory and Alice Bell approach the extreme case of environmental press that occurs in hoarding. Hoarding, the accumulation of "newspaper, paper, containers, clothing, food, books, and trash" (Steketee et al. 178), has been studied extensively as a symptom of obsessive-compulsive disorder but has only recently been addressed specifically among the elderly. Gail Steketee, Randy Frost, and Hyo-Jin Kim have studied adults whose homes are so full of such objects as to significantly impair their physical motion.

> In some cases clutter was knee-high or higher, requiring elderly clients to climb over possessions to reach another location. One client was described as literally swimming over the top of clutter to reach other rooms. Nearly 70 percent of elderly hoarders were unable to use their furniture (for example, bed or sofa), and several elderly clients slept on a chair or a couch because their beds were covered. (181)

Such hoarding would seem to differ from the sort of accumulation I have been discussing. Useless objects such as paper bags can hardly bear valuable memories, yet hoarders cling to them as though this were the case. Steketee, Frost, and Kim found that their clients often "refused entry or claimed that the [visiting health] provider was stealing or throwing away valuable possessions" (6 of 13). It is this slippage from the accumulation of mementos to the hoarding of meaningless trash that is most often considered a sign of mental degeneration among the elderly. At the same time, elderly homeowners' fear that important, if disorganized, mementos will be misinterpreted as garbage animates their determination to retain them.

Marilynne Robinson's novel *Housekeeping* portrays the home life of Ruth and Lucille, two teen-age sisters raised by their schizophrenic aunt Sylvie, who "considered accumulation to be the essence of housekeeping" (180). Robinson shows how Ruth's identity and sense of family history becomes associated with her late grandmother's eclectic collections and her aunt Sylvie's hoarding. Ruth burns her family home when she is forced to leave it rather than let strangers sift through her treasured mementos, basing her drastic action on her awareness of the difference between her own and her neighbors' ability to interpret the objects' meaning.

> [I] could not leave that house, which was stashed like a brain, a reliquary, like a brain, its relics to be pawed and sorted. [. . .] For even things lost in a house abide, like forgotten sorrows and incipient dreams, and many household things are of purely sentimental value, like the dim coil of thick hair, saved from my grandmother's girlhood, which was kept in a hatbox on top of the wardrobe, along with my mother's gray purse. In the equal light of disinterested scrutiny such things are not themselves. They are transformed into pure object, and are horrible, and must be burned. (209)

Ruth so dreads relinquishing this material engagement with her family's past that she would rather destroy the home than hand it over to someone unable to decipher its lost but abiding history. In the eyes of a stranger, the home's familiar spaces and treasured mementos are "not themselves," and without the home environment, Ruth suggests, she will cease to be herself as well. Her vacillation between metaphors, "like a brain, a reliquary, like a brain, its relics," suggests how objects stored in the home facilitate an easy motion between the past and present one finds in thought, in combination with the reassuring materiality of saints' bones.

Although Ruth is a young woman, her statement trenchantly expresses the feelings of many elderly people, who often struggle to remain in their homes not just because their mementos support their identities but because they share Ruth's fear that their treasured objects will be misinterpreted. Steketee, Frost, and Kim found that "[c]ontrary to our expectation that elderly hoarders would have cognitive deficits, providers reported 76 percent to have no problems with cognitive functioning" (181). This striking statistic hints that identification with one's jumbled accumulations does not represent a delusional state, as Baudrillard argues, but is an extension of the normal process of self-representation in the home.

Hoarding amounts to an excessive faith in the power of material objects to convey memories. This same faith makes cleaning out any long-inhabited space painful for us. Each old stuffed animal, dish, and coat casts up a story or tempts us to reclaim one, making us break up the rhythm of work, transforming labor into a series of irresistible reveries. Standing still in the semidark of the attic, we strain to recall some past moments while others burst upon us unbidden, and it occurs to us that if we do discard the object, the memory may never come again. Hadn't that childhood joy been lost to us until we picked up the candy dish? If the mind can't contain all our memories, if it can only cross to the full-bodied past over material bridges, then losing a memento (even a soiled, crumbled one) means losing ourselves.

Perhaps the most notorious literary portrayal of a hoarder is the junk dealer Krook in Dickens's *Bleak House.* By making Krook a retailer rather than a homeowner, Dickens intensifies the absurdity of his attachment to his hoarded possessions. For Krook, who lives in a shop where "[e]verything seemed to be bought, and nothing to be sold" (99), the two strategies of memory we have discussed exchange dynamics: his motion comes to mirror his environment, while his symbolic apprehension of objects becomes a series of smooth but pointless repetitive rituals. Krook's goal in accumulating so many objects is to achieve a sort of mastery over the past, to become the guardian of so many life stories that he achieves power over them. But these vast heaps of memory limit Krook physically, preventing him from moving freely or easily through his dwelling; he has no "smooth routes" and is continually confronted by trapdoors and non-navigable passages. In his attempt to control so many narratives, he ceases to achieve any clear or effective narrative representation of his own life in his dwelling. His motion, rather than a representation of himself, becomes a demonstration of how his environment imposes itself upon him. "The old man [. . .] feebly swings himself round, and comes with his face against the wall. So he remains a minute or two, heaped up against it; and then staggers down the shop to the front door" (338). Dickens describes him as "a bundle of clothes with a spiritous heat smouldering in it" (337), thus literalizing the metaphor of "melding" or "blending" with the environment. However, this sort of blending compromises rather than supports his identity. Like the elders Rubinstein and Parmalee describe, "the boundaries between self and object are blurred" (152), but in this case Krook becomes a "tangible embodiment" of his environment rather than vice versa. He "heaps up" against his heaps. Krook's death by spontaneous combustion represents the grotesque culmination of this process as his boundaries become obliterated, and he smears across the surrounding shambles as "a smouldering suffocating vapour in the room, and a dark greasy coating on the walls and ceiling" (Dickens 511).

Dickens also dwells on Krook's ritualistic manipulation of objects, which in his case enervates the self rather than ritually reinforcing it. Krook obsessively collects documents, yet he is illiterate; the difficulty of "reading" objects for their symbolic import thus becomes literalized. "He is always spelling out words from them [the letters], and chalking them over the table and the shop-wall, and asking what this is, and what that is; but his whole stock from beginning to end, may easily be the waste-paper he bought it as, for anything I can say" (508–9). By continually touching his documents, Krook hopes that their meaning will rub off on him, "infect" him in Belk's terms, and he enacts this desire by touching them and rubbing them repeatedly and by smearing their copied letters in chalk marks on his walls and table. In doing so he is trying to re-create, to literally rewrite, the past, but rather than recuperating stories he succeeds only in enacting a series of fruitless physical habits; his mnemonic objects may be "at hand," but their only impact is on his hands. Belk speaks of the "contagion from the proximity of the object to a special time," and contagion is a dominant concern of *Bleak House:* Krook lives in a district from which smallpox spreads to infect Esther, and he is himself figured as contagious when he spontaneously combusts. This literal contagion of dirt, chalk, dust, bodily fluids, and disease is clearly present in Krook's dwelling, but the contagion of the past is notably absent.

The hoarder's faith in the power of objects to access, and thus maintain, personal history inevitably leads to a sense of paranoid dislocation. Since the rest of society is incapable of interpreting the stories hidden in mess, it simply apprehends such accumulated objects as undifferentiated matter. Krook explains that, to him, all this junk has value and significance that others can't see.

> "You see I have so many things here," he resumed, holding up the lantern, "of so many kinds, and all, as the neighbors think (but *they* know

nothing), wasting away and going to rack and ruin. [. . .] And I can't
abear to part with anything I once lay hold of (or so my neighbours
think, but what do *they* know?)" (101)

While this assertion of the value of what seems like rubbish might apply
to a messy domestic space, it sounds utterly ridiculous when applied to
the junk shop. For Krook, these memories can never be recovered, for
they aren't even his own, yet he clings to the relics all the more tightly,
convinced of their potential meaning. Stewart points out that the object,
with its tantalizing power to unlock a mysterious past, can come to loom
larger than the story it represents. "The souvenir displaces the point of
authenticity as it itself becomes the point of origin for narrative. Such a
narrative cannot be generalized to encompass the experience of anyone;
it pertains only to the possessor of the object" (136). This displacement
of the life event by the object is the basis for Krook's belief that he can
transfer other people's memories to himself. Possessing so many objects
allows him to possess the equivalent number of life stories, whether or
not he understands the memories they contain. He thus represents the
extreme of the common tendency to hold on more tightly to mementos
once their meaning has been lost, or because their meaning has been lost.
Once the storeroom of the brain loses a memory, it can be found only in
the storeroom of the house. Unclassified mess must be retained fully intact
precisely because its owner is no longer capable of successfully classify-
ing it. The great irony at the heart of the novel is that Krook is, for all his
self-destructive delusions, partly right. The packet of letters containing
the truth about Esther's identity, and the key to all the intertwining plots
of the novel, is piled in among Krook's many unread documents. The
hoarder's faith, Dickens suggests, may be at once misdirected and true.

In *Memento Mori*, Muriel Spark portrays what would seem to be the
antithesis of Krook in Alec Warner. This comic novel follows a group of
elderly people, all of whom receive a mysterious telephone call reminding them that they will die. Warner, an aging gerontologist, compulsively
collects and organizes information about his elderly neighbors' mental
and physical degeneration in order to foil the ravages of failing memory.

> Nearly ten years of inquisitive work had gone into the card indexes
> and files encased in two oak cabinets, one on either side of the window.
> [. . .] Presently he rose to fetch the two boxes of index cards which he
> used constantly when working at his desk. One of these contained the
> names of those of his friends and acquaintances who were over sev-
> enty. [. . .] Much of the information on this first set of cards was an aid

to memory, for, although his memory was still fairly good, he wished to ensure against his losing it: he had envisaged the day when he might take up a card, read the named and wonder, for instance, "Colston—Charmian,—who is Charmian Colston?" [. . .] On each was marked a neat network of codes and numbers relating to various passages in the books around the walls, on subjects of gerontology and senescence, and to the ten years' accumulation of his thick notebooks. (58)

Alec's card files serve as an exteriorized memory, allowing for nearly instantaneous intellectual access to the life stories and pertinent personal information of his subjects. His perfectly organized home/office is an extension of the "neat network of codes" on his cards. Rather than smooth routes through living space, Alec moves from card file to notebook to bookshelf and back again, but none of these motions links him to his own memories.

Spark demonstrates how cold and cheerless Alec's life has become. His determination to conquer the disorderly vagaries of materialized memory dooms him to a life without a past of his own. He has no real home, living without family or any personal keepsakes in the "gentleman's chambers" full of notebooks and files. While his files give him access to others' memories (or more accurately the histories of their memory loss), he has none of the treasured objects or quirky arrangements of furniture that would connect him to his own past. Krook lives in a junk shop, Alec in a gerontology library. In both cases the home excessively devoted to asserting power over memory becomes grotesque and compromises, rather than reinforces, identity. At the end of the book Alec suffers the ironic fate of losing his memory to a stroke and moving to a nursing home where he "frequently searched through his mind, as through a card index, for the case-histories of his friends, both dead and dying" (232). Alec's fate inverts Krook's, for while the junk dealer explodes, his identity fully amalgamated with his material surroundings, Alec implodes, his mind cycling endlessly through an incomprehensible inventory of anonymous data without any material referent.

These literary examples dwell on the way environment imposes on the memories of elderly people. I would now like to turn to a young, intellectually vigorous character who would seem to be a master of both memory and environment. Sherlock Holmes, like all great detectives, has the power to manipulate objects so that they "bring the past into the present when the past may have been forgotten or overwhelmed" (Rubinstein et al. 83). Indeed, the essential message of detective fiction is that the past can be made present through objects. In "The Musgrave

Ritual" Holmes recovers a lost piece of family history by manipulating apparently meaningless relics so that they reveal their symbolic import, and by moving so skillfully through an old house that he recovers the life narratives of both the family and the nation.

Holmes tells Watson of one of his first cases: when he is asked by Reginald Musgrave, an aristocratic acquaintance, to investigate the disappearance of the Musgrave butler, who had evinced an interest in an obscure family nursery rhyme, the "Musgrave Ritual." The rhyme is "rather an absurd business" (Doyle 205), yet the family enacts the empty ritual out of a half-superstitious, half-ironic belief in its abiding value. Holmes interprets the rhyme as a code corresponding to physical movements through the house leading to the Musgrave family treasure. He thus performs the method of loci in reverse, reestablishing a lost memory through motion. And what a memory, for the family treasure is "nothing less than the ancient crown of the Kings of England" (212) hidden by Musgrave ancestors loyal to Charles I. Sir Ralph Musgrave had established the ritual as a mnemonic device to assure that the crown's location in the house would be remembered yet kept secret. But the ritual failed, and the crown, with all its historical and personal value, was lost. By literally pacing out the ritual's coded directions, Holmes enacts what Peter Brooks has called "the spatio-temporal realization" (26) of the various enfolded stories, a spatial representation of the life course of both family and nation.

Doyle carefully entwines memory as both narrative and object. The lost history is both the tale of Sir Ralph Musgrave's daring exploits and the crown as heavy, gritty, pure matter. When it is first dredged from the moat, it appears to be "old metal and pebbles" (212). The words "Musgrave Ritual" denote the nursery rhyme, Holmes's smooth navigation of its physical counterparts in the halls of the Musgrave mansion, and the story that Watson writes about his friend. They also correspond to a box of tangible mementos Holmes shows Watson in the frame narrative at the beginning of the story.

> He dived his arm down to the bottom of the chest, and brought up a small wooden box, with sliding lid, such as children's toys are kept in. From within he produced a crumpled piece of paper, an old fashioned brass key, a peg of wood with a ball of string attached to it, and three rusty old discs of metal. (198)

These souvenirs are not, in fact, remnants of Reginald Musgrave's childhood, but Holmes's own personal collection; he used the pegs and string to measure out his route through the mansion, and the metal discs were found with the crown. Now, in the frame narrative, they serve as lightning rods to his professional memory, for Holmes (like the Musgraves) had forgotten his story. Holmes may have a nearly superhuman ability to trace secret histories, but even he needs a box of mementos to bring his own memories to light.

Holmes comes across the box, however, only because he is attempting to organize the huge accumulation of memorabilia that has overrun his flat. Watson complains that

> although in his methods of thought he was the neatest and most methodical of mankind[,] [. . .] [Holmes] was nonetheless in his personal habits one of the most untidy men that ever drove a fellow-lodger to distraction. [. . .] Our chambers were always full of chemicals and criminal relics, which had a way of wandering into unlikely positions, and of turning up in the butter-dish, or in even less desirable places. But his papers were my great crux. He had a horror of destroying documents, especially those which were connected with his past cases. [. . .] Thus month after month his papers accumulated, until every corner of the room was stacked with bundles of manuscript. (197–98)

Sherlock Holmes's cases, which exist for us in Watson's narrative versions, exist for the two roommates as domestic hazards, capable of tripping, poisoning, or wounding them. Holmes and Watson can't go about the business of solving his present cases because his past cases are always underfoot. While his effortless navigation of the Musgrave home enabled him to represent Musgrave family history and British national history, his motion through his own home is blocked as the hoarded relics of his past impede upon his personal boundary. By framing the tale of Holmes's nearly miraculous power over mnemonic objects with a practical demonstration of those objects' physical power over him, Doyle demonstrates that the process of environmental self-representation may become perilous even to the young, strong, and mentally acute.

These literary authors offer their commentary on memory and environment through a series of literalizations: the memory of a cat becomes dirty dishes and bones; a room steeped in memory is also steeped in smoke and soot; the self embodied in the home becomes a body soaking into walls and ceilings. Such literalizations call attention to the perilously literalizing potential of psychological models of identification. When the body and mind become frail, it may be risky for the home to "become" the person (Rubinstein and Parmalee 152) or for someone to have a "bodily awareness" like an "automatic pilot" (Rowles 142). Dickens, Doyle, Lessing, Pym, and Barker essentially argue for the power of the environment to *literally* press against the individual, to assert its own structures of meaning and power, sometimes destructively.

✦ ✦ ✦

I began this chapter by looking at the ambiguous metaphors used to describe self-representation among the elderly. As I have attempted to argue, this ambiguity arises in part from the competing dynamics of mnemonic strategies and from the vulnerability of self-representation to the body's materiality. This ambiguity also arises, I would suggest, from the pressure the environment can place on metaphor itself. The embodiment of memory in the material structures of the home must bear the weight of that materiality. Objects that mirror the self will always tend to become simple, nonsymbolic objects; the life course enacted in the home's spatial flow will always bump up against the material edges of the house. Metaphor is most fragile when its vehicle has greater sensory presence than its tenor. Metaphorical constructions of self, then, will be at great risk in the home, where the vehicle's sensory immediacy imposes constantly on the mind and body. The "self that is embodied in the home" is itself a body as well as a metaphor-creating identity, and in ritually reinforcing itself through self-representation, it may at the same time be placing itself under duress.

The risk posed by accumulation is not limited to the elderly, although it most often appears in its physical form for them. Whenever our memories are transferred onto the objects around us, we take the risk that those objects will turn on us, limiting our lives in some way. To keep rooms free of mess, we must choose some mementos over others, and thus we run the risk of losing the ones we put aside. For every souvenir on the mantle, there are fifty piled in boxes, each holding a memory that may be worth reanimating. Yet if we take the box out and spread the mementos around us on the floor, handling each one to feel the tender influx of the past, we look up to find that the afternoon has gone or the floor is too cluttered to navigate.

For gerontologists and caregivers, understanding metaphorical self-representation helps determine how long the psychological support offered by the home outweighs the hazards of remaining in it. Rubinstein, Lawton, and others suggest that the imaginative lives of the elderly tend to be firmly grounded in the literal material of their own homes and bodies. As such, the pressures and contradictions of environmental self-representation may be desirable, given the alternative of transferring to the unfamiliar, nonmirroring environment of a nursing home or an assisted living facility. The past, both gerontologists and literary authors argue, exists for us in material things; as Bachelard says of the home: "Being reigns in a sort of earthly paradise of matter" (7). We cherish this materiality even if it endangers us: Krook ends up dead, soaking into his accumulated heaps; Holmes discovers the lost crown of England only after finding the body of the butler who sought it before him; Marcia Ivory, Maudie Fowler, and Alice Bell are, like many elderly people, willing to put their own frail bodies at risk in order to remain at home. As living space slides into storage space, the preponderance of our memories threatens to clog our lives, to cut us off from the present, to physically threaten us. "[E]ven things lost in a house abide," Ruth notes (Robinson 209), and in abiding they fill up boxes, rooms, and halls, exerting pressure on the very people to whom their abiding memories matter. The power of accumulation to embody our past selves just when they seem most vulnerable makes us willing to risk a great deal to be in its midst. In order to understand the determination of the elderly to remain at home as long as possible, and thus to judge the best way to ease their transition out of it, we must recognize the importance of materiality to home-based metaphors of identity.

Chapter 3

The Hoarder's House

It is easy to have too many cats. In my family's case, one cat named Lana had one litter of kittens, each of which had a litter or two. Hand-lettered signs advertising free kittens were permanently posted on our fence. The cats tore up the couch arms, infested the beds with fleas, and ripped big chunks out of the Styrofoam soundproofing in my father's office. Scarred, feral strays would storm the house whenever our females were in heat. My parents never considered having them spayed or neutered, partly due to my father's false economy, and partly to my mother's belief that all God's creatures deserved to live freely. She never let us kill wasps or ants, and she once invited a wild raccoon into the house, where he enjoyed a bowl of cat food until my brother chased him out with a base-ball bat.

While it is apparent to me now how unhealthy this situation was, most of my experiences living with the cats were deeply satisfying. I would spend hours patting and playing with them, and I almost always had a cat sitting beside or lying across me. Cats are the most tangibly engaging of pets, with their tendency to rub every surface of their face and back against one's hand, their rhythmic purring, and their oddly appealing scratchy tongues. One of our most ferocious toms would become a true baby whenever he was mortally wounded in a fight, and he would sit on my lap as I did my homework, purring furiously, the heat from his torn back radiating through my clothes. I would gladly have traded my home's roof and four walls for this pervasive and affectionate animal attachment, and while at some level I knew that in society's eyes the cats were destroying my home, in mine they were completing it.

We have seen how the home's space is transformed by the tangible absence of expected bodies and by the tangible presence of treasured objects. I would now like to address our tactile apprehension of domestic companion animals, which stand somewhere between human bodies and objects as somatic repositories of emotional identification. Pet owners are familiar with the uncomplicated companionship inherent in the sound of a dog sighing or the pressure of cat's sleeping back, just as they are familiar with the dirt, hair, and disorder, to say nothing of offspring, that pets can unleash upon the spaces of the home. In this sense, one could describe them as intensified objects, like piles of books that have the power to move and scatter themselves around the house. In another sense, they are like less complex human companions whose reassuring physical presence overshadows their lack of verbal communication, making our relationships with them even more heavily weighted toward the tactile. Like both people and objects, pets serve to support the strategies of identification and self-integration in the home, offering a reciprocally tactile engagement that intensifies the home's safety, peace, and emotional richness. More than either objects or human companions, however, pets pose a particularly potent threat to domestic space through their ability to establish an apprehension of domesticity that relies almost entirely on bodily engagement, making the architectural space of the home either unnecessary or despoiled. In their discussion of Animal Assisted Interventions in mental health, Katherine A. Kruger and James A. Serpell point out the contradictory position animals hold with regard to human attachment.

> While animals may serve as both attachment figures and transitional objects, it is important to note that the roles of attachment figure and transitional object are, by definition, mutually exclusive. "Attachment" implies a long-lasting emotional bond, whereas "transitional" implies a passage from one condition to another and the absence of a lasting bond. (10)

While they ultimately choose the role of transitional object as "more therapeutically desirable," Kruger and Serpell suggest that companion animals tend to blend mutually exclusive categories: animals offer both attachment and transition; they serve as both "figures" and "objects." Moreover, Kruger and Serpell warn that, in some cases, animals have the potential to "serve as a substitute for failed or inadequate human relationships." Their proximity to, yet distinctness from, humans renders pets uncanny; our interactions with them serve as ghostly "substitutes" for the human relationships they threaten to displace.

Studies of the effect of pet ownership on the physical and psychological health of the elderly have come to mixed, sometimes even drastically contrasting, conclusions about the value of companion animals in the home. A well-publicized study by Thomas F. Garrity, Lorann Stollones, Martin B. Marx, and Timothy P. Johnson in 1989 found that elderly pet owners who had recently lost a spouse tended to be in better health and to suffer less from depression, and similar studies in the nineties concluded that pet owners had lower cholesterol and better overall health (Dembicki and Anderson 16). Caregiving programs based on these findings emphasize companion animals' power to solidify the home's domestic stability. Gillian McColgan and Irene Schofield, for example, argue in the journal *Nursing Older People* that "dogs can play an important companionship role for older people, especially when human social circles become restricted. This could have important implications for the kind of community support aimed at people with dementia to enable them to remain in their own homes" (23). As life becomes increasingly centered upon the home, our home-bound relationships with pets become more emotionally valuable. McColgan and Schofield seem to be arguing for pets to assume the position of "substitute humans" that Kruger and Serpell warn against. In effect, without the dog's physical presence, the home would cease to be inhabitable.

By contrast, some other studies have found a correlation between close bonds with animals and antisocial behavior. A recent study published in *Gerontology* suggests that elderly pet owners are less healthy, more frequently depressed, and "less likely to conform to social norms" (Parslow et al. 47).

> An unexpected finding was that owners and carers of pets reported significantly higher levels of psychoticism than non-owners and non-carers, in particular that they preferred to go their own way and liked others to be afraid of them. This outcome has not been reported previously but is compatible with earlier studies that found pet owners liked pets more than they liked people. (46)

Companion animals thus seem to exert contradictory pressures on domestic space. Their presence can shore up a home that is dissolving or precipitate the dissolution of a stable home. For homeowners with many animals, antisocial behavior can take the form of animal hoarding, in which domestic space becomes soiled and overrun by the animals. In this chapter I will look at works by Doris Lessing, Susan Cheever, and Albert and David Maysles, in which focused, somatic animal attachment operates within the home to drain both memory and identity from domestic space. In these representations of animal hoarding and obsessive attachment, respectable, even elegant, homes become socially marginal through the intensification of the relationship between the homeowner and the animals.

Animal hoarding, which had previously been considered merely an unpleasant eccentricity, has in recent years been given closer attention by psychologists, veterinarians, and law enforcement agencies. The Hoarding of Animals Research Consortium (HARC) at Tufts University has defined the syndrome as distinct from other psychological conditions, such as Obsessive-Compulsive Disorder (OCD). Animal hoarders, the consortium claims, accumulate animals beyond their ability "to provide even minimal standards of nutrition, sanitation, shelter and veterinary care." Their homes demonstrate severe overcrowding and very unsanitary conditions, in which animals are exposed to "starvation, illness and death." As the hoarder loses control of his or her home, public officials are often called upon to intervene. A December 2005 *Washington Post* article describes one such intervention.

> "The house was cluttered with feces and urine, and a number of paper plates and a number of paper products used to feed cats were throughout the house," [the Director of the Animal Control Division] said. A number of cats were roaming free, and others were kept in cages and pet carriers. The dead animals, he said, "were on the first floor, second floor, in different places, and there was an outbuilding where they were stored as well." He said some dead animals were stored near cat food in several refrigerators around the house, while others were kept in plastic containers in a shed. Food and water were set out all over the house. (Hernandez B03)

In the hoarder's home, the fundamental distinctions by which we define domestic space are violated. *Washington Post* staff writer Nelson Hernandez lists the various sorts of sanitary and architectural boundaries that have broken down: living cats, dead cats, cat food, plates for cat food, carriers for living cats, containers for cat food, containers for dead cats, refrigerators containing both dead cats and food, and outbuildings containing everything—all are intermingled. Peter Gollub, the Director of Law Enforcement for the Massachusetts SPCA, explains that, typically, "the animals of hoarders are allowed to invade sleeping areas, food preparation areas, bathrooms, and dining areas to an extraordinary extent." Not limited to architectural boundaries, hoarding often involves the violation of the body's boundary through the dissolution of the proper space between bodies. One hoarder reports that she "used to sleep on the bottom bunk . . . but I kept waking up with too many dogs on my chest. They were cutting off my air supply" (Arluke 95). Another hoarder "lived in a six-foot square rabbit hutch with her dozen cats and dogs" (95). In both cases, the hoarders intentionally limit their domestic space and then allow it to be filled by animals until it presses against the body's margin; their bodies become subsumed into a solid mass of animal bodies and domestic objects. It is hard to understand how a person could have "too many dogs on [one's] chest" unless they are tiny dogs and the owner has a very large chest; how many could really fit? One imagines the dogs stacked one atop another, as in the children's book *Go, Dog! Go.* Even when he or she stops sleeping under the dog pile, the hoarder just moves to the top bunk, another layered structure, with the dogs filling the bottom layer. Indeed, layering is characteristic of hoarders' use of space. In one hoarder's house, "a large room [was] stacked to the ceiling with cages, housing hundreds of cats, and, in another, bird cages were "stacked from floor to ceiling in every room" (94).

This solidifying and layering of space blurs categories that define physical identity. It is shocking enough that someone would sleep in a rabbit hutch with rabbits, but why cats and dogs? Why would the hoarder have a rabbit hutch without rabbits? The hoarder's house seems to defy even geographical categories. One is described as a "jungle," there is a frozen alligator in one refrigerator, and "[i]nvestigators also thought they saw an orangutan" (95). The orangutan seems to flit in and out of the imaginary space the house has become, in which any animal can be present and any animal can become any other. Arluke argues that the "confused picture of hoarders" presented by the press reflects "society's confusion" about how to categorize and manage hoarding (92). Judges, social workers, and law enforcement officers are often at a loss concerning who, if anyone, has jurisdiction. I would add, moreover, that in addition to such social category confusion, hoarding effects a fundamental physical confusion about the boundaries of identity. Hoarders have become "more animal than human" (93), as Arluke points out, but animals have also become more like humans, or other animals, or any animal. In the hoarder's house, crucial boundaries between human and animal, and between different types of animals—boundaries that the home serves typically to enforce—have dissolved.

Dirt is simply matter out of place, Mary Douglas argues, but the hoarder's house pushes us to define what we mean by "matter." Animal bodies are always culturally coded as closer to pure matter than human ones; they carry more matter on their surfaces, and they can degenerate into matter very quickly. When animal bodies live closely against human bodies, they spread matter—hair, excrement, parasites—from one body to the next, and this undifferentiated matter bridges the space between bodies. "One of the hallmarks of hoarding seems to be when this extensive 'invasion' involves not just the animals, but the animals coupled with feces, vermin, or some kind of filth" (Gollub). The incorporation of filth, or other bodies, into the body itself represents the endpoint of such boundary blending. "Several articles reported that animal cadavers were discovered in refrigerators. . . . One bag of frozen cats [was] marked 'S. Sauce.' There was some question about whether five bags and a large pot of spaghetti sauce also in the freezer might have been made from cat meat" (94). The hoarder's house is the staging ground for a cultural apprehension of the abject, the perfect site at which to witness the dissolution of the most crucial cultural taboos (animal/human, food/corpse, bed/toilet, flesh/feces) being violated. These journalistic accounts present a carnivalesque imaginarium in which any creature can become any other and where all forms of taboo are violated.

Journalistic accounts of the opening of the hoarder's house emphasize its squalor and the physical deterioration of both human and animal bodies, transforming the hoarder's home into an ignominiously spectacular space. The *Washington Post*'s description of the house is filtered through the perspective of a public official, whose presence at the scene signals a return to social order through the public exposure of the hoarder. In his analysis of journalistic representations of animal hoarders, Arnold Arluke shows how, when the house is opened, newspaper articles unveil the nondomesticated domestic space as a means of both negotiating middle-class anxieties about dirt and disorder and casting the hoarder into public view. "[I]ncidents of animal hoarding make for good news stories because they are so extraordinary, baffling and sad. [. . .] The result is that the hoarders' identities become a matter for public speculation" (86). The *Washington Post* story quoted above follows a fairly typical pattern of journalistic accounts of animal hoarding, which track the perspective of public officials into the hoarder's home; describe the excessive squalor of the house itself; and tabulate living, dead, and sick animal bodies. The reporter then follows the exposed and humiliated hoarder out into the criminal justice or mental health system. Arluke shows how representations of animal hoarding employ a variety of alternating narratives—the crime story, the tale of mental disturbance, the pathetic portrait of domestic ruin (89–92). All of the journalistic genres Arluke describes involve the juxtaposition of the abject and the domestic, which is typical of what might be called suburban gothic, from *Arsenic and Old Lace* to *The Amityville Horror* to *Desperate Housewives*. Like all gothic narratives, suburban gothic focuses on secret domestic spaces and involves the revelation of that secret via the motion through and opening up of architectural barriers. The hoarder's house is always a closed one, to be opened only once and with ghastly drama by public officials, as in the final page of Faulkner's "A Rose for Emily."

In Albert and David Maysles's observational documentary *Grey Gardens* (1975), we are introduced to an elderly woman and her middle-aged daughter, who live in a squalid house overrun with cats. The piquancy of the film, and no doubt some of its cult popularity, stem from the fact that the women aren't just any crazy cat ladies, but Edith Bouvier Beale and her daughter Edie, the aunt and cousin of Jacqueline Kennedy Onassis, and their house is in the exclusive community of East Hampton, Long Island. Like Faulkner's Emily, they are old aristocracy, and their gothic secrets are all the more tantalizing. In the first scenes of *Grey Gardens*, the camera closes in on a newspaper clipping containing the text of several newspaper stories about the Beales that follows the template of hoarding journalism.

> Jacqueline Bouvier Kennedy Onassis' aunt and cousin on Long Island are living in a garbage-ridden, filthy, 28-room house with eight cats, fleas, cobwebs, and no running water—conditions so unsanitary that the Suffolk County Health Dept. has ordered them to clean up or face eviction. [. . .] To reach the house, officials came up a driveway on grounds whose shrubs, trees and foliage resembled an Amazon rain forest. [. . .] [A search warrant had been obtained] by representatives of the ASPCA on the grounds that the Beales were suspected of harboring diseased cats. (*Grey Gardens*)

Several articles are then shown tracking the progress of the Beales' dispute with the town, emphasizing their connection to Jacqueline Kennedy Onassis and featuring photographs of soiled living space. The film thus announces its intention to parallel the journalistic exposé, as it moves into the house, opening successive squalid rooms and private domestic spaces. (Eight cats is almost certainly an underestimate. More than eight can be seen in several scenes in the movie, and the filmmakers' commentary suggests that cats and raccoons overran the house.)

While animal hoarding is not an explicit topic of the film, it is never far from view. Cats appear in most scenes, especially those in Edith's bedroom, where she sits up in bed to eat and talk, with the animals draped across her lap and the surrounding furniture and cat food dishes spread around the room. The animals seem to be soiling or crowding out all of the symbols of family history or personal identity in the household. Pointing to a portrait of herself as a young woman that has fallen to the floor, Edith says, "A cat's going to the bathroom right in the back of my portrait. [. . .] I'm glad someone's doing something they want to do." Feeding the animals seems to be Edie's main occupation. We see her climb to the attic and, as she discusses a missing book, nonchalantly dump an entire box of cat food over an entire loaf of Wonder Bread. "Everything's in the attic," she says with a mixture of pride and bemusement, "everything from sloths, otters, badgers, possums, raccoons." While she is certainly exaggerating, a raccoon does arrive to eat the Wonder Bread, apparently the same animal that has made a hole in the ceiling that Edith points out in the film's opening shots. Most alarmingly, cat food and cat food dishes, pervasive throughout the house, seem to get confused with the Beales' own food. After feeding the cats beside her mother's bed, Edie uses the same can opener on the same soiled table to open a can of liver pâté to feed her mother. In another scene, Edith hands a foil dish to her daughter, and says, "Now don't eat it! Give it to whiskers. You're thin; you want to get thinner." "She's very mean to me," says Edie, carrying the dish to the cat. "I have to be very strict," Edith explains.

For the viewer, the Beales' willingness to jettison their semi-aristocratic past seems both appalling and liberating. Most elderly homeowners struggle to maintain family memorabilia that can mean nothing to anyone else, but the audience is interested in seeing the Beales' old pictures and family mementos. By giving over Grey Gardens (the name of their house) to the cats and raccoons, the Beales detach themselves from their own domestic identity and, in doing so, detach the viewer from the private history of the wealthy, politically connected East Coast families they represent. We catch glimpses of family pictures and hear scraps about Little Edie's life in Manhattan; famous names are dropped and then never mentioned again. We get the impression that their history is, in some important sense, our own, but it has been crowded out by the cats; the cat food dishes; the dirty, dark hallways; and the broken windows.

Gary Patronek, veterinarian and member of the Hoarding of Animals Research Consortium at Tufts University, argues that animal hoarding has less in common with OCD than with attachment disorders, in which relationships with animals "are preferred because they are safer and less threatening than relationships with humans" (Patronek 2). For the Beales, as for many other hoarders, the squalor created by the animals disrupts their ability to store and retrieve their memories within the house. Gollub, observing that hoarders often abandon souvenirs, photos, and memorial objects, argues that the animals come to replace these items.

> Yet those objects are just symbols—for hoarders (and all of us), they're relationships by proxy. I wonder if the hoarded animals and hoarded objects aren't simply new symbols for occasions, memories, etc. Perhaps the hoarder's relationship with the "traditional" symbols gets subordinated to the relationship with the "new" symbols through a process we don't yet understand. (Gollub)

Such a process would involve the replacement of a hoarder's life story, contained within souvenirs and mementos, with more immediate sensory satisfactions. While the memories that objects contain are accessed through some degree of tactile experience, their symbolic or mnemonic connections to an invisible past remain largely imaginary. Animals, by contrast, place the hoarder in a warm, vivid present, teeming with life and perhaps even crowding out the sort of memories objects would retain. Rather than the representations of the self that collected objects offer, collected animals serve as extensions of physical identity, of the visceral, embodied, and atemporal self, that is at odds with the more delicate and complex self of personal memory. Rather than establishing a link to the past, which may have been marked by painful family dynamics, the presence of the animals allows the hoarder to focus on the physical rewards of animal companionship occurring in the present. Because the fame of the Beales family makes their history of intrinsic interest, we find ourselves in the strange position of trying to reconstruct their past from the various objects and pictures left lying around, a past they seem to have abandoned in order to keep tighter hold of their cats.

The newspaper headlines that begin the film place great emphasis on the Beales' Kennedy connection. One of the headlines reads "Jackie's Aunt Told: Clean Up Mansion"; another reads "Jackie Cleans Up E. Hampton [Home]." After a description of the house's squalor, the text trails off the bottom of the screen with "This is the very house [. . .] where Jackie, as a little girl [. . .]." Another passage reads, "Miss Beale [. . .] recalled the earlier, happier times with young Jackie." Moreover, the Beales' accents and physical features resemble their cousin's; as Edie swishes around the moldering porch or greets the Maysleses at the door, her postures and motions seem like a parody of Jackie's political performances. Her shrilly elegant voice evokes both her Social Register training and the shrieking of the cats that surround her. For the viewer, these echoes are sometimes painful, sometimes hilarious, and always disturbing. We are, apparently, watching the "real" Bouviers. The "upside-down and out-of-control performances" of animal hoarders are always somewhat disorientating (109), as Arluke notes, but hoarding journalism typically offers its readers a comfortable position from which to condemn or mock the hoarder's social transgressions. In the Beales' case, their spectacularly debased position as crazy cat ladies is continually informed by reminders of their spectacularly elevated position as society matrons sadly gone to seed. The first story is comic, the second tragic, and their iteration becomes absurd.

The camera often shifts from the shabby exterior of Grey Gardens to the pristine stylishness of the surrounding mansions, emphasizing that the Beales' spectacular position in society has degenerated into a different sort of spectacle. The film thus enacts at the level of cultural history what all animal hoarding implies at the individual level. Hoarding transforms private space into a public concern. For people whose lives are already of public interest, a more complex formulation occurs in which the spectacular, and thus semipublic, wealthy home is transformed by the squalor of hoarding into a normal, and thus private, ruin. One of the most striking things about Grey Gardens is how much it looks like any other messy, crumbling old home. There is no grandeur to this decadence; the Beales eat on paper plates at chipped Formica tables; the overgrown shrubs around their patio look like any overgrown shrubs. Having first become ordinary, it then becomes public; animals and various oddball neighbors wander in and out freely. The Maysleses' camerawork is often disturbingly invasive, finding the women partly clothed or engaged in personal rituals or petty spats. The viewer experiences the disorienting cinematic shifts between a camera that invades a wealthy home to admire and covet and a camera that invades the indigent hovel to pity and recoil. The Beales have abandoned their public role as part of a famous family for a public role as town nuisance through embracing a home life based not on domestic space but on animal attachment.

In keeping with their direct-cinema philosophy, the Maysleses ask almost no questions, so we have to piece family history together from various snatches of discussion. We gradually learn that Edith's husband left her and that she entered into a possibly scandalous relationship with her musical accompanist. Edie's burgeoning career as an actress in Manhattan may have been doomed because of her lack of talent, or it may have been cut short because, as she claims, she had to come home to take care of her mother. The shocking dirt and disorder of the house is a constant visual distraction from their words, however. It is fascinating to watch Edith's facial expression as she holds up a photograph of herself and her young children and asks, "Was I a good mother?" Yet it is almost impossible to avoid looking from her face to the piles of dirty bedclothes, the holes in the walls, and, above all, the cats. A revealing and heartfelt interaction between mother and daughter about Edie's childhood occurs as Edie wanders about her mother's cramped bedroom, opening cans of cat food that are placed on tables cluttered higher than the bed. The camera zooms in on Edie's hands scraping food out of cans as cats swarm the plate. Even if the motion of the cats themselves, and the Maysleses' frequent direction of the camera toward them, weren't enough to pull our attention away, the revulsion we feel at the dirty cat food dishes in the bedroom makes it nearly impossible to focus on Edith's already disjointed reminiscences. We have what amounts to a physiological response to such scenes, a response that crowds out our aesthetic and emotional reaction to the Beales' situation. The film as an investigation of family and psychology is continually undercut by the film as a catalog of abject domestic matter.

We come to understand, however, that the physical presence of the cats is interwoven with the Beales' experience of their own bodies in domestic space. After talking about how cold she had been the previous night, Edith complains, "I was so lonely. She only left me one little kitty to keep me warm." We see here the tension, expressed in continuous minor recriminations, between mother and daughter, the physical discomfort of the women's disordered lives, and the intimate incorporation of the animals into their bodily experience. In *Grey Gardens,* the presence of animal bodies materially grounds the film, continually reminding us of the banal materiality of the Beales' lives. "I've almost died with the fleas in this place," opines Edie as she smears insect repellent on her long-exposed legs. "I can't go on another year. I have to get to a hotel room." As much as we want to view the women as emblems of their social milieu, psychological illness, or media exploitation, their willingness to lie in bed with scabby, flea-ridden cats makes their existence grubbily and pathetically concrete.

The role of the animals, then, is to foreground embodiment so as to negotiate issues of social class, privacy, and public identity. A similar negotiation takes place in Susan Cheever's essay "Little Dog, Big Heart," which portrays dog ownership in terms of class descent. Cheever is best known for her family memoir about her father, John Cheever. While he is a significant American literary figure, John Cheever's place in the cultural imagination has, since his death in 1982, been informed by a series of revelations about his private life, many unveiled by Susan Cheever herself in her memoir *Home Before Dark*. Partly because they so eerily replicated the hidden agonies of his fictional characters, public attention has come to focus on Cheever's secret alcoholism, closeted homosexuality, and diverse family traumas. These revelations are even invoked to comic effect in a 1992 episode of *Seinfeld* entitled "The Cheever Letters." The Cheever family story, like that of the Beales, has become one of American aristocracy's humiliating secrets. Although not a Social Register family like the Bouviers, the Cheevers themselves, as well as the characters in John Cheever's stories, represent upper-middle-class Northeastern intellectual culture in full profile. John Cheever's private peccadilloes are worthy of gossip because in his public persona he seemed to embody what Geoffrey Wolff calls "the suburban proprieties—the crewneck Shetland sweater and khakis, the plumy faux-Brahmin accent, the adoring Labrador at his feet" (1). It is just that adoring Labrador that Susan Cheever undertakes to explain, or perhaps exorcise, as part of her increasingly public childhood story.

"Little Dog, Big Heart," which describes her relationship with her miniature dachshund, is cast as a comic tale of class degeneration. In a description of her dog-owning childhood, she reinforces the Shetland-sweater image of the John Cheever household, in which pedigreed dogs and pedigreed people occupy the grand homes of well-educated, well-heeled suburbia.

> Our dogs were gorgeous creatures with silky coats, fluid movements, and deep, liquid eyes. They came from breeders with WASPy names who lived in large clapboard country houses. These breeders had silver martini shakers and shared our distaste for small dogs and our contempt for pet shops and puppy mills. [. . .] We gave them elaborate show-offy names like Cassiopeia [. . .] and Ezekiel, after a 17th-century ancestor named Ezekiel Cheever. (28)

When it is time for her own children to get a dog, however, she commits a "canine heresy," by buying a "lap dog" at a pet shop. Her son insists on naming it "Cutie," despite her desperate attempts to retain at least the trappings of the cultural elite: "'Why don't we name him Rilke,' I said, 'since dachshunds are German. Or Goethe'?" Unlike the John Cheevers, however, the Susan Cheevers have gone retail and middlebrow.

The essay suggests that the little dog is symptomatic of more profound, and ultimately salutary, lifestyle changes. Her family lives in an apartment that feels "too small for the playing and working and milling around that went on there" (27). In this crowded house, domestic intimacy is happily blended with domestic affection, enabled by Cutie's wagging and cavorting. While the John Cheevers "were not the kind of family who would have had dogs who loved us extravagantly" (27), the Susan Cheevers own a dog "devoted to expressing love, needy love, unmannerly love, blatantly embarrassing love" (28). Cutie sits on laps and sleeps inside occupied sleeping bags, saving the family, through its pushily affectionate physicality, from the emotional distance and domestic alienation that has been so elaborately chronicled in various John Cheever novels, stories, and biographies. The refocusing of domestic space onto animal care, and the invasion of the pet into human spaces, clearly fall well short of the sort of hoarding we see in Grey Gardens. Nevertheless, in its limited way, the essay asserts a similar mechanism of using animal attachment to interrogate the home lives and bodily practice of American aristocrats whose private lives are already a public scandal. In this case, animal attachment counters family discord rather than intensifying it. While Cheever labels her slump from pedigreed Labradors to pet-shop dachshunds a "disintegration" (27), we are meant to understand it as a reintegration of her domestic psychology, which had been scarred by her dysfunctional family of origin.

Ironically, this invocation of an emotionally stunted childhood contradicts the family portrait in *Home Before Dark.* In that work she distinguishes her own family from the wealthier and more respectable Cheever cousins, emphasizing the distance between her father's tumble-down lifestyle and the country-gentleman image the press seemed determined to hang on him.

> The house in Ossining was charming, but after my parents bought it [. . .] the grounds fell into depressing disrepair. [. . .] The brook choked up and the ornamental bridges crumbled. Wisteria vines grew up the fruit trees in the orchard, the yew hedges went wild, and the stone walls disintegrated. It was all they could do, financially, to keep the house in working order. (38)

Like Grey Gardens, the Ossining house embodies a gentility gone to seed. In *Home Before Dark,* as in "Little Dog, Big Heart," dogs enable class failure, breaking at once through physical boundaries and class categories. Home for the holidays from boarding school, Susan Cheever remembers the dogs "grumbling for scraps under the table" (66) and warming her feet in the living room (67). John Cheever, far from the withdrawn patrician with the unloving Labrador sitting decorously by, emerges as an obsessively adoring pet owner, writing saccharine celebrations of "[t]he old dog, my love" (146) in his private journals. He anthropomorphizes his pets shamelessly, referring to them as "'formerly dorgs'—a term he had invented to explain the fact that they were really people temporarily trapped in hairy, rotund bodies" (145), and he composes long letters ostensibly written from one dog to another. While the purpose of the memoir is to show a messier, less idyllic version of Susan Cheever's family of origin than the one publicly in view, the purpose of "Little Dog, Big Heart" is to do the same for her current family. It is ironic that, taken together, the two works so obviously contradict one another; she uses her first, class-disordered, family as the social ideal against which to measure her second family. Both works are a form of exposé, pulling back the curtain on an elevated class tableau to reveal boisterous and emotionally intense family life, with sloppy dogs and sloppily anthropomorphizing humans cavorting at their center. The essay is ultimately a comic, optimistic exposé, while the memoir is darker, more tragic, and more complex; in both cases, however, the dogs' disruption of domestic order and violation of appropriate physical boundaries enables the opening up of a famous family's disorderly, embodied, "real" side. Cheever's animal-assisted memoir functions very much like the Maysleses' animal-assisted documentary.

Albert Maysles comments that the Beales' social status as "American aristocracy" prevented them from going into show business, which led to their "reclusion." "The film has taken them out of that reclusion in the only way that would be suitable to them" (*The Beales*). By employing the documentary as a show-business venue which their social status would not allow them to seek out, the film bridges the gap between show business and high society. The Maysleses thus deliver the Beales from social humiliation by filming them in what most people would consider humiliating circumstances. What film can achieve, Albert Maysles suggests, is the transformative leap from reclusion to celebrity, just the same leap we see in animal hoarding exposés. It is only through their determination to retreat from the world that the Beales fully become a subject worthy of the documentarian's attention.

Similarly, it is only through social withdrawal that the animal hoarder becomes socially visible, and then must be exposed. Hoarders often exhibit a nearly obsessive level of domestic privacy: boarding up windows, refusing to answer doors, and building large fences. Gollub notes the apparent contradiction in such attention to exterior boundaries.

Clearly, hoarders allow the "outer rings" of their space and boundary to be compromised or distorted by their collected objects and their physical environment. Ironically however, hoarders' seemingly endless accommodation to boundary deformation vis-à-vis their animals is counterbalanced by an exquisite sensitivity to the intrusion of outsiders into their domain.

Yet this very withdrawal makes them more apparent to their neighbors. The hoarder's house fails to be fully gothic because it fails to effectively contain the pollution it hides. Rather than a single secret room, or closet, or freezer, the abject has free rein to break down both architectural and social boundaries. A *Tampa Tribune* article from 2006 describes a hoarder's house where "[t]here were holes in the floor big enough for a 60-pound dog to jump through."

Animal hoarding "spreads" outward, even as the hoarder moves inward; the animals themselves, and their dirt, sounds, and parasites, break through the boundaries the hoarder has erected.

They infringe on the lifestyles of neighbors, for example, when the dilapidation of their homes and yards spreads next door, or their animals' defecation and destruction results in unpleasant sounds, sights, or smells that easily offend those nearby. Hoarders also withdraw from neighborhood social life. Many accounts detail their clandestine ways, describing them as loners or reclusive people. (Arluke 111)

Typically, this spreading outward leads to an "invasion" of public officials and journalists, which parallels the invasion of the animals into human space. When the house is opened, journalistic accounts catapult the hoarder from total anonymity to a particularly notorious celebrity. The intense control that hoarders render over their environment and animals is inverted when public officials and journalists intervene. The hoarders cease to be able to control their homes and the way their homes are represented to the outside world. Public exposure is thus cataclysmic for the hoarder's relationship to animals and to space.

Yet, in an odd way, the loss of self that comes about through public humiliation and exposure is structurally similar to what has already been occurring in the hoarder's home. The incursions of public officials who "condemn" the house transform private domestic space into a public concern that must be rehabilitated or destroyed by society. But this transformation has been the hoarder's project all along. The motion of police and journalists into and out of the house make its boundaries porous, just as the animals did. When public officials comment that the house had become a "jungle" or a "zoo," they are simply reiterating the way the hoarder himself has redefined the space as an environment devoid of human structures. The operation of hoarding is always to undermine privacy by breaking down architectural, social, and even physical boundaries. When public officials break open doors, arrest hoarders, and, in some cases, even bulldoze the houses, they are simply reifying the dissolution of private identity the hoarder set in motion.

✣ ✣ ✣

In the previous chapter I addressed the extension of memory into surrounding physical objects which can, especially among the elderly, result in accumulation. Animal hoarding is distinct from this sort of mnemonic accumulation as its emphasis is on physical extension of the self rather than memory. The relationship between the homeowner and the home becomes transformed by animal hoarding even more than by object hoarding. While accumulated objects may limit motion through the home, accumulated animals almost always compromise both motion and health. This striking contrast between the power of animal life and the increasing weakness of domestic space is a hallmark of animal hoarding. Even when the animals themselves are sick (which is often the case), the sheer number of them overpowers their environment and its human inhabitants.

If a cluttered home can be seen as moving toward being a junkshop (like Krook's), a home full of animals is moving toward being a zoo, a morgue, or a garbage dump, none of which are private. One of the alarming elements of accumulation is that the home becomes increasingly privatized: the objects have meaning only to the owner; the public space becomes crowded with private items; and the floor space becomes literally smaller. Animal hoarding, by contrast, threatens to make the space so squalid as to be no longer a home, and thus no longer private in any sense.

Doris Lessing's story "An Old Woman and Her Cat" portrays the way animal identification breaks open and dissolves the home's spaces and structures. The story tracks the declining years of Hetty Pennefather, an aging widow whose allegiance has shifted from her domestic space to her cat; Hetty's living situation and health degenerate until she dies of exposure in a condemned ruin. The story portrays Hetty's social marginalization as tragic, but it also represents the real pleasure and emotional fulfillment Hetty derives from the abandonment of domestic order and her attachment to her animal.

Hetty Pennefather is a widow living in a council flat in London who is distanced from her children and seems to have no real friends. When she quits her retail job and starts selling used clothes from an old pram, her semi-itinerant lifestyle makes her feel happier and freer. Hetty describes herself as "half gipsy," and when she finds a stray kitten and brings it home, the cat, Tibby, becomes an embodiment of her pleasure navigating the urban landscape: "he ranged about that conglomeration of staircases and lifts and many dozen flats, as if the building were a town" (431). Hetty is ejected from her council flat when she begins to eat things the cat dragged in.

> The neighbours were gossiping that Hetty had "gone savage." This was because the cat had brought up the stairs and along the passageways a pigeon he had caught, shedding feathers and blood all the way; a woman coming in to complain found Hetty plucking the pigeon to stew it, as she had done with others, sharing the meal with Tibby. (432)

Lessing's portrayal emphasizes both the cat's navigational power and the thoroughness of the contamination he represents. We follow the pollution inward, down the halls, to Hetty's apartment, into her kitchen, and finally into her body. Her neighbor discovers her performing a parody of acceptable domestic ritual, as the flat takes on the air of a witch's kitchen. Hetty seems to relish her transgression. "'You're filthy,' she would say to him [the cat], setting the stew down to cool in his dish. [. . .] 'Decent cats don't eat dirty birds. Only those old gypsies eat wild birds'" (432). Hetty's lack of embarrassment over such boundary crossing, and her self-conscious mockery of social mores in her grotesque endearments at the cat's "dirty" behaviors, demonstrate her social marginalization.

When she takes up residence in one room of an abandoned building, Tibby extends her motion outward into the landscape.

> She was in the ground floor back, with a window which opened onto a derelict garden, and her cat was happy in a hunting ground that was a mile around this house where his mistress was so splendidly living. A canal ran close by, and in the dirty city-water were islands which a cat could reach by leaping from moored boat to boat. On the islands were rats and birds. There were pavements full of fat London pigeons. (431–32)

The cat becomes an extension outward into the landscape—a stronger and more successful version of Hetty as he scavenges, circumnavigates the urban environment, and fends for himself. If we apply the paradigms of navigation and amalgamation from the last chapter, the advantages of Hetty's open home become clear. With a lifestyle spent mostly on the streets, navigation presents fewer difficulties, and amalgamation is detached from the home and becomes portable. The cat, who is a navigator par excellence, serves as an avatar of the home's dissolution, and Lessing makes the creature admirable and impressive, consistently emphasizing his strength, health, and virility.

As long as both of their bodies work relatively well, Hetty can be happy with her cat and can enjoy the physical pleasures a disordered urban existence offers. At its best, Hetty's life with Tibby seems more fulfilling than her young married life. Like the clothes she begs from her neighbors and then sells, the cat is "all reward and no cost" (433). Moreover, in its very violation of standards of cleanliness, the cat offers Hetty literal sustenance. In the story, the human-animal relationship thus serves as an alternative to middle-class domestic ideology. The caregiving and control of pet ownership, which represent middle-class notions of order and sustenance, is always balanced against the disorder and dirt created in the home by pets. The balance need shift only slightly for dirt and disorder to gain greater control, as is the case with animal hoarders. But Lessing also shows how the aesthetic appeal of disorder itself, which pets help intensify in the home, can sometimes challenge domestic aesthetics based on cleanliness and privacy. Hetty feels that she is "living well, even without her pension" (433); the festive, mobile, "gipsy" image Hetty maintains of herself offers her the psychological support many elderly people find in domestic objects. Rather than filling her house with personal memorabilia, she creates an aesthetically pleasing environment using other people's castoff clothes: the "little room was soon spread, like her last, with a rainbow of colours and textures and lace and sequins" (431).

When the abandoned house is demolished by a gentrifying developer, Hetty is faced with the choice of giving up her cat or giving up her spot in a nursing home. She ends up inhabiting a derelict structure that is utterly lacking in the practical requirements of a home.

> There was no glass left anywhere. The flooring at ground level was mostly gone, leaving small platforms and juts of planking over basements full of water. The ceilings were crumbling. The roofs were going. [. . .] Here she made her home. [. . .] Tibby, who was cramped after making the journey under the clothes piled in the pram, bounded down and out and vanished into neglected undergrowth to catch his supper.

He returned fed and pleased, and seemed happy to stay clutched in her hard thin old arms. She had come to watch for his return after hunting trips, because the warm purring bundle of bones and fur did seem to allay, for a while, the permanent ache of cold in her bones. (437–38)

This image of the cat's warm bony body pressing into Hetty's frail sick one is the first moment in the story when we actually see Hetty holding the cat. By placing it immediately adjacent to the description of the "bombed" ruin Hetty has to inhabit, Lessing demonstrates how drastic a choice Hetty has made. She has exchanged domestic comforts, indeed necessities, for the physical and emotional rewards of attachment to the animal. The structure has so many broken architectural boundaries—ceiling, roof, glass, floors—that it has ceased to function as any sort of shelter. So many domestic boundaries have been broken that her life is in danger. She responds by clutching the cat closer, thus breaking social boundaries concerning species-appropriate intimacy, as though to become unified with the sort of physical vitality that requires neither walls nor ceilings. Rebekah Fox, a cultural geographer who has studied pet ownership, notes that such boundary crossing, and the perilous balance between social position and physical intimacy it involves, are endemic to pet keeping.

> The intimacy is something that some people may be embarrassed to admit for fear of stigmatization or disgust at the close-lived nature of the relationship with another species, which is seen as crossing moral or social boundaries. Whilst it is accepted that humans and animals will engage in close physical contact, boundaries for this vary greatly even within the same society or family. (533)

Lessing's story suggests that Hetty's attachment to Tibby renders the cat a sort of incubus, draining the life from his owner, forcing her to give up society and shelter for his sake. Gradually freezing and starving to death, she spends her last nights "with the animal held against her chilly bosom" (438). Hetty's death scene emphasizes how her connection to the animal has sapped her own body and collapsed her home to the cocoon of rags encasing her.

> In the comparatively dry corner of the windy room, away from the gaping window through which snow and sleet were drifting, she made another nest—her last. She had found a piece of plastic sheeting in the rubble, and she laid that down first, so that the damp would not

strike up. Then she spread her two blankets over that. Over them were heaped the mass of old clothes. [. . .] She heaved herself into the middle of this, with a loaf of bread near to her hand. She dozed, and waited, and nibbled bits of bread, and watched the snow drifting softly in. (439)

Like the animal hoarders who crowd themselves into hutches to sleep with dogs on their chest, Hetty retreats to increasingly smaller and less domestically controlled spaces, until the walls of her home are only rags a few inches from the edges of her body. Her fatal choices of an open, messy, "gipsy" living environment are the direct result of choosing the animal's body as the defining feature of her domestic life.

Hetty's children have abandoned her, and she has no apparent connections to her past. Unlike seniors who are attached to their homes, she shifts dwellings easily and without regret. Her only possessions are the cast-off clothes which she buys and sells. Unlike Krook, however, she seeks to claim no history through them; they simply immerse her in the variety and fluidity of an urban commercial environment. Hetty exists in a deracinated present, and her relationship with the cat becomes primary in part because of his ability, like hers, to easily break free of the social ties that domestic space represents. The childless pram becomes an image of her alienation from family history and society; she carries her cat in it as she moves to her final "home."

Patronek notes that for hoarders, the self is primarily deposited not in the past but in the physical presence of their animals.

[Pets] become central to the hoarder's core identity. The hoarder develops a strong need for control, and just the thought of losing an animal can produce an intense grief-like reaction. Preliminary HARC interviews also suggest that hoarders grew up in chaotic households, with inconsistent parenting, in which animals may have been the only stable feature. (Patronek 1)

Patronek's emphasis on control, stability, and attachment suggests that the hoarder's identity is supported through physical attachment to the animal rather than to environmental identification. One could say that the animal hoarder allows his house to degenerate because the physical relationship with the animals creates a sense of home. The pollution of the architectural home is simply an embodiment of what has already occurred psychically, as the animal hoarder has detached his identity from the home environment and attached it to the animals. When this rejection of the domestic occurs within the home itself, as in animal hoarding, it destroys the home. Lessing, like the Maysleses, identifies the liberating qualities of an antidomestic bond between humans and animals, without underplaying its costs. Hetty resists the social services that would limit her "gipsy" life with Tibby, clutching the animal so close that her frozen body becomes its den. The Beales allow their home to degenerate into an extravagant inversion of the high-society celebrity culture they inhabit. Both works operate by inviting the viewer or reader into private space that at once fascinates and repels.

Donna Haraway casts such repulsion as a playful political critique in *The Companion Species Manifesto: Dogs, People and Significant Otherness*. Her arch description of her dog, "Ms. Cayenne Pepper," is a rumination on the transgression of physical space between dog and owner.

> I'm sure our genomes are more alike than they should be. There must be some molecular record of our touch in the codes of living that will leave traces in the world, no matter that we are each reproductively silenced females, one by age, one by surgery. Her red merle Australian Shepherd's quick and lithe tongue has swabbed the tissues of my tonsils, with all their eager immune system receptors. Who knows where my chemical receptors carried her messages, or what she took from my cellular system for distinguishing self from other and binding outside to inside?
>
> We have had forbidden conversation; we have had oral intercourse; we are bound in telling story upon story with nothing but the facts. [. . .] We make each other up, in the flesh. Significantly other to each other, in specific difference, we signify in the flesh a nasty developmental infection called love. (2–3)

The passage distances and appalls, even as it invites and comforts, the reader. While Haraway wants us to know she is having fun, there is a clear political valence to this glorification of a dog whose saliva can "colonize all my cells" (1). Although "reproductively silenced," human and animal breed through a transfer of bodily substances, figured as saliva, bacteria, viruses, and sexual fluids. Their molecular exchanges, which may be miraculously transforming DNA or may be an infection, create a new biological entity. Their companionship, which binds through a dissolution of inside and outside, can effect a form of communication "in the flesh" that supersedes language, even the language we are reading. While she doesn't explicitly address the home, Haraway's attention to boundary definition points to the sort of physical attachment that all the authors we have looked at figure in opposition to domestic space. Later in the same passage, Haraway refers to humans and dogs as "co-travelers." The physical bond that companion animals create with humans seems inevitably to be expressed as an itinerant union that pulls away from, or pulls apart, the home, leaving us exposed and homeless.

In the chapter that follows I will continue my analysis of animal attachment by looking at homeless pet owners, for whom the home as architectural structure has been fully superseded by their physical attachment to an animal companion.

PART TWO

HOMES WITHOUT WALLS

Intercorporeal Domestic Space

Chapter 4

Homeless Companions

I probably should have known it was a bad idea to take the dog along on my honeymoon. Not because it interfered with romance or because my wife was jealous (we were both as besotted with Jess, our black-and-white Springer Spaniel, as we were with one another), but because it rendered us social outcasts. Since we weren't able to go into any stores or restaurants together, we got in the habit of staking out the best park benches so that we could sit, read, and eat in public. We eyed the local street musicians and homeless people with territorial antagonism. On our last night, we finally decided to go out for dinner. Carefully selecting a restaurant with shady parking, and waiting until well after sundown, we insisted on sitting where we could see our car, its windows cracked wide, with Jess inside. In the middle of dinner we were confronted by a woman from the next table, who told us she planned to report us to the police for leaving our dog in a hot car. In one stroke, we had gone from honeymooners to fugitives.

The only lodging that would take a dog was a pleasant but run-down bed-and-breakfast with lumpy beds and holes in the screens. Bed-and-breakfasts are always ambiguously domestic, since they are somebody's home, just not yours, but Jess's presence made it seem homier. We spent most of our time hanging around the B & B reading beat-up paperback novels and talking to the owner. She told us about her usual guests, mainly military personnel and power-company employees, as we sat in the kitchen eating sweet, greasy homemade donuts with Jess at our feet. She told us about her husband's cancer as we sat in lawn chairs, swatting mosquitoes, Jess panting nearby. On the whole, it didn't feel like a vacation; it definitely didn't feel like a honeymoon. We had the odd feeling that we had moved, which seemed strangely appropriate given our new state in life. Jess had made us at once more and less socially marginal, more and less at home.

In this chapter I will investigate the writings of homeless pet owners, who, in the process of representing the psychological and practical aspects of homelessness, redefine domesticity through their embodied relationship to a pet. The possibility of creating an alternate version of domesticity based on intimate embodied contact with an animal presents significant challenges to legal and cultural norms. Living in public with an animal companion triggers deep social anxieties about how the body's relationship to the landscape should be enforced by private-property and housing legislation. Not surprisingly, other forms of social disempowerment, especially poverty, make this challenge even more daunting. In some cases, alternative domesticity can empower the homeless, offering emotional stability and practical security, but in others, the bond with an animal intensifies a spiral of marginality and social alienation. Rod Michalko and Lars Eighner portray their physical interactions with their canine companions as a form of alternative domestic embodiment. In John Steinbeck's road memoir, *Travels with Charley,* the essential familiar dynamic that makes travel strengthen, rather than undermine, identity is the bond between dog and owner; Kelly Reichardt's 2009 film *Wendy and Lucy,* based on the Jon Raymond short story "Train Choir," shows the devastating impact of that bond being severed. In these works, discourses of homelessness are interwoven, and sometimes interchangeable, with those of disability. Such is especially the case for Michalko, who is himself blind and has written extensively in the field of disability studies, but the disabling of the homeless body also emerges as a trope in Eighner's and Reichardt's work. Intimate bodily encounters may result, they suggest, in the combination or transformation of both bodies, and such tactile remolding forces the pet owner to recast his or her body image in the context of cross-species companionship. Because the homeless cannot participate in traditional conceptions of home, they undertake to create somatic homes in motion; their corporeal interchanges with their dogs fulfill those aspects of embodiment fundamental to domesticity. In doing so, they interrogate the way that home and homelessness are defined and policed in contemporary American society, and they liberate domesticity from four walls.

In a study of everyday pet-keeping behaviors, cultural geographer Rebekah Fox points out the importance of tactile engagement to the "embodied intimacy" people share with their pets.

> [P]et-human relationships cross understandings of the human-animal
> divide through the embodied intimacy of their everyday relations.
> [. . .] The relationship with pets is a very tactile one, providing both
> human and animal with physical contact and affection. [. . .] For many
> this pleasure seems to be mutual, with both animals and humans enjoy-
> ing the simple satisfaction of being together and engaging in play and
> close physical contact. (532–33)

The specific example she gives is of Christine, whose Pyrenean Mountain
Dog jumps into bed with her after her husband leaves every morning.
"I like this time snuggling up to the warmth of a furry body beside me"
(533). Fox argues that such affectionate snuggling contrasts significantly
with anthropomorphic models of emotional bonding with pets, in which
the animal's behavior is interpreted in terms of human emotion. Tactile engagement itself creates a sense of well-being for pet owners, while
other forms of interaction, usually involving the visual observation of the
animal's behavior, require an extra interpretive step. People who identify
love, grief, boredom, or excitement in their pets typically describe these
behaviors visually. Elizabeth, another of Fox's subjects, describes how
her cat expresses grief after her husband dies: "He seemed disturbed and
uneasy, hanging around the house and following me as if he thought I
might go away too" (532). Elizabeth is comforted by her cat's behavior
just as Christine is by her dog's snuggling, but Elizabeth must ascribe
human emotion to the animal in order to receive such comfort. Christine's response is based entirely on tactile sensation; the "warmth of a
furry body" in a specific relation to hers is enough.

Fox uses her findings to challenge what she considers reductive
discussions of anthropomorphism, which rely upon overly rigorous
categorization of human and animal. "Such non-verbal, non-cognitive
interaction again challenges human social and conceptual boundaries,
but perhaps in a less human-centred way, valuing animals for their own
characteristics rather than trying to define their 'personhood' through the
recognition of human-like attributes" (533). Anthropomorphism ceases
to be problematic, Fox suggests, when we understand it as an embodied
experience. Nobody is philosophically vexed by the fact that it feels good
to pat a dog and the dog enjoys it too. Fox identifies tactile qualities as
animals' "own characteristics" and identifies visually observed or "recognized" behaviors, such as following, sitting, or looking at an owner in
a particular way, as "human-like" attributes. In "The Animal That Therefore I Am (More to Follow)," Jacques Derrida describes such an anthro-

pomorphic interchange with his cat, which "looks at me in my bedroom, or in the bathroom" ("The Animal" 378). As Donna Haraway notes, their emotional exchange, their "regard" for one another ("Encounters" 102), is enacted through the gaze: Derrida is "faced with a cat that continues to see me, to watch" ("The Animal" 381). Derrida proceeds to argue, however, that this visual interchange is buttressed by a form of physical relating, of "being-with," based on pressure: "being *alongside,* being *near [près]* would appear as different modes of being, indeed of *being-with.* With the animal. [. . .] [T]hey express a certain order of the being-huddled-together *[être-serre]* (which is what the etymological root, *pressu,* indicates[,] [. . .]) the being-pressed, the being with as being strictly attached, bound, enchained, being-under-pressure" (379–80). The affectionate pressure Christine experiences when she is "huddled-together" with her dog in the morning offers a less anthropomorphic, because less visual, way of relating to her pet. Ralph Acampora, in his critique of Levinas's "homo-exclusive portrayal of face-to-face encounter," makes a similar distinction between the visual and tactile apprehension of animals.

> Concentration on the face tends to reinstate an anthropocentrist gaze that takes the eyes or seeks ocularity as the reflective surface of a morally weighty soul denied to other animals. [. . .] [An alternative] form of relating, namely *fellowship,* might enable us to broaden our corporal attention and moral imagination, and to become aware of whole-body encounters and their ethical significance. (225–26)

Elizabeth and Derrida derive anthropomorphic comfort from watching their cats move about the house and interpreting the animals' gaze as revealing an emotional bond, while Christine's comfort comes from bodily contiguity. Such "whole-body encounters" between humans and their pets occur easily and frequently in the home. Domestic companion animals, what we sometimes call "house pets," might more accurately be called "body pets." Their ability to comfort and sustain us through tactile intimacy doesn't require architectural space as a staging ground, as visually perceived anthropomorphic comfort does.

In the previous chapter, we saw how choosing an intimate, boundary-crossing relationship to an animal over standard domestic organization could put the home at risk. Hetty Pennefather's death scene could be the nightmarish intensification of Christine's morning snuggle. Fox's and Ralph Acampora's arguments suggest that the relationship between animal and domesticity need not always be pernicious. It should be possible to imagine a vividly embodied animal-human connection that transcends or redefines domestic space without ruining the pet owner's life. Implicit in Fox's portrayal, however, is the same sort of shifting of emphasis from architectural space to bodily relation that is apparent in Hetty's dependence upon Tibby. The site of the domestic experience is not the room but the bed, and not the bed so much as the position that two bodies occupy upon it.

The bed might, in fact, be the best place to begin redefining the home based on corporeal rather than architectural engagements, as it is central to the legal definition of homelessness. The McKinney-Vento Homeless Assistance Act, the most significant piece of federal homelessness legislation, defines a homeless person as "as an individual who lacks a fixed, regular, and adequate night-time residence" or "an individual who has a primary nighttime residence" that is either a shelter or "a public or private place not designed for, or ordinarily used as, a regular sleeping accommodation for human beings" ("Federal"). Homelessness, and thus home, depend entirely on where you sleep; having a home means sleeping within a permanent and substantial architectural structure. If Christine snuggles with her dog in a car or a tent rather than in a family house or apartment, she is homeless, even though the feeling of domestic intimacy and stability their cuddling creates is the same. Any attempt to reconceptualize the home in terms of corporeal unions, especially those involving sleeping, would run counter to the legal definition.

Legal definitions of homelessness are closely related to those of disability, Robert McRuer argues, because the cultural construction of domestic space in twentieth-century America involves the exclusion of the disabled body. "[F]ar from emerging as the 'private' counterpart to the new and public able-bodied identity, disability [. . .] was more firmly linked to ideas of pathology, loss, lack, and isolation and was opposed to the intimacy and security associated with (heterosexual and able-bodied) domestic space" (93). The home as an "orderly, managed" (91) space represents the orderly managed body and thus requires the disorderly or disabled body as its homeless counterpart. It is important that in being pushed out of the home, the disabled are denied not just order and security but also "intimacy." If intimacy can operate only within the normative architectural home, then the homeless and disabled are doomed to live a life without it. In direct opposition to this view, Michalko and Eighner portray a version of disabled and homeless domesticity structured entirely around the bodily intimacy they share with their dogs.

In his analysis of his relationship with his service dog, Smokie, Michalko offers a political elaboration of McRuer's point about the disabled body's cultural exclusion from the home, arguing that blindness represents a form of cultural exile in relation to the "homeland" of the sighted world.

> [Blind persons] will always be, to some degree, homeless in the land of sightedness. Being at home with blindness can only mean that one is reconciled to a "home away from home." [. . .] All of us move and live "between" the private and public realms. We have private homes in our public homeland and we live in between these homes. But blind persons carry their private homes with them in a way that sighted people do not. The home of blindness cannot be left behind when a blind person enters the home of sightedness. [. . .] When we see blindness in this way we see it as a home unworthy of habitation. (99–101)

The physical condition of blindness has, as a cultural corollary, an inevitable redefinition of the physical qualities of home. Blindness brings about a psychological state of itinerancy in which home ceases to be geographically located and becomes something that one must "carry." Because this moving home is consistently defined in relation to the sighted home, the itinerant home of the blind is "unworthy of habitation." This mixed metaphor—a home that cannot be left behind but also cannot be lived in—suggests the profound alienation from social relations that Michalko attempts to describe.

In *The Two in One,* Michalko argues for an apprehension of home that, while in motion, sustains and maintains his identity. "Smokie has given me a glimpse of my homeland from the point of view of home-in-blindness. I am 'in home' with my blindness and, with Smokie's help, I carry this home gracefully through the homeland of sightedness" (123–24). Smokie reestablishes a sense of home, not by reestablishing an architectural structure, but by making the mobility inherent to the blind apprehension of home into something graceful. Michalko's book thus theorizes the relationship between home and the dynamic interaction of bodies. Living in a body that does not participate in the somatic relations to architectural space through which sighted people define certain structures and landscape locations as home, Michalko experiences a sense of home through somatic engagement between his own body and his dog's.

In *The Two in One,* Michalko attempts to interrogate social conventions about the relationship between sight and blindness and between owner and pet. Forced to define the landscape that surrounds them in the terms established by sighted culture, he argues, blind persons can only conceive of their experience in what amounts to a foreign language. His relationship with Smokie allows for the reinterpretation of cultural assumptions that place human, nature, blind, and sighted in particular places on a hierarchy of power. "Smokie and I do not merely inhabit a common natural and social world; we depend upon one another for our existence, and together we construct and re-construct the world. Smokie and I are, almost literally, extensions of each other, and the interpretive chain that we inhabit takes the form of a circle" (5). Michalko's ability to reinterpret these social dynamics operates through a physiological apprehension of space defined by extension rather than perspective, more by tactile association than visual placement. Inhabiting, being placed in a particular habitat, is opposed to constructing and reconstructing, in which the physical environment is dynamic and continually negotiable. Rather than inhabiting a visually comprehensible world, man and dog come to inhabit an interpretive process, and their power to interpret this world derives from their physical connection.

This mode of inhabiting is made necessary, Michalko argues, by a fundamental contrast between the sighted and the blind in their understanding of absence. Sighted persons rely on the phenomenological principle that invisible objects could be seen if they were physically present, before the viewer's eyes. Blind persons, on the other hand, experience all objects as "always-already present despite their always-already absence. The homeland of the 'sighted world' is never absent insofar as it is experienced in the ubiquitous sense of 'omnipresence'" (100). This omnipresence is not the numinous cloud of a deity but the endless labyrinth of hard-edged or fast-moving bodies that the blind need to negotiate, aided by their physical attachment to a guide dog. To inhabit such a dynamically omnipresent landscape requires that one break down distinctions between human and animal, as well as body and landscape, a process that Michalko describes as *our coming in touch with our world* (184).

> At one time, I am master; at another, Smokie is. Now I am handler, now he is. On one occasion, I take ownership for decision-making; on another, Smokie does. Recall that Smokie and I both lead and follow one another. This is a fluid relation that does not apply when leader and follower are understood as static and completely separable entities. Thus mastery, handling, and ownership are situated phenomena and not ontological ones. Our situation originates in our commitment to being in touch with our world. (184–85)

Because successful motion through their landscape can occur only through a multitude of minute negotiations of their bodies, which depend on silent, "ineffable" communication, the power dynamics between them become "situated phenomena and not ontological ones." The social power of owning a dog, of being its master, is of less importance than the social empowerment Michalko experiences through physical motion, which allows him to "master and handle the social world." When communication between man and dog is "fluid," physical motion across streets, over curbs, and past obstacles also becomes fluid. Because their "situation"—their posture and position in relation to one another—is constantly changing, the sequence of "situated phenomena" that comprise a walk down the street undercuts any clear ontological identification of leader and follower, master and servant.

Michalko's use of the term "situated phenomena" seems an odd way to describe motion, suggesting as it does definitive location; but fundamental to the sort of physical experience Michalko describes is a sequence of physically situated engagements that string together into fluid arcs. "Everything Smokie does comes to me through the harness. I feel each of his steps and I step with him. I feel every variation of speed, every change of direction, the most subtle variation in the path Smokie is taking, and I feel myself moving with the subtle smoothness and grace that Smokie gives me through the harness" (122). The human-animal relationship brings the otherwise unconscious aspects of physical motion to the fore, but, more to the point, the instinctive or unconscious operation of joints and muscles that occurs in walking takes on a rich emotional valence when two physical beings have synchronized their motions together. Because they can move together, their identities cease to be static and are also in motion.

Michalko's emphasis on "fluidity" discourages the reader from constructing a visual image of himself and Smokie, which might involve halting or ungainly movement. In fact, much of Smokie's job involves stopping, or blocking, his owner "to avoid a carelessly moving pedestrian, a cyclist, or even an automobile" (122). Yet Michalko represents their motion as sinuous and graceful. The landscape itself takes on fluidity when Michalko walks with Smokie. The very obstacles that limit his ability to move through the world are swept away by the metaphor; he and Smokie seem to flow, or even float, down the street. Ironically, in placing emphasis on the embodied situatedness of his bond with Smokie and rejecting its ontological definitions, Michalko makes the obstacles to his motion less embodied, and they become an abstraction—"the social world." A similarly contradictory formulation inheres in his definition of their motion as "in touch with our world." Smokie allows Michalko to walk without relying on a cane or other extensions of his sense of touch, and he prevents him from excessive touching—tripping on or bumping against objects. When they walk together, they are "in touch" with the world by navigating around obstacles and touching only the clear, safe spaces. Michalko adopts the musical metaphor of counterpoint to describe this motion.

> As we move through our world, Smokie and I are not merely side by side. We move together as one, touching and imagining both each other and our world. Our harmony comes from the contrapuntal relation of the two-in-one. We depict a world to each other generated by our difference and sameness. We communicate this world to one another through the ineffability of the togetherness found in distinction. (185)

This musical metaphor illustrates how their distinct bodies and abilities gracefully reinforce one another. As in musical counterpoint, balancing asymmetries combine to create harmony. The human-dog combined body is not a pairing but a unification that exists first and most importantly in the invisible acts of imagination and "depiction." Michalko clearly is not suggesting an exterior depiction, in words or pictures, but a form of private, unspoken yet fully apprehended representation occurring through touch and motion. They "construct and reconstruct" (5) this depiction of space as they move through it together.

That safe space surrounding Michalko and Smokie, created by their union, is the real subject of his portrayal of movement, as his subsequent metaphors of dance and football playing suggest.

> Smokie and I move in and out of pedestrian traffic in the same graceful, well-choreographed way. [. . .] Moving with Smokie invariably conjures up my days as an athlete on the football field. I followed my blockers with the same precision with which I now follow Smokie. Running through a field of defenders, I looked for any semblance of an opening and moved through it twisting, turning, stopping, and starting. (123)

Both dance and football involve the vigorous navigation of bodies relative to other bodies, without their necessarily touching. In the football comparison in particular, Michalko's goal is not to be touched. He is not an offensive lineman or a tackle but a tight end, relying on his teammates to create a space through which he can carry the football. Michalko is carrying something much more consequential, however: "with Smokie's help, I carry this home gracefully through the homeland of sightedness" (124). Michalko's body becomes "in tune" with itself, like a dancer with the music, through the graceful creation of adjacent space, and this space serves the same function as the space within the home through which we define ourselves domestically. In the home, the phenomenological distinction between vision and sight is intensified; sighted homeowners have greater-than-normal confidence that all visually absent objects can still be found in the next room. It follows that the "omnipresence" that characterizes the apprehension of blind persons, in which no object is more visually present, and thus none more visually absent, would also be intensified. According to Michalko's reasoning, a blind person would be able to imaginatively transport, or "carry," all of the objects that make up his domestic identity more easily than a sighted person. While at home, a sighted person perceives the space around him as saturated with familiarity because every object his eye falls upon carries memories, and every object around the corner or down the hall will do the same. Once he leaves home and less-familiar objects fill the visual field, surrounding space becomes alien and noncomforting. For the blind, however, the omnipresence of familiar and unfamiliar objects makes public and private space equally familiar. While this can be isolating, as Michalko notes (101), it also means that the blind can more easily perceive the space adjacent to their bodies, even when in public, as richly familiar, or domestic. Smokie's perfect partnering creates such space and thus creates a home that can be carried.

Eighner's *Travels with Lizbeth* portrays his experiences as a homeless man, living in and moving through various Southwestern cities in the late 1980s. Like Michalko, Eighner investigates the creation of domestic identity in public space through his physical attachment to his dog. Michalko demonstrates the condition of being at home in blindness; he struggles to create for his reader a sense of the homelessness implicit in his disability. Eighner struggles to convey the physical limitations associated with homelessness, which he renders as a form of disability. The book offers a polemical meditation on the politicized economic landscape in relation to the homeless body, and his intimate association with Lizbeth both mitigates and intensifies his political disenfranchisement. *Travels with Lizbeth* is, in large part, a description of Eighner's logistical difficulties moving through the landscape. He must find safe places to sleep, sit, and stand in a landscape that persistently designates his bodily presence as unlawful. He spends his days establishing himself in relatively safe benches or public seating areas. His dog Lizbeth always accompanies him, and their attachment often limits his motion.

Lizbeth had her disadvantages. I could not go some places with her.

Usually I had no safe place to leave her. Individuals and institutions who might have helped me alone could not consider the two of us. She is not an especially bright dog, and even so I regret not having trained her to the extent of her abilities in her youth. I often averted disaster only by anticipating her behavior, which is to say, I suppose, she has trained me. (*Travels* xiii)

Lizbeth's presence elaborates the normal difficulties of itinerant mobility, pushing Eighner further into the social margin, in part because her lack of training makes it necessary for Lizbeth to remain *physically* attached to him most of the time. He must worry not only about where he can go but also about where they can go in combination and how that combination will be maintained. While Michalko emphasizes Smokie's expertise and training, which allows for the social integration of the man-dog pair, Eighner dwells on Lizbeth's imperfections. Not very bright, not well trained, she is on the margins of the dog world just as her owner is on the margins of human society. Smokie's excellent training, on the other hand, allows him and Michalko to undercut the social discourse of "mastery" and become partners in their seamless movement. Lizbeth's lack of training also undercuts mastery, but in a chaotic, physically inconvenient way. The dog has "trained," which strongly suggests "restrained," Eighner, making their movements together clumsy and difficult.

> I did not much want to negotiate Hollywood Boulevard with Lizbeth and the gear, but I did not want to wander around in the hills after dark. I was concerned that Lizbeth might misbehave in the crowds, but once I saw what the neighborhood [. . .] was like, I was glad to have her with me.
>
> Where the Hollywood Freeway passes under Hollywood Boulevard I found a weedy spot on a corner and sat down with Lizbeth on the gear. I had walked my limit with the gear and thereafter we moved at intervals from one bench at a bus stop to another. Lizbeth, on the other hand, was still feeling frisky because for most of the distance we had covered she had walked on sidewalks or grass. (71)

He has the choice between "negotiating" and "wandering" and has to settle for the ungainly dance of moving from bench to bench. His own body is not a perfect match with Lizbeth's; his exhausted stasis contrasts comically with her manic friskiness. Unlike Michalko's grace of motion with Smokie, Eighner and Lizbeth move in jerks and starts, at different speeds on different surfaces. He must continually make difficult decisions because of Lizbeth's presence, and the story of their travels is the story of these calculations and the anxiety they cause. While Michalko portrays his relationship with Smokie as a sequence of physical adjustments and exchanges—"I feel every variation of speed, every change of direction"—Eighner's attachment with Lizbeth requires a series of imperfect decisions: "I did not much want [. . .] but I did not want. [. . .] I was concerned."

Eighner's anxiety about Lizbeth parallels his relationship to the social landscape. The needs of his body—for sleep, rest, food, occasional sex and cigarettes—must be balanced against the material limitations of his circumstances. He needs to make judgments about where he can keep his usually exhausted, sometimes sick, self comfortable without attracting the police or irritating the public. His body becomes an inconvenient obstacle to his progress, something that makes easy motion impossible. Since Lizbeth and he are, in Michalko's words, "almost literally, extensions of each other" (5), her body becomes an extension of his physical difficulties.

> I found no place to tie Lizbeth and I took her with me across the boulevard to a liquor store. There I tied her to the gear and went in to buy cigarettes. [. . .] In the liquor store I had to wait in line. Sure enough, a man who had not realized Lizbeth was affixed to my bags tried to grab one of them. Lizbeth snarled. I left my place in line and went outside where I saw the man fleeing down the boulevard. Encumbered by the gear, Lizbeth had managed to pursue him only twenty yards. (72)

Eighner's writing emphasizes that, like Michalko and Smokie, the power dynamics between him and Lizbeth are "situated phenomena and not ontological ones" (Michalko 185). They are situated in a hostile social landscape, however, that breaks and blocks their negotiation of space. Every element of this scene bespeaks both physical encumbrances and the social and psychological encumbrances that result from them. Eighner worries about losing both dog and gear, so he ties both together. In theory, Lizbeth will protect the gear and not run away; tying them together makes them safe. But Eighner knows that the dog could still escape and the gear could still be stolen, and in fact both things nearly happen because he is blocked by the line at the liquor store, which is itself a manifestation of legal control. Where Michalko disembodies the landscape through metaphors of musicality and fluidity, Eighner renders the precise locations and postures that make up the physics of social disempowerment. Lizbeth and the gear constitute the "home" Eighner carries with him, but dragging, rather than carrying, might be a more appropriate description. The image of Lizbeth dragging the gear as Eighner watches from across the street points to the mutually reinforcing problems of encumbrance and attachment.

As its title suggests and as I mentioned earlier in this chapter, *Travels with Lizbeth* gestures toward John Steinbeck's *Travels with Charley* in portraying a writer's wanderings in America accompanied by his dog. But Steinbeck's book is an optimistic celebration of the free exploration of a unified homeland. For Steinbeck "the road away from Here seems broad and straight and sweet" (3); it has none of the jerky, circuitous trajectories of Eighner's interstate travels. As David Chichester notes, there is a strong American tradition equating embodied mobility, especially automotive mobility, with democratic freedom (57). Steinbeck's America is a freedom-loving nation that can best be appreciated from the perspective of itinerancy.

> My plan was clear, concise, and reasonable. [. . .] I discovered that I did not know my own country. I, an American writer, writing about America[,] [. . .] had not heard the speech of America, smelled the grass and trees and sewage, seen its hills and water, its color and quality of light. [. . .] So it was that I determined to look again, to try to rediscover this monster land. (5)

Such voluntary homelessness is a whimsical undertaking; Steinbeck calls himself a "casual turtle carrying his house on his back" (6). He runs no risk of being arrested, lost or marginalized, except to the extent he wants to be. In fact, his main concern is that he might be recognized as a celebrity and thus be forced back into the cultural center. Far from being unemployed or forced out to tramp, Steinbeck's trip represents a sort of easygoing literary research.

While *Travels with Charley* is a fairly conventional travelogue, Steinbeck's description of himself as a "practical bum" and "a wayward man" (3) are attempts to elide himself with what John Allen calls "the tradition of the romantic, adventuresome hobo as represented by Jack London, W. H. Davies, and other tramps, as well as the Beat Generation" (140). As Allen points out, such narratives tend to portray itinerant homelessness as a choice, or an adventure, and thus to diminish the social significance of those forced to live on the street. Given Steinbeck's status as the creator of the iconic homeless family, the Joads, this seems particularly ironic, and at certain points, *Travels with Charley* does seem oddly like a saccharine reworking of *The Grapes of Wrath* with plenty of money and a better truck.

Steinbeck devotes significant attention to his custom-made camper, "a beautiful thing, powerful and yet lithe" (6), which provides him the ideal combination of comfort and freedom. Unlike a trailer, which "is difficult to maneuver on mountain roads, is impossible and often illegal to park" (6), there is nothing ungainly or inconvenient about Rocinante, as he calls it; the camper fits perfectly into the landscape, and both he and Charley fit perfectly inside it. Charley easily "retired into a carpeted corner under the table" (27) or "curled up in his place under the bed" (141), the perfect canine counterpart to Steinbeck's "clear, concise and reasonable" domesticity. Charley takes his place in relation to the camper rather than in relation to Steinbeck's body; their relationship is significantly less contiguous or embodied than Eighner's or Michalko's, in large part because the trailer works successfully as a miniature, but fully functioning, domestic structure.

Studies of pet ownership consistently find higher levels of "animal empathy and attachment" among homeless pet owners than among their "securely housed" counterparts (Taylor et al. 219). Eighner's book investigates the physical reification of this attachment, with close attention to the social and logistical difficulties it entails. The fulcrum of these difficulties is the leash. Eighner describes in great detail the logistics involved in linking the bodies together.

> I had installed another snap on Lizbeth's leash, making one on each end. This had proved handy in many ways. In camp I could extend Lizbeth's range by attaching a strap of whatever I had to a tree and snapping her leash onto that. When we left camp, I had nothing to untie, but had only to unsnap the leash. I could fix her easily to dumpsters when I needed both hands to go through the contents. (*Travels* 206)

The double-snap leash becomes an umbilicus between Eighner and his dog who, ironically, seems far more limited in her motion than most housedogs. He rarely lets her run free but for the most part keeps her tied to himself or his immediate surroundings. By replacing the handle with a second snap, Eighner diminishes his haptic connection to the animal; he cannot feel or communicate with the dog's body through the leash, as Michalko does through Smokie's harness. Yet Eighner clearly spends more time physically attached to Lizbeth than Michalko does to Smokie. Rather than interchange, the double-snap figures the constancy and pervasiveness of their connection; Lizbeth is less a partner than an appendage, an actual element of Eighner's body. "[A]nyone who has had to sleep by the side of the road in some wild place may appreciate that an extra pair of keen ears, a good nose, and sharp teeth on a loud, ferocious ally of unquestionable loyalty have a certain value that transcends mere sentiment" (xiii). Lizbeth offers not just dog's eyes and dog's teeth but an "extra pair" for Eighner, or, more accurately, for the man/dog amalgam they have become through constant attachment. This bodily extension allows even poorly trained, disorderly Lizbeth to succeed at Smokie's complex job: "For the most part we went to the bamboo after dark and left it at dawn. In this Lizbeth was very useful for it was often too dark for me to find our place in the bamboo by my own senses" (223). Lizbeth's extra eyes see for Eighner in the "wild place[s]" he must move through. The animal-human composite body is well suited to an existence that occurs literally on the margins of society, "by the side of the road."

Homeless pet owners interviewed by Lynn Rew describe a similar physiological bonding with their animal companions. Rew's study was designed to determine whether pet ownership diminished loneliness and improved social skills among homeless teens. Rather than describing their emotional bond with the animal, however, the teens emphasize the animals' intimate, sometimes boundary-crossing, physical proximity. "They climb in your sleeping bag with you and keep you company. [. . .] They know you need a lick across the face" (130). Often, the animal's body is closely identified with, or imaginatively overlaid upon, the owner's. One girl explains that "you have a lot of responsibility for a dog. Even in my muscles and shoulders because when you're hitchhiking you have to carry like 20 pounds of dog food with you" (129). Her emotional bond with the dog, and the socially ameliorative responsibility she gains through this bond, are both manifested in her "muscles and shoulders." Eighner offers an even more elaborate melding of bodies, suggesting that he and Lizbeth share unconscious nervous and muscular responses and that their bond is not just physiological but autonomic.

> A few experiences like that [being threatened while sleeping in the open] and I think anyone would have to stop and think if forced to choose between his dog and his own arm. [. . .] To say I trusted Lizbeth in matters within her purview would hardly express it. Do I "trust" my fingers to hit some key (if not precisely the right one) as I type? After a while I relied on her without really noticing that I was. I did not hear with her ears, but I read the indications of what she heard from the fur on the back of her neck without having to think about it. ("Lizbeth" 16)

Lizbeth responds to and communicates with Eighner unconsciously; she moves to protect him, like an arm, and helps him express himself, like a finger (a particularly resonant comparison for a writer). She has become incorporated into his body image, and he can interpret her bodily responses "without having to think about it," as though they were his own. Yet the protection Lizbeth offers can also be understood as a terrible compensatory sacrifice; the first sentence of the passage suggests both that Lizbeth is as valuable as an arm and that by choosing her he must become a sort of amputee.

Lizbeth thus can be seen as both enabling and disabling Eighner. She offers him physical security, expanding and intensifying his bodily powers and offering him a unique and rewarding form of bodily companionship. At the same time, she disables him by making his motion through, and practical action within, the landscape difficult. She excludes him from the shelters and social service organizations that might help him adopt a more traditional lifestyle. Tanya Titchkosky, in her analysis of discourses of disability, suggests, however, that the "inclusive" social services Eighner has to relinquish are themselves disempowering. "[E]ach and every programmatic attempt to institute inclusion is, at one and the same time, making disability materialize in particular ways [. . .] [such] that disabled people are reproduced as an exclude-able type" (149–50). For Eighner to accept the help of shelters that wish to include him in normative society would be to identify himself as marginal, homeless, disabled. By preventing him from doing so, Lizbeth makes him more marginal in society's eyes and also excludes him from society's system of definitions. Eighner offers an alternative way of understanding able-bodied identity, in which Lizbeth's "keen ears [. . .] good nose, and sharp teeth" are incorporated into his own body image, empowering him to maintain his (socially disempowered) lifestyle of sleeping by the side of the road. Understood in terms of normative domesticity, Lizbeth forces Eighner into the legal position of a homeless person; understood in terms of embodied intimacy, Lizbeth and Eighner together create a more successful domestic environment than he could ever find in a shelter.

The power struggle between social and personal definitions of disabling and enabling, homelessness and domesticity, is the central concern of Reichardt's film *Wendy and Lucy*. The film portrays a few days in the life of a homeless woman, Wendy, and her dog, Lucy, when their car breaks down in a small Oregon town and their tenuously maintained lifestyle falls to pieces. At the start of the film, Wendy and Lucy exemplify the same sort of mutually supportive embodied unit as Michalko and Smokie or Lizbeth and Eighner. As they walk together or sleep in Wendy's small car, their bodies move in unison and fit comfortably against one another. The film addresses the practical and emotional impact of their physical separation. Eighner and Michalko suggest the power of the human/dog physical bond to hold off the worst forms of social disempowerment; Reichardt's film shows us how the breaking of such a bond intensifies them.

Wendy and Lucy opens with the two companions walking contentedly beside the railroad tracks, weaving back and forth, responding to verbal and physical cues that demonstrate their habitual corporeal bond. The fragility of this bond immediately becomes apparent, however, when Lucy disappears, and Wendy finds her after darkness falls, at a bonfire created by young vagrants who are riding the rails. Although they are friendly, many seem drunk or potentially dangerous, and they are clearly more socially marginal than she. Rather than her own safety, however, Wendy's primary concern is that she will be separated from Lucy. She shifts position, trying to get closer to the woman patting the dog, clearly anxious that she might not release her. Reichardt's camerawork emphasizes the placement of bodies in relation to one another; the strange faces and actions of the vagrants as they tell stories of working in Alaska, where Wendy hopes to find a job, are secondary to Wendy's slow repositioning of arms and legs to reclaim Lucy.

This scene, with its focus on physical contiguity and posture, serves to foreshadow the main action of the movie, which follows Wendy's search for Lucy after they are separated. Wendy ties the dog in front of a grocery store before going in to shoplift dog food and, like Eighner when he ties Lizbeth outside the liquor store, has to check on her through the window. Stepping out of the store to comfort Lucy, she is caught with unbought food and is arrested. We see the dog, still tied up outside the store, grow smaller in the rear window of the police car. At the police station, Wendy incessantly watches the clock. In a film that has no action sequences, and in which almost nothing takes place, these scenes are surprisingly suspenseful; we cringe at every little delay, knowing the dog is vulnerable and uncared for. Returning hours later to the grocery store, Wendy's worst fears are realized, and the visceral pain of the separation is rendered on her face for the rest of the movie. Reichardt so successfully positions our attention upon the felt bodily loss of the dog that even when Wendy is nearly assaulted by a mentally ill vagrant as she tries to sleep in the woods, we comprehend her danger in terms of Lucy's absence; if Lucy were there she wouldn't be in danger of robbery, rape, murder.

Wendy's search for Lucy, which occupies the rest of the film, requires her to undergo successive somatic losses, reiterating the fundamental loss of her companion. As in Eighner's memoir, Wendy's physical limitations become the imagistic leitmotifs of the film. She must walk miles to the pound and then walk more miles around the city, taping up homemade signs. When a kindly security guard suggests that the dog may return to a piece of clothing that smells like her, the camera dwells on Wendy's hands tying her few pieces of clothing to street signs, bushes, and fences, as though she is leaving pieces of her body behind. Disability is a visual trope in the film; motorized wheelchairs move through the background in many scenes. Because she has to sleep in cars and change her clothes quickly in cramped public restrooms, Wendy's young, fit body becomes hunched and twisted. As she wanders through the landscape, she must lug a large backpack and a bag of clothing and bedding, which makes her movement hobbled and jerky. While in the first few scenes we see how Lucy, like Eighner's Lizbeth, limits Wendy's movements by pulling on the leash or needing to be tied up outside, it becomes apparent that Lucy's absence is even more disabling.

In the story, the loss of the dog is rendered as an amputation. "The ache of Lucy's absence was like a limb being severed over and over again" (230). This is the same trope used by Eighner when he imagines a choice between Lizbeth and his own arm. Because the dog limits Wendy's mobility and creates practical and financial burdens for her, such an amputation might be considered salutary. Wendy ends up in jail only because she is shoplifting dog food, and the endless walking, waiting, and dealing with logistical problems all result from losing Lucy. In her discussion of "overcoming stories," Titchkosky analyzes an article in *Kidzworld* magazine about a child named Rudy who undergoes a voluntary amputation in order to participate in mainstream childhood activities. "'Despite having no legs Rudy plays football, runs track and has even competed in several triathlons'" on his prosthetic legs.

> The remarkable notion that a five-year-old has decided to amputate his legs [. . .] [gains] sensibility and even ordinariness under the organizing force of the overcoming story. Thus, Rudy is depicted as overcoming his body's confinement to a wheelchair by deciding to amputate his legs and by using prosthetic devices. His decision, as well as the devices he uses, are taken up by the narrative as the artifice of the overcoming story makes it seem as if it is Rudy's five-year-old body that is calling out the demand. (188)

Such a gory solution to the problem of disability enforces the cultural assumption that the disabled body is valueless, "emptied of life" (164), Titchkosky argues. The amputation of Lucy or Lizbeth from their owners would be a positive step toward enabling their owners' return to normative status, no matter how painful. Wendy's determination to become physically reunited with Lucy represents a stubborn refusal to overcome the physically and socially disabling effects the dog has on her body.

Reichardt's portrayal of Wendy's search for Lucy also suggests that, for the homeless, the landscape of exurban sprawl that now characterizes much of America is itself disabling. She must wander with her belongings from donut shop to parking lot to railroad siding, never finding a welcoming public place to rest. This leaves her physically and psychologically exhausted; she leans and slumps against any surface she can find. In an interview about the film, Reichardt makes explicit this elision between physical disability and the landscape of "sprawl just outside a city." "I felt like I had a clamp on my head for about a year. Location has so much to do with that. Just the constant sounds of traffic, of getting away from nature in every way. Of getting locked in. [. . .] It's a soulless, in-between place" (Van Sant). The landscape of parking lots, rental houses, and vacant lots that Wendy moves through tortures and distorts the body like a "clamp on [the] head." It also imprisons her, "locks" her in to a powerless way of moving. The film alternates between exteriors, in which Wendy is always in motion but never moving freely or gracefully, and locked enclosures, such as the dog pound, the police station, and the chain-link fence, topped with razor wire, that surrounds the car lot.

This imagistic elision between imprisonment and disability is consistent with the cultural and legal history of homelessness. Rosemarie Garland Thompson notes that "the history of begging is virtually synonymous with the history of disability. Much of American disability legislation has attempted to sort out this conflation, termed by Tom Compton the 'vagrant/beggar/cripple' complex" (35). In his analysis of the historical rhetoric associated with homeless legislation, Ken Kyle notes that under English vagrancy laws, which form the basis for current American homeless legislation, "homeless people might be labeled 'the idle,' 'vagabonds,' 'beggars,' 'criminals,' and a little later as 'rogues'" (77). This cascade of terms involves a logic of substitution in which the body's motion through a nondomestic landscape implies its failure to perform able-bodied work and its reliance upon others for financial support, leading to its criminality and ultimately imprisonment. The film shows Wendy's progression through these stages, which are intensified, rather than mitigated, by her physical attachment to her dog. A vicious cycle is created when she loses her home in a fire, must travel to find work, and resorts to petty crime to feed Lucy. Shoplifting leads to her arrest, Lucy's incarceration in the pound, and subsequent cycles of vagrancy and social marginalization. In an extended scene at the pound, the camera moves torturously from cage to cage to cage, focusing relentlessly on the dogs, all of whom are incarcerated and hoping for a companion, and none of whom are Lucy. Each subsequent view into a cage represents Wendy's dashed hopes and serves as a further image of her social imprisonment.

The discourses of domesticity, attachment, disability, and criminality all come together in Eighner's memoir in a chapter entitled "Lizbeth on Death Row." As he sits with Lizbeth at a public market, Eighner is approached from behind by a blind student, who pokes Lizbeth with his cane. When she growls in response, the student calls the dogcatcher, and Lizbeth is taken to the pound. Eighner constructs the scene so that his attachment to Lizbeth first bespeaks peaceful domestic affection and then, suddenly and ineluctably, social disempowerment and incarceration.

> The Christmas season was upon the market. [. . .] [I]t was busy enough that Lizbeth and I could not sit on the benches around the planters. [. . .] When I sat on the sidewalk at the market to knit, I put the leash around my waist and snapped the usually free end onto her collar. As I am uncommonly stout, this left Lizbeth only a little slack. When the weather was cool, of course, she did not want much slack. She got on my lap and curled up, and somehow I managed to knit. So it had been many days that we visited the market. (*Travels* 206–7)

Eighner is knitting a sweater for himself from yarn donated by a local housewife. The domestic character of his physical bond with Lizbeth is foregrounded. Eighner becomes the maternal homemaker, knitting placidly, with Lizbeth curled up on his lap and connected to his round stomach by the leash umbilicus: a tranquil Santa with a Christmas fair proceeding behind him. Eighner goes to great lengths to establish the spatial dynamics of the ensuing accident. "If the student had been feeling the sidewalk with his cane he would have hit my leg with it. But instead he was waving the cane through the air about a foot from the ground, and so, with an accuracy a sighted person would have had difficulty matching on purpose, he poked Lizbeth in the face" (207). Both Eighner and the blind student are socially marginalized, and both are portrayed as having a disability. Eighner's attachment to his dog, and his need, as a homeless person, to establish a public location that he can occupy, make him vulnerable. Because the market is crowded, he cannot sit on a bench, so he takes up residence on the sidewalk. Because he is engaging in domestic behavior in a nondomestic setting, he becomes a hazard and, ultimately, risks destroying the very unit of dog and man that the scene seemed to celebrate. When the police arrive to take Lizbeth to the pound, Eighner's attachment to Lizbeth puts his social and physical disempowerment nakedly on display. "I held her in my lap as she licked the tears from my cheeks. I cried that she was all I had. [. . .] When I got up I could hardly stand" (210). His attempt at domesticity in public is to blame for the catastrophe. Sleeping in public can land one in jail; knitting in public is a comparably transgressive attempt to redefine domesticity on the street, an act that can land you, as Eighner describes it, "on death row."

When Lizbeth is taken to the pound, Eighner begins to identify himself as homeless and, subsequently, as a criminal. "According to the rules, Lizbeth was now a *bite dog*. If I could not redeem her, she would die. I would be allowed to see her only once; now or later. I decided I wanted to see her right away. If I could not get the money I might get a gun, and if so I would want an idea of the layout of the place" (211). As with Lucy, Lizbeth intensifies the sequence of equivalences whereby her owner is designated as homeless, vagrant, and criminal. Eighner's determination to undertake an armed prison break of the pound may be ironic, or it may not. The story demonstrates how sudden his shift into disempowerment and potential criminality occurs. One moment Lizbeth and Eighner are sharing a warm and sustaining domestic interchange in the market, peacefully coexisting with society, and a few hours later Eighner is plotting a desperate, if rather absurd, criminal act outside of Lizbeth's "cold concrete cell" (211).

The dog pound has such imagistic resonance in stories of homeless dog owners because it highlights a crucial distinction between homeless pets and homeless humans. In much of the United States, pets without homes are illegal. Homeless pets are placed in pounds or shelters en route either to a "good home" or to being killed. Dogs embody a short circuit in the process from homelessness to criminality, thus revealing an underlying social anxiety about homeless persons themselves: that anyone without a home can swiftly descend to a point where he is at least socially, and perhaps legally, sentenced to death

Interestingly, Eighner reserves his greatest contempt for the blind student, whom he portrays as "shrieking curses" and whose physical disability he equates with mental problems. "I knew that some forms of blindness caused by brain damage can be accompanied by a personality disorder" (207). One might assume that Eighner would empathize with a person who, like himself, is socially marginalized, but the opposite seems to be true. This may have to do with the student's participation in a strategy of social inclusion; he is practicing walking with a cane as part of his instruction at a "blind school," and he is accompanied by an able-bodied aide who seems to be infantilizing him. Eighner, by contrast, relishes his marginality; despite his benign, grandmotherly appearance in the market, he fancies himself a Texan Mme. Defarge: "I liked to imagine I was knitting while the heads of yuppies rolled past my feet" (206). Eighner's combative tone may also derive from the fact that both he and the student are competing for a valuable, and limited, resource—the control of sufficient space to allow for physical self-determination. Michalko discusses the value of canes in allowing blind people independent mobility. "The search for a guide is a search for a way to move through the world with freedom, and for a way to come to know the world in the process. The cane allows this kind of freedom" (116). While he ultimately chooses Smokie as a guide, Michalko identifies a cane as serving some of the same purposes as a guide dog by extending its owner's haptic knowledge of the environment. The freedom gained through the use of a cane is the freedom to move on one's own terms, to create an alternative space structured by one's body. Eighner's attempt to establish a domestic space on the sidewalk, however modest, represents another, competing, non-normative configuration of public space. One blind teenager whom Michalko interviews offers a more obstreperous analysis of cane use, one that might serve as the blind student's response to Eighner. "Crowd control, that's what I call my stick. When I go down the street, people get out of my way in a hurry. Then sometimes I go from side to side on the sidewalk. You know, some sighties probably think I'm drunk. But I'm just looking around" (116). While the student gains knowledge of surrounding space through his cane, he also clearly takes satisfaction in asserting power over that space. Dubbing his cane "crowd control" places him in the position of the police rather than of the drunken lout the sighted world perceives him to be; he thus reverses the elision between disability and criminality, placing the "sighties" in the position of a disorderly crowd in need of control.

Lizbeth and Smokie enable their owners to configure public space in relation to their own, non-normative bodies. For all its perils, the presence of the dog allows for a crucial imaginative empowerment that its removal would dissolve, as *Wendy and Lucy* portrays. At the end of the film, Wendy is briefly reunited with Lucy through a chain-link fence, their physical contact limited to a single dog kiss. The loss of her car, most of her money, and, above all, the domestic unit that her combination with Lucy represented signals her degeneration to a lower level of itinerancy and social alienation. In the film's last scene we see her huddled figure through a freight-car doorway; she has become one of the frightening vagrants she encountered in the film's first scene. In giving up Lucy, she has, in fact, given up and has become what she only appeared to be at first: truly homeless.

While Eighner can't fully escape the stigma of homelessness, he can live with it in part because his mind is never fully present in his bodily experience.

> No one will ever know if I become senile. Since childhood I have had the tendency to be absentminded, abstracted, and off in another world. Thus, I not so much became accustomed to minor physical discomforts as often failed to notice them. Perhaps this was not all to the good, for had I been less abstracted I might have been driven to measures that would have altered my situation in one way or another. (*Travels* xi)

Eighner is clearly ambivalent about his tendency to be "abstracted," alluding to it self-deprecatingly and expressing regret for its effects on his life. Yet the narrative impels us to recognize its value; both his travels and his attachment to Lizbeth emerge from this limitation. There is an element of pride in the phrase, "No one will ever know if I become senile," which carves out a unique space for Eighner's subjective experience. Similarly, Lizbeth, who is "not an especially bright dog," remains happily incognizant of her homeless condition. "[Lizbeth] did not know she was homeless. She did not know there was such a thing. She was a dog. For all her dog brain knew, she was the dog of a hunter or nomad" ("Lizbeth" 19). Eighner's cognitive blockages leave him in a state of peaceful dissonance with standard versions of domesticity and personal satisfaction. Eighner's embracing of insensibility and cognitive inattention seems in sharp contrast to Michalko's vivid theoretical engagement. His and Smokie's physical motion is also a process of intellectual interpretation; they "construct and reconstruct the world" (5) as they move; the physical space they "inhabit" is also an "interpretive chain" (5). Yet Eighner and Michalko are, ultimately, making similar claims about the inaccessibility, and the resulting value, of their experience; they hold out "another world" to the reader which we cannot access. Michalko writes that "the independence I get from Smokie includes this natural movement of my body. [. . .] Yet independence is more than that, for blindness is not merely the absence of the visual; it is also a presence" (123). Michalko's culturally excluded body is included in the combined body he and Smokie share when moving, and this creates a presence out of the absence that normative culture identifies with blindness—a presence only they have access to. While Michalko can attempt to describe their bodily contiguity using metaphors of music, dance, and sports, their relationship is fundamentally tactile, and thus uniquely private, although performed in public.

Titchkosky argues that narratives of overcoming disability offer textual enactments of exclusion by which the disabled body "is included as an excludable type, functioning as a scene of annihilation and understood as a life incompatible with life" (139) while the normative body "shines forth without ever having to be directly spoken of" (164). Eighner's and Michalko's narratives of somatic bonding, conversely, allow the life-affirming, intimate experiences of their corporeal connection to their dogs to emerge while at the same time asserting the inaccessibility of this experience to the reader. I use the term "accessible" advisedly, as it is the common language of the mechanisms of inclusion Titchkosky critiques. Fox argues that the human-animal bond offers alternatives to the "human rational subject" as the basis of subjectivity. "The intimate embodied nature of the human-pet relationship can challenge such ways of defining subjectivity, through other types of relationality and connection, which are not purely based upon notions of language and intelligence" (535). Eighner's and Michalko's experiences of domestic union with their dogs are radically different from society's definition of domesticity and, as Fox suggests, rely upon modes of relating that can't be fully expressed in language. Kari Weil points out that animal studies and disability studies share a focus on "a larger, less circumscribed, and less rational way of knowing" practiced by "beings who are removed from 'normal' sociolinguistic behavior" (89). By choosing to write books about this nonverbal connection, however, Eighner and Michalko put the reader in the position of accessing this connection through the medium of language. Eighner makes no attempt to overcome his cognitive failures, and in doing so he undercuts his own text's ability to bridge the gap between his experience and the reader's. He staunchly refuses to portray his experiences as representative or even significantly expressive. "I still think my experiences were atypical, but I have come to disbelieve in typical homelessness. [. . .] I do not pretend to speak for the homeless. [. . .] I do not know many of the homeless" (*Travels* ix–x). Michalko's theoretical analysis of blindness empowers him, or any other blind person, to redefine his disability through subjective bodily experience. "Smokie and I are different from most of our respective species by virtue of our togetherness as a dog guide team. Smokie and I live *in* this differentiation. [. . .] Smokie and I move through our world *alone together,* focusing on one another in the midst of the plurality of our world and its many blindnesses" (183, 187). Their choice to be physically attached, to be a "team," focused upon each other, isolates them socially even as it creates a space of differentiation they can inhabit together.

Eighner follows Lizbeth's lead in rejecting any standard of domesticity other than physical comfort. "She was permitted to sleep behind her master's knee, and to lick his face in the morning. The truth was, most of the time she was perfectly happy, so far as a dog can be happy" ("Lizbeth" 19). His close proximity with Lizbeth requires Eighner to accept her minimalist, embodied definition of home as the hollow of her master's knee. This definition amounts to a nondefinition, a declaration of ignorance, relative to the architectural structures society calls homes. Her happiness with such a limited home reveals the limits of her "dog brain." Eighner's human brain is intensely aware of his social disempowerment, and the difficulties that result from it, but the guilt he feels about not providing a home for her is, he ultimately decides, "anthropomorphizing" and a waste of time. First he interprets her pulling toward their campsite as a desire for home, but he gradually comes to understand that this is a short-term habit, like her tendency to jump in any open car door after several months of hitchhiking. When they walk past a shack where they lived together for two years, she shows no interest. Lizbeth's imagination cannot encompass the concept of an architectural home, and she finds the immediate tangible comforts of soft surfaces and adjacent bodies far more important. "She seemed not to suffer much, so long as we had a bedroll for her to lie upon. She liked softness and warm places. She seemed to be compensated for all the discomforts of our new life by being constantly near me" (*Travels* xii). She has, in Michalko's terms, fully escaped the cultural apprehension of living in a foreign homeland by not being able to understand it. What she can understand is tactile pleasure; corporeal companionship; and a soft, warm place to sleep.

Chapter 5

The Healing Touch

My father had degenerative arthritis and was also accident prone; as a result, our home was frequently a place of noisome convalescence. He was once dragged down the driveway by the car, and, while avoiding more serious injury, he had huge patches of skin scraped off his whole right side. These scabbed up gradually but had to be regularly smeared with antibiotic salve. Given his fragile surface, physical contact, especially anything approaching a hug, was completely out of the question, and we had to be careful rubbing past him in the hall or brushing by his chair lest we accidentally graze away some of the slowly healing flesh.

A more extensive convalescence occurred when a staph infection after hip replacement surgery left him with a large, gaping wound that had to heal open. My mother dressed it twice a day for several months, but sometimes this dressing would break loose at the dinner table or in public. On one visit to the zoo, the smell of fresh blood drew the attention of the big cats, who pressed their faces to the bars and licked their chops as he passed by. My father faced them down, waving a crutch a few feet from a lion's nose and declaring, "Not today, buddy." While we were glad to have him home from the hospital, his arrival transformed our domestic habits. We moved his bed into the "family room," which now became a center of potential contamination, and thus off-limits. Bloody bandages turned up in every garbage bin, among other places; broken pieces of him seemed to be scattered throughout the house.

The wounded body spreads out into the home, disordering space and threatening to touch the bodies around it, especially those caring for it, with tangible corruption. In the previous chapter, I investigated how bodily contiguity can serve as the basis for domestic experience, replacing architectural structures. This chapter will investigate the home that is rendered uninhabitable by illness in order to unveil a similar dynamic, one in which the corporeal bond between patient and caregiver reestablishes domestic stability. Because the patient's broken body has the potential to compromise the caregiver's body, however, the same corporeal bond that establishes domestic sustenance can expound the confusion of identity brought on by illness. In the writings of home health care workers Nesta Rovina and Rebecca Brown, and those of nursing home aide Thomas Edward Gass, healing through touch represents a particularly perilous act, a disempowering, self-corrupting compassion that subjects the healer not just to the practical danger of the disease but also to the profound psychic confusion and anxiety that accompany it. Such corrupting confusion is also apparent in the biblical discourse of abomination, particularly leprosy, and in Sophocles' plays. By analyzing these writings in the context of Julia Kristeva's and Mary Douglas's theories of the abject, I hope to demonstrate both the heroic aspects of embodied caregiving and its power to establish domestic space where the ailing body's crumbling edge meets the hand that seeks to sooth it.

In *Tree Barking*, her memoir of her career as a home health therapist, Rovina encounters not just pain and suffering but unremitting domestic squalor. "Linda lay on a hospital bed. Behind it was a relic of a chair, covered with stained blankets and sheets. The air was stuffy, the carpet underneath stuck to my shoes. A commode was placed next to the bed. I was thankful that someone had poured out the contents" (128). Serious illness disrupts the boundaries within the home, centralizing the use of space in a way that is analogous to what occurs in the homes of the elderly. Especially in small houses, the central living space typically becomes a sickroom. A hospital bed and perhaps a portable toilet are moved into the living room, occupying the center of the floor since the normal furniture is usually left in place. The most private bodily functions thus become fully public, even spectacular, to those entering the home. The functions of the various rooms are compacted into one, as though the walls of the house were broken open and the rooms flowed together.

Much of Rovina's job involves reestablishing spatial order by providing patients with walkers and bathing chairs or giving them training in how to get into and out of baths and beds after surgery. Consequently, she inevitably encounters the home at its most chaotic. This interpenetration of domestic functions poses a threat not only to the patient but also to the caregiver. Rovina describes many homes in which the boundary-breaking necessary for nursing the sick precipitates complete domestic breakdown, exposing her to various kinds of waste.

> The place was dark. I stumbled over empty soda cans, newspapers strewn all over, ashtrays overflowing with cigarette stubs, phone cords, plates of dog food, and the inner cardboard tubes of toilet paper until I reached a room where a cheery-looking lady in her forties sat on the edge of a bed. The sheets were stained and bore scorch marks of cigarettes, and what surely were bits of dried feces. (31)

The disorder emanating outward from the patient's body encroaches upon and disrupts Rovina's motion through the home and threatens to pollute her body through contact. While she deals principally with injuries and cardiovascular or respiratory disorders, not contagious diseases, she portrays the homes she encounters as rife with contagion. The darkness means she must feel her way, recognizing soiled objects by physically touching them. She does not simply stand on the carpet; the carpet "stuck to my shoes." Between houses she yearns to reestablish her body's sanitary boundary by reinforcing her skin and clothing. "Onward, but first I needed to return to the office to scrub my hands and arms, because the sanitizer I normally use did not feel sufficient. I would have liked to boil my clothes in lye as well" (132). The blending and disorder of rooms caused by illness brings about the blending and disorder of bodies. Since the sick body is already broken open, Rovina fears that her own body's boundary will also rupture and become blended with the bodies of her patients.

Animal hoarding and the hoarding of objects is also common in the squalid homes she visits. As is always the case with hoarding, domesticity is disrupted, and this disruption is intensified by the homeowner's illness. The vital functions of daily life, such as eating and cleaning, are both more difficult and more essential because of the homeowner's health problems, and such functions are thoroughly undercut by the category shifts typical of hoarding.

> I entered homes full to the brim with newspapers dating back to when the inhabitants were born, piled high on every available surface, blocking access to passageways and rooms. Mouse droppings on kitchen counters provided an obstacle course for armies of ants. The plumbing did not work, toilets were backed up. [. . .] Cages of finches were in

the shower and bathroom as well, leaving the bird-loving residents nowhere to bathe. (166)

Rovina is appalled by the trash and animals in the house, and by their power to compromise the health of her patients, but she also experiences them as an assault on her own body. Because she is allergic to cats and birds, she "sneezed, coughed, and spluttered" (166) through interviews, becoming sick herself as her own body is invaded. At times she has to limit interviews or have the animals removed before she can begin her work. Pollution through touch is her pervasive anxiety. When a patient invites her to sit on the bed, she demurs, knowing she can't say what she is really thinking: "There is no way I would sit on that bed of yours without being able to bathe immediately afterward, preferably in disinfectant" (31).

The assault on the caregiver's body in Rovina's portrayal of in-home caregiving is also central to Gass's description of health care work in a nursing home setting. In *Nobody's Home: Candid Reflections of a Nursing Home Aide,* Gass portrays the nursing home as a sort of surreal, anti-domestic space in which all conventions of home life are inverted, and all categories become interchangeable. The result is that the aide's body and the resident's body are invariably brought into intimately polluting contact. Ironically, this is particularly the case in what ought to be the center of cleanliness—the shower room, where "neglected turds" litter the floor because the "open-bottom seating device" used for bathing the residents tends to "provoke an unfortunate evacuation reflex" (125–26). While all bathrooms involve the paradoxical combination of sanitizing the body and enabling its excretions, the nursing home residents' physical frailties intermingle with these purposes to appalling effect. Their "stripped bare" bodies, the "open-bottom" seat, and their unreliable orifices all bespeak the dissolution of proper boundaries, and the aide's body inevitably ends up soiled by this dissolution. Gass's description of the first bath he administers as a trainee is a grotesque comedy of errors in which every sort of bodily contortion and boundary dissolution takes place.

> I finally persuaded [Laura] to go along with me step by step, being very respectful of her modesty. Then just after I lifted her onto the shower chair, the examiner said, "look down." I had her shit all over my brand new white Reeboks I was so delighted with. I wiped off the mess, changed rubber gloves and washed my hands while craning my neck around the shower wall to keep an eye on Laura. [. . .] Then she shit again—more rubber gloves and washing again, then another shit.

Finally I got the water on and she screamed it's too hot, then it's too cold, then too hot. [. . .] I handed Laura a washcloth, but in doing so I knocked the soap dispenser off the shower wall with my elbow. I fumbled to put it back up, but the plastic brackets had broken. [. . .] I put a huge glob [of shampoo] on a washcloth and rubbed it in Laura's hair. I said to Laura, "Boy, this shampoo sure doesn't lather very well." The examiner asked, "Did you read the label? That's body lotion." [. . .] I dressed her and went to clip her toenails, putting on my drugstore reading glasses to see more clearly what I was doing. The rubber glove on my left hand got caught in the right hinge of my glasses but I dared not release her foot with my other hand. (10–11)

While he begins by carefully maintaining appropriate postures to protect Laura's privacy and keep her safe, the complex logistics of washing an infirm, incontinent, and hypersensitive body gradually renders his own actions comically inefficient. He twists and reaches, craning his neck to keep an eye on her, breaking a soap holder with his elbow. His own bodily failures intensify the problem, when his lack of reading glasses causes him to mix up lotion and shampoo. Initially, Gass maintains clear sanitary protocols, changing gloves and washing hands repeatedly, but eventually the relentless iteration of Laura's incontinence defeats him. Gass claims that most aides come to view feces as "'just stuff,' as undifferentiated matter, seminal, stinky peanut butter" (9), and in his portrayal, everything in the scene becomes gradually undifferentiated. The nursing home "bath" enacts a thorough redefinition of the word; the combination of water, soap, lotions, feces, flaking skin, and bodies creates an amalgam of abjection in which everyone involved is bathing. Even the ultimate distinction between body and corpse is subverted. When Gass first steps into the bathing room, his response is "Wow, do we have our own autopsy table in here?" (125). The nursing home represents the absolute extension of category blending seen by Rovina in the homes of the sick.

In their unflagging caregiving in the worst possible circumstances, Rovina and Gass demonstrate great devotion to and empathy for their patients. Yet their unfailingly candid portrayals force the reader to confront the inevitable elision between care of the sick and disgusting physical contact with the abject. Caring for sick bodies inevitably leaves us splashed, soaked, and spattered by their uncontainable elements. Except in rare cases, close, habitual contact with the infirm elderly or the gravely ill will leave traces of their bodies upon that of the caregiver. Such contact gradually compromises the psychic, as well as the physical, integrity of the caregiver in ways that both Rovina and Gass suggest can be at once emotionally devastating and spiritually rewarding.

Martha Nussbaum notes that in order to meet "Aristotle's require-ment that the person acknowledge similar vulnerability" (*Upheavals* 318), compassion must be reciprocal, since "the attachment to the concerns of the suffering person is itself a form of vulnerability." Here I would like to employ "attachment" in its material sense by investigating those moments when caregiving requires one to touch a leper, when contact with a diseased body's crumbling margin becomes necessary for healing or tending the sick person. Such portrayals of the healing touch offer two related but somewhat contradictory dynamics. The crumbling of the body's edge represents the fluctuation or dissolution of the afflicted per-son's identity. At the same time, acts of healing or soothing the afflicted that involve touching their bodies tend to expound the confusion of iden-tity brought on by the illness, so that both caregiver and sufferer become blended or enigmatic. While identity is compromised in both cases, the healing touch involves admixture rather than loss. This union is hardly sentimental; such physical mingling with a profoundly sick person will inevitably render both bodies undifferentiated, like Gass and Laura, thus polluting the healer.

✣ ✣ ✣

In order to clarify the psychic implications of pollution, I would like to turn to the biblical portrayal of leprosy, which most theorists of the abject identify as the founding cultural portrayal of abomination. The Bible's descriptions of leprosy are infamously unscientific; leprosy has been identified as many diseases, from psoriasis to syphilis. It is clearly a con-dition that visibly compromises the skin surface, causing it to decompose, and threatening to crumble or spill onto those nearby. J. Keir Howard describes it as "not so much a discrete medical condition, but rather what might be called a 'religious syndrome'" (68). Douglas sees the diagnosis of leprosy not as medical practice but as part of a "doctrine of sacred contagion" in which the disease is elided with all bodily discharges (187). The cluster of images used to describe biblical leprosy portrays an incom-prehensible and unstoppable assault on the identity through the body's edge. As the victim's margin crumbles, his body participates in a similar assault on adjacent bodies. Leprosy enacts a frightening dissolution of the very principle of individual identity, serving as an embodiment of psychic uncertainty about the self. Perceived visibly, leprosy appears as a polluting mark on the normal skin, and representations that emphasize its polluting qualities define it in terms of visible patterns. When vision gives way to touch, however, the disease become less definable and more threatening.

"Let her not be as one dead, of whom the flesh is half consumed when he cometh out of his mother's womb" (Numbers 12:12). With these words, Aaron pleads that his sister Miriam be healed of her leprosy. The leprous body is at once dead, being born, and a diseased adult; its horror emerges, for Aaron, from its inconstancy. The verse resonates with mutually canceling formulations: Miriam is like a child who is already dead when born, so never alive. She is like a rotted corpse, half-returned to dust, but also a new baby. The opening of the mother's body to bear life mirrors the opening of the child's body which brings death. The phrase "Let her not be" requests a cancellation of a condition that seems unclear: Let her not be dead? Let her flesh not be consumed? Let her not be contaminated like a newborn?

In its elision of birth, death, and disease, the passage demonstrates Kristeva's reading of biblical leprosy, which defines abomination in terms of "admixture," especially "flow, drain, discharge" (103). Douglas also emphasizes the fluidity of the leper's body: "[God's] power over the waters is the favorite sign of his greatness. The body that releases its waters in a disorderly way is not a faithful model of the world he made" (191). Kristeva's and Douglas's emphasis on the effluence of the leper's body reflects the disease's association in Leviticus with fluid discharges; the chapters on leprosy are sandwiched between discussions of uncleanness caused by running sores and reproductive fluids. As Douglas notes, the prevailing imagery of Leviticus 13 is that of the skin surface in flux: "The Levitical writer is particularly interested in the ebb and flow of the disease. [. . .] The diseased pustules of leprosy are described as spreading, erupting, and blooming" (184, 188). William Miller also notes the proximity between the reproductive and the abject: "Images of decay imperceptibly slide into images of fertility and out again" (40).

Douglas uses architectural language to describe leprosy's boundary-breaking. The disease creates a "breach of the body's containing walls" that threatens "the integrity of the living being" by going "counter to God's creative action when he set up separating boundaries in the beginning" (190). This architectural metaphor is borne out in Leviticus, where the leprous body spreads its pollution outward to the materials of the home.

> Then the priest shall come and look, and, behold, [if] the plague be
> spread in the house, it [is] a fretting leprosy in the house: it [is] unclean.
> And he shall break down the house, the stones of it, and the timber

thereof, and all the mortar of the house; and he shall carry [them] forth out of the city into an unclean place. (Leviticus 14:44–45)

Leprosy's power to rupture the body becomes reified in the home, which is not only disordered, like those Rovina enters, but completely disassembled and scattered. Once the body's "containing walls" are breached and leprosy has spread to the walls of the house, the home cannot be purified; it can only be broken apart and carried away.

Yet Kristeva and Douglas mitigate their own argument by relying upon a visual discourse inherent in Mosaic Law itself which defines admixture through figure/ground distinctions. Kristeva also portrays the skin as a boundary, the clearly outlined visible edge of the coherent self.

> Chapters 13 and 14 of Leviticus locate impurity in leprosy: skin tumor, impairment of the cover that guarantees corporeal integrity, sore on the visible, presentable surface. [. . .] [T]he disease visibly affects the skin, the essential if not initial boundary of biological and psychic individuation. From that point of view, the abomination of leprosy becomes inscribed within the logical conception of impurity to which I have already called attention: intermixture, erasing of differences, threat to identity. (101)

Kristeva puts great emphasis on the fact that identity's limits are visible limits. Threats to identity attack the visible surface of the body, its cover, which must be "clean and proper in order to be fully symbolic" (102). As Gail Weiss explains, Kristeva considers the abject "precisely what makes the coherent body image possible because it marks the boundary between the body image and what is not" (89). The skin is a marked boundary, coherent because visibly defined by abject ground.

The Levitical descriptions of leprosy are designed to establish just such a clear figure/ground pattern for this alarmingly equivocal condition. Of course, there are good practical reasons for defining leprosy in visual terms. Priests trained to diagnose leprosy must be able to do so without touching it; nearly half the verses in Leviticus 13 begin with the phrase "And the priest shall look." Leprosy thus becomes a pattern on the skin; it is described almost entirely in terms of color and sheen.

> And if in the place of the boil there be a white rising, or a bright spot, white, and somewhat reddish, and it be showed to the priest [. . .] And if it spread much abroad in the skin, then the priest shall pronounce him unclean: it is a plague. But if the bright spot stay in this place, and

spread not, it is a burning boil: and the priest shall pronounce him clean. (Leviticus 13:19–23)

The skin becomes a canvas or screen on which eruptions appear as spots or regions of color. The priest apprehends breaking, spreading sores as a series of static marks with clear limits. There is, quite literally, a bright line on the leper's body defining the edges of his corruption.

William Miller points out that the sense of touch is the source of most of the language we use for disgust, because "it is easier to come up with words to describe disgusting sensations when these are moist, viscid, pliable. [. . .] [E]ven the scabby and the crusty borrow their disgusting-ness from the fact that they are formed from the coagulation of viscous substances" (60). Unlike the eye, which must establish borders in order to see at all, the tactile sensorium excels at apprehending intermediate conditions: crumbling, weepy, or ichorous states. In *Gifts of the Body,* her fictionalized account of her work as a home health worker, Brown must engage with a ruptured skin surface in which distinctions are not so clear. As she rubs salve on the sores of an AIDS patient named Keith, visible distinctions slide into haptic ambiguity.

> The salve was thick, opaque, yellowish jelly. It came in a big, wide-mouthed plastic jar. It didn't smell like anything. The first time I went there and opened the jar I saw the tracks of someone else's fingers where they'd gone in to get the salve. I don't know why it frightened me so much, but it did. I was afraid to look at him. His sores were dark purple and about the size of quarters. The edges of them were yellow and his skin was dark brown. The sores weren't running or oozing or scabs because they always had this salve on them. (117)

Like the Levitical priest, Brown apprehends Keith's body as a palette of colors. One of these colors, the yellowish substance at the edges of his sores, is indistinguishable from the salve, however, and she can't eval-uate the condition of his sores because of it. The yellowish substance defines the disease and makes it undefined; the salve becomes the ooz-ing outward of sores that, because the salve is there, aren't oozing. The "wide-mouthed" plastic jar seems as much an open, oozing body as Keith's. Brown is not afraid of touching someone with AIDS (she handles AIDS patients for a living), but she becomes frightened as she looks from the salve to Keith and back, registering the lack of distinction between his disease and its treatment, the slippery matter of his body and of the ointment. She can't tell by looking where Keith's sores end, and when she touches him, his edges become even less distinguishable. "I changed gloves several times when I was doing the salve because my gloves got coated with it, and also with his hair, which was very tight and curly and fell out easily, and with flecks or patches of skin" (118). If Keith's identity depends upon his body having a solid boundary, then Brown is doing more harm than good; like the disease, her touch breaks apart his surface, pulling away his defining dark brown skin and tight, curly hair. The gloves, which ought to serve as the boundary of Brown's body, become "coated" with Keith's body as salve, scab, sore, skin, hair; her touch shatters his edges, creating a no-man's-land of bodily rubble that they share.

Mosaic Law defines leprosy and other bodily impurity in visual terms in order, I would argue, to avoid the confusion associated with a more tactile apprehension of contamination, such as the one Brown experiences. The best-trained Levitical priest cannot diagnose leprosy by touch and would not try to. Touching would not allow him to define the color or sheen of the sores or hair. Dryness and scaliness would be somewhat apparent, but touching could disrupt scabs, burst boils, or expose raw flesh. Since the appearance of "raw flesh" (13:14–16) rather than scabs marks someone as unclean, the priest's hands could alter the diagnostic signs. Detecting leprosy by touch would not only be impractical but also require the priest's body to come into pervasively and even invasively intimate contact with the leper.

This potential for the caregiver's touch to disrupt bodily integrity precipitates a profound dissonance in the practice of medicine, especially nursing, in which the process of healing an easily wounded body can be performed only by another body which may accidentally harm it. Dolores Krieger, a professor of Nursing at New York University, pioneered the practice of Therapeutic Touch in the 1970s. Based on the belief that energy fields surrounding the body can be manipulated by a therapist's hands, the practice has had a controversial history. The two major research studies of this therapy were a 1984 study on premature newborns and a 1994 study on burn patients at the University of Alabama. Critics of Therapeutic Touch point out that the name itself evades clear definition. "Whereas the original protocol was based on actual physical touch, subsequent research claimed that similar results could be obtained without touching the patient" (Courcey). Joan Turner (who ran the University of Alabama study), Ann Clark, Dorothy Gauthier, and Monica Williams explain.

The name therapeutic touch is really a misnomer because actual touch or physical contact with the patient's skin is not necessary. The technique can be implemented by holding the hands 2–5 inches from the patient's body since the therapy is based on the assumption of a human energy field which extends beyond the skin. Not having to touch the burn patient is an advantage because it avoids the discomfort sometimes associated with direct touch. (12)

Thus both critics and adherents of Therapeutic Touch point to the verbal distortion inherent in its name. For Courcey, the apparent self-contradiction of a touch that is not a touch suggests the unempirical slipperiness of the therapy. For Turner et al., the "misnomer" points to the practical value of a therapy that liberates caregivers from the disquieting somatic engagements we see between Brown and her patient Keith. Where an actual touch could harm a burn victim or a premature newborn, touching an immaterial extension of the body's boundary overcomes the difficulties for both patient and nurse that Brown enunciates.

Mosaic Law, like Therapeutic Touch, addresses anxieties about edge contamination by vigorously asserting that tangible diagnosis and healing is unnecessary and even counterproductive. The 2-to-5-inch energy field that Therapeutic Touch establishes around the body operates as a thickened bodily border, a medical buffer zone that can be manipulated instead of the body. Turner et al. describe the therapy administered during the University of Alabama study as follows:

During TT, the practitioner replenishes depleted energy and clears and rebalances the energy flow in the injured person through conscious intent and hand movements which re-pattern the energy flow. [. . .] Using hands held with palms facing the subject and, 2–5 inches from the subject's body, the TT practitioner assessed the energy field and implemented techniques such as clearing, directing, or balancing the energy flow, based on the assessment. (12)

Turner et al. emphasize how hands-on the practitioner must be, using "hand movements" to direct, balance, and repattern. Wrestling with bodily energy flows, like wrestling with an angel, seems at once physical and invisible. It is clearly not enough to use "conscious intent"; the hands themselves are deployed, as if they are going to touch the body, but they remain "facing" the body's surface, as if looking at it. Therapeutic Touch thus remakes the body's edge as a distanced area that can be seen but not touched, while touching occurs in an invisible, intangible realm.

For Gass, who must literally wrestle his nursing home residents into and out of bathing chairs, diagnosis can only be a literally hands-on process.

> Showering also provides a good opportunity to check for impactions and various skin conditions. We wash under the folds of fat and flabby breasts and between mangled toes. We check for bruises, rashes, scrapes skin tears, sores, abrasions, contusions, and fungus-infected toenails. (126)

The shower room at Gass's nursing home is certainly a place where we would find what Douglas calls "[t]he body that releases its waters in a disorderly way" (191). But for Gass, unlike the Levitical priest, diagnosis necessitates haptic engagement with this watery, compromised form. Sometimes the skin is scraped or torn open, sometimes it is impacted or overgrown, and sometimes it is just "flabby." These bodies are never clean and proper, and Gass must touch all of their ruptures and distortions. He must be alternately gentle and muscular, touching bruises carefully, but trimming toenails forcefully, since "[m]any, perhaps most, residents have a fungus that makes their nails grow bulky and difficult to trim with a standard clipper" (126). These infected nails are disgusting because, as Miller would argue, they are both dead and teeming with fungal life. The ghastliness of the passage describing Miriam's leprosy derives less from the contrast between abject mark and smooth skin than from its suggestion that leprosy pulls the body into an intermediate, fluctuating condition between identifiable states. Admixture is certainly the fear in leprosy, as Kristeva suggests, but not simply the admixture of clean skin and clearly defined patches of corruption. In tangible terms, leprosy involves a far more pervasive and disorienting admixture involving the complete loss of the self's definable edge, like the "mangled," scraped, ruptured, and distorted forms Gass washes as a matter of course.

Anyone trying to diagnose such an edgeless state by touch would begin to apprehend his or her own body as edgeless. Rovina describes her encounter with Mae, an elderly woman who has been given what seems to be a meaningless, incomprehensible diagnosis. "*Tree barking?* I wondered whether the nurse who had referred me had made a mistake when writing the diagnosis. [. . .] What on earth was 'tree barking'?" (1). She discovers that the term refers to a form of chronic dermatitis that swells and ruptures the skin, rendering Mae's bodily margin, like Miriam's, both dead and alive. "The skin stretched over those calves was gnarled, tough, and furry-looking, full of crevices and nodules, like the bark of an ancient decaying tree. An odor of sweet rotting flesh and decay emanated through the cracks and fissures" (2). Mae's skin, broken open to the world, is like a tree as much as it is like a corpse. Later in the book, describing her own response to a particularly stressful patient interview, Rovina portrays caregiving as a sort of emotional flaying that tears apart her own skin. "Each time I saw them there, my flesh felt like it was withdrawing, leaving me raw, exposed, and vulnerable" (84).

This migration of wounds from patient to caregiver is also apparent in Jesus's miraculous healing of the "woman having an issue" in Mark 5. The woman's intent is to take Jesus's power without his willed consent by sneaking up and touching him. Remarkably, it works, which seems to suggest that Jesus's power can be physically activated. The question of Jesus's relative agency in this encounter has theological implications that are beyond my discussion here, but Jesus's sudden, shocked response does strongly suggest that even for Christ, the act of healing those whose physical edges are compromised calls one's own shape, and one's own identity, into question. Jesus's primary response is not outrage but confusion: "Who touched me?" Why is Jesus confused? If he knows power has passed out of him, why doesn't he know to whom it has passed? Mark's version emphasizes the private, corporeal experience of the miracle: "she felt in her body that she was healed of that plague. And Jesus, immediately knowing in himself that virtue had gone out of him, turned him about in the press" (Mark 5:29–30). The healing takes place in an intimate, secret space where touching and being touched are interchangeable.

While Jesus is quick to deny the material dynamics of healing by touch, declaring that "thy faith hath made thee whole" (48), the woman clearly acted not simply on faith in Jesus's power to heal but also on faith in physical contact with that power. "For she said, If I may touch but his clothes, I shall be whole" (Mark 5:28). Many others in the crowd pressing against Jesus believe he can heal them, but the woman has the greatest faith in the power of his touch alone, perhaps because she is the one who is forbidden to touch him. Unclean discharges or issues are dealt with in Leviticus 15, immediately after the discussion of leprosy. The majority of the chapter focuses on the importance of avoiding contact with the clothes, bedding, saddles, and so on, of one so afflicted. Most importantly, one should avoid their touch: "And whomsoever he toucheth that hath the issue, and hath not rinsed his hands in water, he shall wash his clothes, and bathe himself in water, and be unclean until the even" (Leviticus 15:11). The woman must know, then, that in touching Jesus she is breaking Mosaic Law; forbidden the healing touch, she takes it anyway, trespassing on the sacred body and performing the part of the healer reserved for God's anointed. Yet despite the profound inappropriateness of her behavior, Jesus validates the woman's priestly function when he says, "thy faith hath made thee whole; go in peace, and be whole of thy plague" (Mark 5:34). The second, redundant, phrase sounds like the words that will affect the miracle, but, as he himself admits, Jesus is too late; she has already performed the miracle herself. Physical contact between the healer and the healed has reversed their roles. As soon as she touches him, her wound is closed and his is opened; the "fountain of her blood" stops flowing from her as "virtue" starts flowing "out of him."

Such a confusion of roles is inevitable when the priest's role ceases to be one of diagnosis and becomes focused on healing through touch. As she spreads salve on Keith's sores, Brown is disturbed not only by the crumbling of his body but also by the "tracks of someone else's fingers" in the salve, attesting to the corporeality of a third person who touched it and then touched Keith, and suggesting that people whose bodies come in contact with Keith's skin become, like the sores themselves, multiple and pervasive. When she applies the salve, "it was like there were four different people there. The two people having the normal conversation and the person touching the body with the salve and the person with the body with the sores" (121). Brown cannot legally distribute medicine, but the salve "wasn't really a med so much as something just to comfort: it couldn't heal anything" (118). The salve does not, in other words, partake in a discourse of health or purity that attempts to define the edges of the sore or of the body, as, for example, the gloves do. It is not surprising, then, that application of the salve results in the apprehension of comforter and comforted as contiguous and interchangeable.

When Brown treats bedsores for Connie, one of her elderly clients, she experiences a similar blending. Here Brown does not focus on the lesions; Connie's entire body has become so frail that it seems to Brown as though its anatomical structures are becoming amorphous.

> Connie's muscles felt like putty or like something in a sack. Her skin hung off her like crepe paper. [. . .] When I touched it, it was completely smooth, and it completely gave to me. Sometimes I couldn't believe the skin was alive, I couldn't believe it was part of her. [. . .] When I went to clean up, my hands felt strange. I felt like there was something tingling inside my skin or hanging from the tips of my fingers. It felt like the fibers of underwater plants, like everything was underwater, I was, and Connie was, breathing and all, but even when we weren't touching I could still feel something pulling and pressing around my body like a current of water around us. (156–59)

Like Jesus, Brown can tell that her own body has been altered some-
how, but she can't tell whether the change is "inside my skin" or outside, "hanging" from her flesh. The phrase "hanging from the tips of my
fingers" is at once grotesque and tender; it is the tips of her fingers that
have massaged Connie's putty-like flesh, which now seems to adhere
to Brown's fingers, deforming them and rendering them clumsy. Like
Miriam's, Connie's skin seems both alive and dead, and she passes this
ambiguity to Brown. Shifting to a second metaphor, that of underwater
plants, Brown ceases to portray the body's edge at all; instead, she and
Connie are entirely undifferentiated, suspended in a fluid continuum,
buffeted by an invisible power they can perceive only by touch, like two
giant hands "pulling and pressing." While much less unhygienic than the
"bath" described by Gass, it shares the sense of pervasive amalgamation,
of muscular interaction leading to a sinuous, but still vividly material,
synthesis.

Such labor is perilous and disorienting; embracing a person whose
margin seems corrupted or in flux can appall or terrify. The smoothness
and the purity we like to believe characterize our bodily margin are sac-
rificed by caregivers who confront bodily surfaces drastically different
from their own. Because of their daily interaction with the basic needs
of those they care for, home care workers and nursing home aides will
always be most thoroughly soiled by bodies that unpredictably release
their waters. The caregiver's body becomes, in its way, a record of the
patient's symptoms. Gass suggests, moreover, that the most frightening,
and also the most enlightening, aspect of the healing touch comes in recognizing the common frailty shared by caregiver and resident.

> We are all infirm. We all have cancer and dementia, and we are all
> dying. [. . .] Appearances are deceiving. I know what it's like to be in a
> state of shock, and while my interior experience was then quite sweet,
> the outer appearance of my body was a real mess. In the long view,
> surely I am no different and essentially no better off than the worst of
> these unfortunates. (5)

Gass comes to understand his own identity through its loss. His empathy
for the residents he works with allows him not only to understand their
suffering but also to recognize that, inevitably, his own identity is subject
to the vagaries of age and physical failing. The caregiver's willingness
to touch, even embrace, another polluted body leads to a confusion of
symptoms, and ultimately of selves.

✣ ✣ ✣

In his plays *Philoctetes* and *The Women of Trachis*, Sophocles places the healing touch in the context of heroic culture, contrasting traditional martial heroism with the complex heroism of caregiving.[1] Both plays present a victim of suffering who was once defined by his physical heroism and a loved one who must choose between a similar heroic career and the debasing duties of a caregiver. By focusing on skin afflictions that pollute and destroy identity, Sophocles offers a detailed rendering of how the victim's pain and bewilderment elicits a "terrible compassion" from the caregiver, a compassion that represents a different form of heroism.

Philoctetes is marooned on the isle of Lemnos because of his oozing, festering foot, which threatens to pollute the religious rituals of the Greeks. Receiving a prophecy that only he, bearing Hercules' bow, can conquer Troy, the Greeks send Odysseus with Achilles' son Neoptolemus to try to bring Philoctetes back. From the start, the play identifies the island as an antidomestic space; Lemnos is "desolate, / no one sets foot on it; there are no houses" (Grene 2–3). On this "shore without houses or anchorage" (220), Philoctetes occupies "an empty hut, with no one there. / And nothing to keep house with" (31–32). Odysseus and Neoptolemus identify Philoctetes' cave home by listing the lack of domestic objects, the only notable items being "some rags [. . .] drying in the sun / full of the oozing matter from a sore" (38–39). Sophocles thus elides social exile, the dissolution of the home, and the loss of bodily integrity in both practical and psychological terms. He describes at length how finding food and water becomes an arduous task, as he "must drag my foot, / my cursed foot. [. . .] I crawled and miserably contrived to do the work" (288–89, 293–94). The chorus sets up a series of equivalences between the exile's isolated self-care and his psychological fixation on his illness. Because he has "no one to care for him" (171), he "always suffers the savagery of his illness" (170); because "he makes his bed without neighbors" (183), his "thoughts are set continually on pain" (185). The difficulties of living this way turn the home itself into a spatial manifestation of his affliction. Emptied of all domestic structures that might mitigate or distract from his suffering, it is a "Hollow in the rock, hollow cave [. . .] Passageway,

---

1. Citations are from David Grene and Richmond Lattimore, eds., *The Complete Greek Tragedies, Vol. 2: Sophocles* (Chicago: University of Chicago Press, 1992), translated by David Grene (*Philoctetes*) and Michael Jameson (*The Women of Trachis*); and from Seamus Heaney, *The Cure at Troy: A Version of Sophocles'* Philoctetes (New York: Farrar, Straus and Giroux, 1991). The names of the translators of *Philoctetes* are given in parentheses along with the line numbers for Grene's translation, and the page numbers for Heaney's, for clarification and comparison.

crowded with my cries of pain" (1081–88). While the homes Rovina visits have begun to lose spatial distinction, and thus their power to sustain their owners' suffering bodies, Philoctetes' home is so lacking in the physical solace which domestic items allow that it contains nothing but his pain.

This emptying out of the home is consistent with the imagery of opening and emptying that Sophocles uses to portray Philoctetes' illness. When the pain of his suppurating foot comes upon him, Philoctetes cries, "I'm all blood again. / I'm open deeper than ever. It's pouring out. / It's here again. Circling for a kill. / Why me? Gods curse this foot" (Heaney 43). There's a cruel redundancy in asking the gods to curse a foot that hurts because it has already been cursed, the mirror image of Jesus's compassion when he speaks healing words to a woman who has already been healed. Philoctetes asks for the curse in order to establish a boundary between the foot and himself, to render the foot impure and outcast from his body in the way he has been cast out of Greek society, but the distinction between himself and his foot is belied at the beginning of the same passage, where his whole body become identified with the sore: "I'm all blood again / I'm open deeper than ever."

The circularity of such psychosomatic self-definition is enacted in the play's emphasis on circling. Philoctetes describes the illness as a beast hunting him, presumably following the blood trail left by itself. The chorus's description of Philoctetes also engages in such corporeal fluctuations.

> He crept round like an infant.
> He wept. And when he hunted
> For herbs to soothe the foot
> The foot wept as he dragged it.
> His trail was blood and matter. (38)

He weeps because of the foot even as the foot weeps; as he hunts, he leaves the trail of a hunted beast, a trail along which his sickness will hunt him. "Your wound is what you feed on, Philoctetes" (61). Philoctetes has lost himself in his pain. The disease which has isolated him on the island isolates him even more profoundly within his self-distorting agony.

In order to redomesticate Philoctetes, Neoptolemus must become a different sort of hero from his too-famous father, one whose great work involves touching and soothing. He arrives on the island like Brown or Rovina arriving at a patient's home, offering Philoctetes both practical help and a compassionate touch. The entire play, with its intimate focus on Philoctetes and Neoptolemus circling toward one another like lovers, emphasizes the importance of physical proximity to healing. At the climactic moment of his illness Neoptolemus' compassion emerges in the words, "You most unhappy man / you that have endured all agonies, lived through them, / shall I take hold of you? Shall I touch you?" (Grene 760). Philoctetes initially responds by letting Neoptolemus hold his bow, the only object remaining from his past heroic life, which then becomes a material bridge between the men. Neoptolemus' willingness to touch not just the bow but also Philoctetes' body, despite the "black flux of blood and matter [that] has broke / out of his foot" (823–24), constitutes the emotional climax of the play.

> *Neoptolemus:* I have been in pain for you; I have been
>   in sorrow for your pain. [. . .]
>   Do not be afraid. We shall stay.
> *Philoctetes:* You will?
> *Neoptolemus:* You may be sure of it. [. . .]
> *Philoctetes:* Give me your hand upon it
> *Neoptolemus:* Here I give it you,
>   To remain. (805–15)

Philoctetes' shocked awareness that he will not, as before, be left behind, and that he has found someone willing not only to help him but also to touch him and care for him, flowers outward in this quick exchange of lines before the men finally take each others' hands. Neoptolemus' self-denying decision to choose his oath to Philoctetes over his orders involves not just returning the bow and telling the truth but also, as Mary Whitlock Blundell points out, relinquishing the sort of glory expected of Achilles' son (219). To stay beside this mad, sick, reeking friend, he accepts a life of anonymity and perpetual corruption. "A kind of compassion / a terrible compassion, has come upon me / for him" (966). Truly, the compassion will be terrible in its grandeur and in its relentless difficulty. Neoptolemus imagines Philoctetes as a physical extension of himself, rotten foot and all. "There's something in me he touched / From the very start. I can't just cut him off" (Heaney 43). By choosing to care for Philoctetes, Neoptolemus must partake of his combined bodily dissolution and social exile.

The play's equation of illness and exile thus progresses to one of caregiving and exile; Rovina makes the same comparison throughout *Tree Barking*. Being herself deracinated from South Africa, her country of origin, and then from Israel, her spiritual homeland, she experiences

America as a place of exile, and her sense of exile as a wound. "My own roots remain bleeding and severed in the red South African earth" (3). Arthur W. Frank argues that, inevitably, physicians must tell "a diaspora story" because healing requires one to relinquish any monolithic identity (*Renewal* 104). Rovina argues that, in her case, the divided consciousness engendered by South African apartheid doomed her to a perpetual state of self-exile, thus allowing her to participate in her patients' sense of self-dislocation. Moving in and out of the lives of her patients, as an itinerant laborer, a foreigner, a white woman in communities of color, she is an outsider in almost every possible way. Interacting with her patients as "both a participant and a stranger[,] . . . I always feel somewhat apart, my own internal apartheid" (8).

Gass also points to parallels between his own unclear social identity and the loss of self experienced by the residents he interacts with. Nursing home residents, he argues, are in a continual state of identity loss and reclamation, due to dementia and to the nature of institutional life. Two roommates have a terrible fight but forget about it the next day. A husband and wife live down the hall from one another, but no one, including the couple themselves, seems to be aware of this. Caretaking also places Gass himself in a social netherworld. He endures the sneers of his nephew, who calls him a "baby-sitter" (9), and keeps clothes in his car so he doesn't have to wear his scrubs in public. The distortions of identity for both patient and caregiver are apparent in the perfectly modulated title of his memoir, *Nobody's Home.* The phrase seems to be a truncated version of "the lights are on, but nobody's home," which would apply to many of the nursing home residents. But it also reminds us that the facility is no kind of home; nobody would ever choose to live there, as it cannot sustain any sort of authentic domestic life. As a result, it becomes the home to a sequence of nobodies—both residents and aides exist in a twilight world of social marginalization and indeterminate identity.

Rovina, Gass, and Brown all engage in self-deprecating rhetoric that foregrounds their sense of personal and social exile and seems to downplay the effectiveness of their work. When asked by strangers if he is a doctor, Gass replies, "'No, I'm a butt-wipe in a nursing home'" (9). Rovina feels powerless to address the social problems she witnesses every day. "The only answer I had to these weighty questions was that I had absolutely no idea" (84). Brown points out that the salve she spreads on Keith's wounds was "just something to comfort: it couldn't heal anything" (118). All of these caregivers seem to believe that their caregiving is inglorious, inconclusive, and ineffectual, yet they continue with their work. A comparison between the two translations of *Philoctetes* I have been using here suggests the odd contradiction between insignificance and power that comes from touching the ill. Seamus Heaney translates Neoptolemus' declaration of empathy as "I'm here. I'm here. / But I'm useless" (43). David Grene's version reads "I have been in pain for you; / I have been in sorrow for your pain" (805–6). To be in close physical contact with those who suffer is often to be both useless and in pain, to comfort them by blending ourselves with them without any hope that they will be cured. The uncertainty of touch also emerges in its uncertain value. The example Christ sets in touching lepers can't be simply that, given the chance, one ought to miraculously heal the sick. Rather, we see in Jesus's confused words "Who touched me?" an admission that anxiety and uncertainty always accompany compassion.

Sophocles ultimately argues, however, that the choice of caregiving, with all its attendant anxiety and alienation, is a heroic choice. The true nature of heroism is explicitly addressed in *Philoctetes* when, at the end of the play, Hercules' ghost appears to reconcile Neoptolemus' duty and compassion. Hercules had been Philoctetes' mentor in his youth, and the bow that Philoctetes now bears was given him by his master. When Philoctetes refuses to return with Neoptolemus and conquer Troy, Hercules' ghost steps in to reintegrate him into society. The ghost tells Philoctetes that "the tasks and sufferings that were mine / [. . .] All this must be your suffering too, / The winning of a life to an end in glory, / Out of this suffering" (1419–23). The parallel seems rather vague since Philoctetes has never had to endure the muscular, glorifying labors of Hercules. But it is his heroic sufferings rather than his heroic tasks that Hercules requires of Philoctetes.

Twenty years before writing *Philoctetes,* Sophocles had devoted an entire play to Hercules, but not to his labors. *The Women of Trachis* portrays Hercules' agonizing death, his skin eaten away by the skin-dissolving Nessus coat. The coat is soaked in the blood of the centaur Nessus, whom Hercules killed with arrows dipped in the Hydra's blood. Those observing Hercules' affliction emphasize its ability to blur the line between inside and outside, pure and impure, body and nobody. "[T]here comes to torture him / A murderous confusion, / Sharp points brought to burning heat" (836–40). The poison's source is itself a blending of already-blended beasts: the Hydra's blood mingled with the semihuman centaur's "soak in" to Hercules, blending their bodies with his and dissolving his identity into "a confused mass" (698). Hercules experiences his affliction as a welter of sensory contradictions: "the malignant tearing scorches me" (1082); "it feeds on me again, / it has sprung out, it blooms" (1088–89). The pain tears, scorches, eats, and flowers. Like Philoctetes' body, Hercules' has become "all blood." He cannot recognize his form, cannot link his own body to familiar appearance or deeds or lineage, and, in his own eyes, ceases to be.

> my hand, my hands,
> O my back, my chest, O my poor arms, see
> What has become of you from what you once were.
> [. . .] I am nothing,
> Nothing that can even crawl (1089–1108)

His fundamental identity as a monster slayer has dissolved with his dissolving skin; the greatest heroic body of his age becomes undifferentiated flesh.

When the ghost of Hercules speaks to Philoctetes of their shared great suffering, then, he is not comparing their military or muscular feats. He is acknowledging that both men have known the fleshly, self-distorting agony of becoming monstrous and untouchable. In both plays, moreover, Sophocles suggests that an even greater heroism can be found in the act of assuaging such suffering. In *The Women of Trachis*, Hercules asks his son Hyllus to burn his body; Hyllus responds with disgust: "You are asking me / to be your murderer, polluted with your blood" (1206–7). Hercules' blood, now blended with that of monsters and breaking forth from his body, would pollute anyone who touched it. Hercules corrects his son, redefining pollution as healing. "I ask you to be my healer, / the only physician who can cure my suffering" (1208–9). When healing rather than purifying becomes the standard, the hero must accept that he will be polluted, and in taking up his father's charge Hyllus becomes a different sort of hero than his father. Rather than destroying impure monsters, his job is to embrace another's physical impurity. Hyllus remains profoundly uncomfortable: "So wretched, so helpless am I, no matter where I turn" (1243). In accepting these labors, he also must accept the uncertainty and guilt that go with them—emotions that never accompanied his father's heroic tasks. Nevertheless, Hyllus take up his burden, manifesting his heroism in his willingness to touch his father's corrupt body even though doing so leaves him frightened and doubtful. Like Gass, he becomes a "butt-wipe" for his father's ignominious death, bound to cover his own body with pollution. And like Rovina, he has "absolutely no idea" if what he is doing will really help.

In the later play, Sophocles recasts the story, making Philoctetes, rather than Hyllus, the final caretaker of Hercules' broken body (Grene 799–803). The heroic bond they share is thus explicitly associated with the bond between sufferer and caregiver. By casting Philoctetes in Hyllus' role, Sophocles suggests a progression from physical strength to weakness, from heroic action to heroic caregiving, passed from one generation to another. When Hercules' ghost addresses Neoptolemus, he exhorts him to such heroic caregiving, in which "he shall guard you, you him" (1437). Rather than the man-slaying heroism of Neoptolemus' father, Achilles, he must practice a humbler and more self-compromising, although no less physically difficult, heroic endeavor. The image of Hercules' bow arcs through both the plays. It begins as Hercules' weapon of purification but is polluted by the combined sufferings of Hercules and Philoctetes. It comes to represent the tactile joining of Neoptolemus and Philoctetes, a union through touch that is compassionate because of the hero's willingness to become corrupted. Neoptolemus' caregiving allows Philoctetes to finally leave his realm of isolated suffering and return home; "home" is, in fact, the play's last word. Similarly, *The Women of Trachis* takes place "before the house" of Hercules. In one sense it is darkly ironic that the hero bound to travel the world risking life and limb finally returns home to suffering and death. But the play also suggests that suffering itself makes Hercules' home necessary; home is where we return when our heroic bodies fail. Or, rather, the relationship with an empathetic caregiver facilitates the return to, or re-creation of, a home even for those who seem permanently exiled.

Both Rovina and Brown also suggest the power of empathetic caregiving to reestablish homes that have been lost or forgotten. Mae's broken, bark-like skin and "rotting flesh," while repellent, invoke in Rovina a tactile memory of an actual tree she used to climb as a child in her native South Africa. Attending to Mae's affliction, she experiences a sudden visionary return to her childhood home.

> Lulled by the heat and her voice, I floated to our backyard in South Africa. I leaned against my beloved mulberry tree, reading Enid Blyton's book *The Faraway Tree*, about a wondrous tree growing in an English country garden. [. . .] I felt the rough bark of the mulberry tree, warmed by the African sun, against my back. (3)

Mae's broken body breaks open Rovina's past, giving her a vividly somatic apprehension of belonging. To be home, for Rovina, is to feel the rough bark "against her back." Unlike the homes of many of her other patients, Mae's home is nurturing and supportive. Rovina describes Mae's legs as "a part of her security, her rootedness." While apparently decayed to the point that they are nearly dead, Mae's legs are materially and metaphorically linked to the solidity of her home, which contrasts starkly with Rovina's own "bleeding and severed" family and cultural roots. Rovina even suggests that the disability they cause makes her domestic life more stable and rewarding. "Because it is hard for her to leave her home, longtime friends and community members come to help her clean her house and bathe, and to shop for her. Young children drop by to visit, to mow her lawn, and to run errands" (3). Mae's home becomes the center of community life, and her legs, broken and rotting as they are, lie at the center of her home. The compassion they elicit has the power to incite, even in a rootless wanderer like Rovina, a physical sensation of domestic identity. Rovina chooses Mae's condition as the title of the book largely because as she progresses through the many dysfunctional homes of her clients and moves through the devastated landscape of Richmond, California, the process of caregiving creates an apprehension of home for her. "To contribute to others is my reason for being here. Because of this work, I no longer feel like a stranger in a strange land, separate from all that surrounds me" (193).

Brown's work as a home care worker is more directly focused on ordering and maintaining the home itself than is Rovina's. She cleans and cooks and straightens up her clients' houses or apartments in addition to helping her clients with personal needs. In doing so, she sometimes revives memories and domestic engagements that have been dispersed by the homeowner's illness. When she comes to clean Rick's house, Brown expects to share a pleasant moment with him over coffee and their favorite cinnamon rolls. Instead, she finds that Rick's health has declined cataclysmically. He is lying in the living room on a futon that is "usually up like a couch" (6) but has now been flattened to make a sickbed.

> I got onto the futon. I slid on very carefully so I wouldn't jolt him. [. . .] I pulled my body close to him so his butt was in my lap and my breasts and stomach were against his back. I pressed against him to warm him. He pulled my hand onto his stomach. I opened my hand so my palm was flat across him, my fingers spread. He held his hand on top of mine, squeezing it like the quilt. I could feel the sweat of his hand on the back of mine, and of his stomach, through his shirt, against my palm. (7)

Brown positions herself so that their bodies are fully contiguous, with as many surfaces as possible touching. While the embrace is clearly tender, Brown also emphasizes its muscular intensity; she "pulled" and "pressed" against him, and Rick "pulled my hand" and "squeez[ed]." They seem to be trying to wring their separate bodies into a single, clenched form. His sweat soaks through, blending clothes and skin.

After Rick is taken to the hospital, Brown remembers that the same futon had been the sickbed of Rick's partner, Barry, before he died; being embraced by Brown had simply switched Rick's position in the caregiving bond. "They'd pull the futon out like a bed and watch [a movie] from there and pretend they were at a bed-and-breakfast on vacation. Rick would make something fabulous and they'd eat it together. That was when he was still trying to help Barry eat" (9–10). The futon was at once sickbed and marriage-bed, site of corruption and of uncomplicated domestic pleasure. By lying on their futon, Brown had been able to re-create that domestic order, to return Rick to the home he had with Barry through their brief, but still powerful, physical embrace. Sitting down to eat the cinnamon rolls in Rick's empty apartment, she is both part of Rick's home and an outsider. Her physical presence and kindness have reanimated the domestic emotions of the space, just as her cleaning has reestablished domestic order. By using her body, she has re-created the essential human touch that defined Rick and Barry's life at home.

Caregivers are often called upon to serve as physical surrogates for family members, touching and holding sick bodies until loved ones can, or because they can't. As Keith is dying, Brown attempts to keep him calm and stable until his mother arrives from the airport. "I leaned over the bed and took him in my arms. I held him as tenderly as I could. 'Keith,' I said, 'your mother is coming.' [. . .] I held him until his mother arrived. Then I put him in her arms" (127). The posture of caregiving, like that of giving birth, is ungainly and strenuous; Keith looks at her "the way a baby does when it opens its eyes for the first time" (126). While Brown's words may be soothing, it is the physical act of holding him that communicates most effectively. Santanu Das notes that portrayals of battlefield caregiving that gesture toward the maternal embrace also tend to deemphasize verbal exchange, suggesting that "[p]hysical extremity can lead to a bodily intimacy and immediacy that is perhaps inimical to linguistic representation" (194). A hospital bed in the living room centralizes the function of health care, but it can also centralize empathy and emotional bonding. It is disturbing that Rick's futon is pulled out, signifying his illness, but the embrace he and Brown share on it reanimates the tender domestic life that took place in the home he shared with Barry. Like the homes of the elderly, those of the gravely ill need to tell their owner's story. In the elder home, that story can become overwhelmed by objects; in homes disordered by illness, the story is swamped by the immediate necessities and by-products of the failing body. For those who suffer from dementia or who can no longer communicate, the only story left may be the simplest kind: two lovers embrace; a mother holds a child. Such stories can only be told with the body, through the sense of touch. The caregiver creates a space in which that story can be told and offers a body to help tell it, even when doing so is perilous and terrifying.

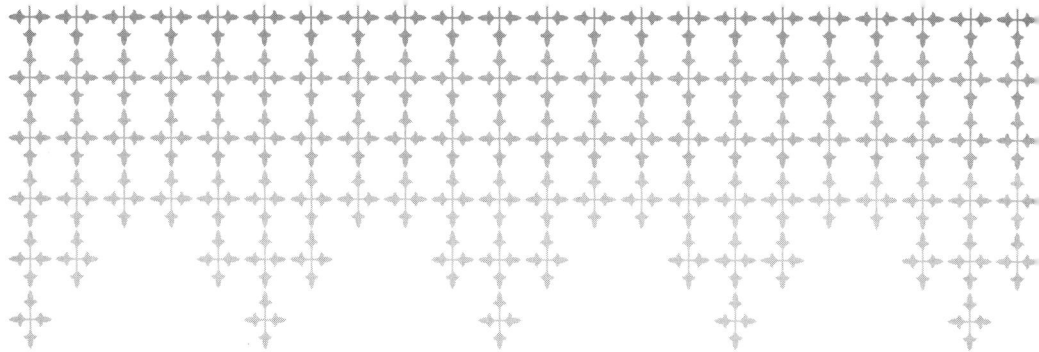

PART THREE

HOME AT THE BODY'S EDGE

Domesticity as Somatosensory Boundary Definition

Chapter 6

The Language of Pressure

In the Sermon on the Mount, Jesus advises his followers, "enter into thy closet, and when thou hast shut thy door, pray to thy Father which is in secret" (Matthew 6:6). As a child, I thought he meant this literally. Every night I would creep into the closet in my bedroom, kneel down between the hanging shirts, and close the sliding door behind me. Kneeling on board games and sneakers was uncomfortable and strange, but I remember feeling a profound sense of spiritual sustenance, as the hanging clothes pressed against my face and back, moved slightly by my breath. In the ensuing years, I have poked fun at myself for such slavish fealty to the King James Version. But remembering that comforting sensation of physical enclosure, intertwined with spiritual comfort, allows me to place myself precisely within my childhood home and my childhood faith.

Gaston Bachelard celebrates the daydreams available in corners and closets but nevertheless belittles the withdrawal to such spaces as an "indigent solitude": "this purely physical contraction into oneself already bears the mark of a certain negativism. Also, in many respects, a corner that is 'lived in' tends to reject and restrain, even to hide, life. The corner becomes a negation of the Universe" (137). For people who live with the sensory hyperarousal typical of Autism Spectrum Disorders, the negation of an overwhelming universe can sometimes be essential to maintaining a coherent sense of bodily identity. Low-sensation environments, such as dark closets, can moderate boundary anxieties and support the self by impeding painfully intense sensory responses. "Occasionally, I enjoy sitting in the bedroom cupboard, closing off from all outside disturbances" (102), writes Wendy Lawson in *Life behind Glass: A Personal*

Account of Autism Spectrum Disorder. Dawn Prince-Hughes, in her memoir of growing up with undiagnosed Asperger's syndrome, describes how she would calm the fears she experienced while shopping. "My strategy for survival was to hide inside the clothing racks. [. . .] [T]he feel of the soft fabric and the clothing's dark colors (I picked my racks carefully) and the lack of light would help me calm down. I always felt safer in the dark" (21). Prince-Hughes is describing a common behavior among children with Autism Spectrum Disorders in which a low-sensory environment is combined with "pressure seeking" at the body's margin. Autistic children will often wrap themselves in blankets, climb under mattresses, or hide in closets to help reinforce their fragile sense of somatic boundary (Grandin, *Thinking* 58).

Throughout the preceding chapters, I have argued for models of domesticity that collapse toward the body's edge. Sharing of embodiment between humans and animal companions, and between caregivers and patients, offers the tangible sensations of comfort and security we experience at home. For pet owners and caregivers, embodied interchange is fundamental to this experience of domesticity. In this chapter, I would like to investigate an alternate version of domesticity that is both tactile and private. Sylvia Plath and Temple Grandin are writers whose work is preoccupied with the vulnerability of the body's edge and who explicate a form of tactile domestic experience that shores up, rather than breaks down, the body's felt boundary.

For both Plath and Grandin, the sensory key to domestic comfort is tactile pressure, which defines and reinforces bodily coherence. The normal architectural spaces of the home fail to provide this pressure; the architectural spaces they seek out—tunnels, chutes, crevices, and passageways—minimize the space between the skin surface and walls and deemphasize visual stimuli. Both writers portray this pressure-based domesticity through the representation of real or imaginary animals: bees in hives, worms in tunnels, cows in feedlot walkways. Plath and Grandin find in animals a fitting alter ego, or alter body; the portrayal of themselves as animals becomes a way of conveying their alienation from the dominant discourses of gender, enablement, and neurotypicality. Unlike Lars Eighner or Rod Michalko, Plath and Grandin do not primarily interrogate the social implications of their haptic engagement with actual animals; rather, they employ the imaginative identification between their own bodies and the bodies of animals to assert the significance of tactile experience. The beehive or cow chute would seem the antithesis of human domestic space management, yet Plath and Grandin undertake to transfer the apprehension of tactile pressure experienced by animals in such spaces to the human domestic realm. The animal's body thus serves as a starting point in redefining the nature of domestic identity.

In the discussion that follows I hope to demonstrate how Plath and Grandin triangulate animal identification and architectural space to redefine domestic experience as located immediately adjacent to the body. The anxiety-laden hyperarousal that leads them to configure domestic space around pressure seeking represents an extreme of the equation between tactile enclosure and domestic comfort. While we all want our homes to enfold and nurture our bodies, people who suffer from boundary anxieties consider such a supportive embrace its main function. I am not suggesting that pressure seeking is exclusive to people with Autism Spectrum Disorders or that Sylvia Plath herself was autistic; instead, I hope to use the heightened boundary-based experience of home enunciated in both Plath's and Grandin's writing to elevate the often underplayed significance of immediate tactile sensation in the embodied dynamics of domestic space.

In every version she tells of her own life story, the founding moment of Grandin's coherent identity occurs on an Arizona cattle ranch, when she climbs into a cattle "squeeze chute."

> I asked my Aunt Ann to press the squeeze sides against me and to close the head restraint bars around my neck. I hoped it would calm my anxiety. At first there were a few moments of sheer panic as I stiffened up and tried to pull away from the pressure, but I couldn't get away because my head was locked in. Five seconds later I felt a wave of relaxation, and about thirty minutes later I asked Aunt Ann to release me. [. . .] This was the first time I ever felt really comfortable in my own skin. (*Thinking* 59)

Ironically, this seemingly brutal confinement in a powerful mechanical device, with its metal poles and electric motors, sets Grandin free by creating a sense of bodily integrity she formerly lacked. The squeeze chute, which is a V-shaped device powered by an air compressor, is used to hold cows still while they receive vaccinations. Grandin explains that for her, and for the cows, feeling this sort of intense pressure is comforting; "deep pressure is a calming sensation for just about everyone. [. . .] The squeeze chute probably gives cattle a feeling like the soothing sensation newborns have when they're swaddled, or scuba divers have underwater. They like it" (*Animals in Translation* 4–5; hereafter cited as *AT*). Autism makes it difficult for her to control her emotions, but the squeeze machine represents an exteriorized manifestation of control through pressure. Prince-Hughes explains her longtime affection for small hiding places as a desire for a solid boundary. "Containment silently reminded me of my physical boundaries—never solid and always in danger of disappearing" (127). Grandin proceeded to build her own squeeze machine, which became the centerpiece of her domestic space. An industrial device incorporated into the home offers emotional sustenance by collapsing domestic space to the body's edge. Like hoarders who seek out high-density spatial relationships with objects or animals, Grandin's definition of domesticity focuses on the body's margin. Rather than extension into or exchange with another body, however, Grandin dwells specifically on the apprehension of pressure in defining the ideal domestic space.

Hypersensitivity to touch is common among people with Autism Spectrum Disorders, and there is increasing evidence that deep pressure therapy can significantly diminish the anxiety it creates. Experiments using a device similar to Grandin's squeeze machine "reported significant physiological and behavioural changes, which were taken as supporting the proposal that deep pressure touch reduces arousal" (Blairs et al. 215). Other studies have used weighted sheets or blankets and a "therapeutic vest that delivers a portable hug" ("Novel" 8). The language of parental affection, of hugging or "swaddling" (8), is the most common way to describe this sort of therapy. In one study, Sharon Blairs, Susan Slater, and Douglas Hare successfully reduced the aggression and anxiety of a thirty-one-year-old autistic adult (known as "B") by re-creating soothing sensations from the subject's childhood.

> B's mother reported that when he was a child and became upset, she would hold him on her knee, giving him a big hug. She was also able to identify that as a youngster he would always choose to wear a tight coat (that he had outgrown). [. . .] Staff on the unit reported that B was "only really happy" at night when he was tucked up in his bed (bedclothes tucked in tight around him). (216)

Blairs's protocol involved the patient being regularly "tucked in" to his bed by hospital staff. "A top sheet was laid over [him], covering his body from the shoulders to his ankles. This was then tucked in tightly under his body. [. . .] A second folded sheet was laid over his torso and also tucked in under his body" (216). It is important to distinguish this sort of neurological re-creation of the maternal hug sensation from a psychological return to childhood. For B, being tucked in soothes him not because it makes him feel the same emotions as his childhood experience but because it generates the same neurological response. In their study of tactile sensation in Asperger's syndrome, Sarah-Jayne Blakemore, Teresa Tavassoli, Susana Calo, Richard M. Thomas, Caroline Catmur, Uta Frith, and Patrick Haggard explain:

> The somatosensory system has also been divided into a discriminative pathway subserving tactile perception, and an affective pathway subserving emotionally significant touch. Our measure of tactile threshold pertains to the discriminative rather than the affective pathway. Therefore, hypersensitivity to suprathreshold tactile stimuli in people with AS is not merely a matter of excessive dislike of a normal percept, but rather reflects a percept which is itself unusually intense. (12)

The hypersensitivity to touch that makes it difficult for some autistic people to wear rough clothing or shake hands, like the comfort Grandin and B feel from deep pressure, is not due to a simple dislike of rough clothing or to the pleasantness of childhood emotional associations. Rather, it is in the first case an intensely amplified sensory response and in the second a form of pressure-based stimulation designed to soothe that hypersensitivity. Bruno Bettelheim's now infamous misinterpretation of autism as a psychological withdrawal in response to "refrigerator" mothers relies upon an emotional, rather than a somatic, apprehension of the maternal embrace. Being wrapped in tight sheets is effective not because it gives B warm memories of his mother's hug but because the sensation of deep pressure it creates soothes him, just as his tight coat did when he was younger and just as the squeeze machine does for Grandin.

A psychological interpretation of the experiment would suggest that being tucked in "returns" B to the comforts of his childhood home. A neurological or somatosensory reading would say that it brings his home to him, by placing his body's edge in the same tactile relation to its surroundings as he experienced in his mother's arms or his childhood bed. If the home is equivalent to this set of sensations, it is, in a sense, portable, like the weighted vest that serves as a "portable hug" ("Novel" 8). The home's architecture and spatial aspects are less important than its immediate tangible surfaces. For Grandin, her living room does not feel like home until she sets up her squeeze machine in the middle of it, and then it is the space inside the squeeze machine, and more precisely the surfaces of her body being pressed upon, that represent domestic comfort to her. It is fairly common to describe a room filled with large couches and soft cushions as "homier" than a room with only hard surfaces and straight chairs; the tactile pleasure of having one's body enfolded by soft, supporting surfaces intensifies the room's domesticity. Grandin's placement of the squeeze machine in her home is simply an extreme tipping of this balance toward tactile experience; the tactile sensation itself establishes the space as homey, regardless of any of its other formal or spatial dynamics.

In her early journals, Sylvia Plath describes the tight fit of her childhood home, which wraps her up like a maternal hug. Unlike B, who craves the deep pressure of his mother's arms, Plath's response suggests both affection and antipathy.

> Some people have to have silence and peace when they write. I am in a bad position, looking at writing from the point of view of celestial inspiration. My fat fleshy grandmother sits in the corner, breathing loudly, sewing on the coat I will wear tomorrow. The ice box clicks and whirrs. From the downstairs bathroom comes the bristly sound of my brother brushing his teeth. If I were going to be realistic, I would not say much more than "It looks like an ad of the middle-middle class home." Yet somehow I don't give a damn about the scraped place on the yellowed and finger spotted wallpaper. I don't care too much that the rug in the dining room is blueflowered and has the threads showing where the chairs are scraped across it, or that the chair seats, once shining maroon with satin stripe, are now darkened and greasy with food stains. [. . .] It's funny, but now I'm home, and no matter how many mansions I will see, I won't care about the shabbiness of this dear little house. (*The Unabridged Journals* 53; hereafter cited as *UJ*)

The coat Plath's grandmother sews for her serves as a synecdoche for the home itself, which fails to offer the uncomplicated somatosensory comfort that B's tight coat provided him. Plath's home surrounds her with an overwhelming sensory blanket which is at once comforting and maddeningly claustrophobic; she describes her family as "people I know by sight, by sound, by touch, by smell, by flavor" (56). Plath presents her home in culturally iconic terms—"an ad for the middle-middle class home"—while at the same time unveiling the irritating, claustrophobic, and grubby bodily dynamics of domestic life. The grease, dirt, and wear brought on by fleshy, wheezing, tooth-brushing family members leave every surface in the house "scraped" and worn down. Habitual somatic engagement with the spaces and surfaces of the home is comforting but also overwhelming. To be in this tight space is to "know instinctively, like the rat in the maze, that this door opens . . . this of all the doors . . . my feet know this is the door" (56). Muscle memory and tactile abrasion are the perceptual foundation of home life, Plath suggests; the feet, rather than the eye, identify the right door, and we scrape our way between its narrow passages. The rat image also suggests that the home is a form of trap—a shabby, cramped cage.

These passages reveal deeply contradictory feelings about the physical proximity incumbent on domestic life. Plath associates the authentically rewarding affection her family offers with being crowded, rubbed, and wrapped up, but she is also alarmed and anxious. Joyce Davidson, a feminist geographer who studies women with boundary anxiety, notes that highly populated spaces may create just the sense of entrapment and anxiety Plath exhibits. "People literally populate space with their own presence and constructions, causing it to become charged with their noisy, odiferous, colourful and tactile spatiality" ("A Phenomenology" 655–56). If one "lacks the ability to assert [one's] own subjective spatiality in the face of the spaces of others" (656), then the home can be a sustaining, enforcing space. When the home itself is the crowded, overstimulating space full of beloved but overwhelmingly present family members, however, the body's vulnerability would seem painfully intensified, inciting the desire for an even more private space.

Throughout her career, Plath expresses this anxiety as a struggle to find a private space in which to engage in artistic creation; she initially frames the above description of her home in relation to having "peace when [I] write." In contrast to the overwhelming claustrophobia of the home, Plath often imagines an ideal work space, characterized by privacy and sensory comfort. In her portrayals of her childhood home in Wellesley, her college dorm at Smith College, and her English country house in Devon with Ted Hughes, Plath attends to the specific spatial relation between her body and the home's spaces and furnishings in order to imagine a space that seamlessly integrates artistic productivity and domestic life.

> Here I sit in the deep cushioned armchair, the crickets rasping, buzzing, chirring outside. It's the library, my favorite room, with the floor a medieval mosaic of flat square stones the color of old book-bindings. . . . [R]ust, copper, maroon leather chairs with the leather peeling off, reveal a marbled pattern of ridiculous pink. The books, all that you would fill your rain days with, line the shelves; friendly, fingered volumes. (*UJ* 20)

The sensory pleasures of the library environment, its settled intellectual peace where everything is pleasing and at hand, impel her, rather anomalously, to musings on the limitations of marriage and the self-betrayals

of sexual desire. "Isn't it better to give in to the pleasant cycles of reproduction, the easy comforting presence of a man around the house? [. . .]
I spiral back to me, sitting here, swimming, drowning, sick with longing" (20). While she is physically comforted and nurtured in the deeply
cushioned library chair with "friendly" volumes within reach, when she
imagines that same body in its social context, she experiences a panicked
sensation of swimming and drowning. The home life that will result from
giving in to social expectation, in which her space will be crowded with
children and "a man about the house," seems like an alarming contrast
to the rich, cultured privacy of the library. While at Smith, she writes to
her mother:

> I still can come up to my own private room, with my drawings hanging
> on the walls . . . and pictures pinned up over my bureau. It is a room
> suited to me—tailored, uncluttered and peaceful. . . . I love the quiet
> lines of the furniture, the two bookcases filled with poetry books and
> fairy tales saved from childhood. At the present moment I am very
> happy, sitting at my desk, looking out at the bare trees around the
> house across the street. (*Letters Home* 40; hereafter cited as *LH*)

Plath portrays her room as both a return to childhood and a launching
pad for her adult intellectual life. The room is "tailored" like a suit, to
fit her body snugly and reinforce her identity without having the overwhelming sensory stimulation of her mother's house. The somewhat
monastic freedom she experiences derives from her ability to control the
space so that she is buffered from the many people and responsibilities
surrounding her.

These passages demonstrate what will become a common spatial formulation for Plath—the comfortable, private study, or often just a chair or
desk—walled off from an anxiety-laden world of familial struggles. Like
elderly homeowners, Plath engages in a form of "environmental centralization" in which home space becomes narrowed down to a single room,
or even a single chair or sofa, that meets all of the homeowner's domestic
needs. Environmental centralization is typically associated with sickness
or old age, when the body's limitations make such flexible usage necessary. Plath, however, idealizes such bodily limitation as the interweaving
of domestic and artistic identities, even as she recognizes its contradictory and disabling aspects.

Plath seems to have imagined her parents' young adult life as an
idyllic vision of how to integrate intellectual and domestic activity.
In 1934, Otto Plath published *Bumblebees and Their Ways,* a version of

his dissertation; his wife Aurelia was closely involved with the work's composition and editing, although she received no credit. The book embodies her parents' intellectual exchange, a textual communion contemporaneous with Plath's conception. Aurelia and Otto Plath met as student and teacher, so editing and writing together was foundational to their marriage and endemic to their home life. Aurelia Plath describes how her husband's work became the center of their home in Jamaica Plain: "seventy plus reference books were arranged on top of the long side-board; the dining table became his desk" (*LH* 12). These were details of family history that Sylvia must have known, and the book would have loomed large, perhaps even larger than her beloved poetry books, among the "friendly fingered volumes" (*UJ* 20) on the library bookshelves. In "Among the Bumblebees," a fictional account of her childhood relationship with her father, she portrays herself passively engaging in her father's professional life in yet another big comfy chair. "Alice followed her father into the den and went to sit in one of the big, slippery leather chairs near his desk. She liked to watch him correcting the papers he brought home from town in his briefcase" (*Johnny Panic* 308; hereafter cited as *JP*). She thus fantasizes a father/daughter professional writing bond that offers both physical privacy and emotional communion; she is near him but in a separate, enfolding chair. This was a sort of domesticity Plath was to pursue unsuccessfully throughout her life. But even here, physical propinquity seems to be terrifying. "The light of the study lamp circled his head with a crown of brightness, and the vicious little red marks he made on the papers were the color of the blood that oozed out in a thin line the day she cut her finger with the bread knife" (309). Her father's presence is soothing, but it immediately invokes anxiety about her identity, registered as fear for her skin's soft, vulnerable boundary.

Bumblebees itself offers a striking representation of domesticity in the animal world that seems to gesture toward Plath's desires for privacy and bodily self-determination as well as her preoccupation with boundary vulnerability. The book, which quickly became a definitive study of the species, argues that bumblebee behavior is more vigorous and dynamic than had been previously supposed. One behavior it deals with extensively is queen hibernation. Unlike honeybees, which live in large hives that survive through the winter, the ground-dwelling bumblebee hive dies off; only the queen survives by hibernating in a narrow tunnel underground and reemerging with the warm weather. Chapter 9 of *Bumblebees*, entitled "Hibernation," takes issue with other entomologists who claim that the bees hibernate in east- or north-facing banks, which provide shelter from the harshest weather. Otto Plath's field research leads him to the conclusion that young bumblebee queens "hibernate in the soil near the entrance to the maternal nest" (92), usually "in a small cavity, connected to the nest by a narrow passage" (88–89). To prove his hypothesis, he observes a group of young queens preparing for winter close to their mother's nest.

> On September 26, more than forty of them were busily at work digging their *hibernacula* in the sod surrounding the nest entrance. [. . .] Near each one of these was a cavity, about one half of an inch in diameter. A few of the mounds were examined, and in almost every one a young queen of *B. impatiens* was found at a depth of about two or three inches. [. . .] [Later, in February] [t]he piece of sod was broken up with a pick, and during this operation three queens of *B. impatiens* were obtained. [. . .] [Q]ueen No. 2 was feebly moving when first noticed, while No. 3 appeared to be dead. During the ten-minute walk home, I carried queens No[s]. 2 and 3 in the hollow of my hand, and by the time I entered my room, queen No. 3 also began to show signs of life by slightly twitching her tarsi. (88–90)

The passage offers an empirical, but nevertheless touching, rumination on the social and material structure of home. Plath's scientific task is to prove that the young female bees, to put it anthropomorphically, love their mothers. Their irresistible attraction to the home of their birth leads them to dig tunnels near it, even if this exposes them to harsher weather, as though its very proximity would keep them warm through the long winter. The passage celebrates family ties and what seems like a resurrection. The bees at first "appeared to be dead" but in a few minutes show "signs of life" as if they were only waiting for the spring.

Sylvia Plath's poem "The Beekeeper's Daughter" portrays just such a young queen bumblebee, placing emphasis on the enclosure and privacy of its personal resurrection (*The Collected Poems* 118; hereafter cited as *CP*). The poem portrays a young girl accompanying her father to care for his honeybee hives; like "Among the Bumblebees" it offers an idyllic fantasy of inclusion in the part of her father's life she could only read about in his book. The account is clearly imaginary, as Otto Plath never kept honeybees and Sylvia was at oldest a newborn during the period of his field research. The poem ends with a description of a young bumblebee queen emerging from the ground, witnessed by the young girl who kneels down to see it more clearly.

In burrows narrow as a finger, solitary bees
Keep house among the grasses. Kneeling down
I set my eye to a hole-mouth and meet an eye
Round, green disconsolate as a tear. (lines 14–17)

The passage emphasizes both the narrowness and the homeness of the bumblebee's tunnel where she can "Keep house" in peaceful independence, retreating to her private tomb to rise again at Easter time. This tunnel seems like the perfect solution to domestic overstimulation. While adjacent to the home, it is still its own private sanctuary and has the low sensory combination of darkness and pressure ideal for reinforcing the body's edge. Plath has found, in her father's writing, a representation of ideal domestic space management that maximizes family communion while minimizing sensory overstimulation. Bachelard writes that "[b]y allowing the imagination to wander through the crypts of memory, without realizing it, we recapture the bemused life of the tiniest burrows in the house, in the almost animal shelter of dreams" (141). Plath retells her past so that the tiny animal shelter becomes a domestic model for private identity, family unity, and rebirth.

The hibernaculum can also be a crypt, however. In 1953 Sylvia Plath attempted suicide in her Wellesley home, climbing into a crawl space off the basement and taking sleeping pills. In *The Bell Jar* (1963), she offers this fictionalized account:

> Behind the oil burner, a dark gap showed in the wall at about shoulder height and ran back under the breezeway, out of sight. The breezeway had been added to the house after the cellar was dug, and built out over this secret, earth-bottomed crevice. [. . .] It took me a good while to heft my body into the gap, but at last, after many tries, I managed it. [. . .] It was completely dark. I felt the darkness, but nothing else, and my head rose, feeling it, like the head of a worm. (160)

The verbal parallels to Otto Plath's portrayal of bumblebee hibernation are apparent: Otto Plath's "small cavity in the soil" becomes a "secret earth-bottomed crevice"; both extend out in a narrow tunnel from the mother's home. When Esther Greenwood is removed from her hibernaculum, the light feels like a "chisel cracked down on my eye," recalling Otto Plath's pick. The hard chisel and harsh sunlight seem to assault Esther's soft, wormlike body, which presses against the edge of the dark tunnel, feeling "the darkness, but nothing else." After emerging, the young queens "move feebly," "try to avoid the scorching rays of the sun," and "fall into a sleep-like stupor" (88, 91), while Esther "tried to roll away from the direction of the light, but [. . .] I couldn't move" (163). Late in her revisions of *The Bell Jar*, Plath changed her heroine's name from Victoria to Esther, a name gesturing toward Easter, the day of resurrection on which "The Beekeeper's Daughter" also takes place. Esther is also the Bible's most appealing young queen. Reading this passage in relation to Otto Plath's work calls into question the common critical reading of Esther's, and by extension Plath's, suicide attempt as what E. Miller Burdick calls "the ultimate fatal female retreat" (877) to the womb. The textual parallels point to Plath, figuring her suicide as a form of hibernation that imagistically intertwines her father's work, her family home, and her own sense of tactile domesticity. While it would be foolish to suggest that Plath actually believed she would be hibernating when she took sleeping pills and climbed into the crawl space, it seems equally unlikely that the parallels between her suicide attempt and the images in her father's book are a coincidence, especially since she describes bumblebee hibernation in her poems. The choice of location is inflected by her father's writing, by her own preoccupation with somatic enclosure, and by the desire to reimagine the grave as a domestic space, capable of family reunification in which darkness, closeness, and pressure define the body's relationship to its surroundings.

Plath also elides her father's grave with a hibernaculum in "Electra on the Azalea Path" (*CP* 116–17), the poem she wrote a few days after visiting his gravesite in 1959.

> That day you died I went into the dirt,
> Into the lightless hibernaculum
> Where bees, striped black and gold, sleep out the blizzard
> Like hieratic stones, and the ground is hard—
> It was good for twenty years, that wintering—
> As if you had never existed (lines 1–6)

Otto Plath was buried in Winthrop, Massachusetts, where the family had lived during his fatal illness. The visit represented a homecoming of sorts; Plath suggests that the trip revives family memories that her Wellesley home could not, since Otto "never existed" there. Plath visited the grave six years after her suicide attempt in Wellesley, but a fictional version of the graveside scene occurs immediately before Esther's suicide attempt in *The Bell Jar*, emphasizing the continuity between the two evocations of self-burial. Here she is a bee rather than a worm, specifically one of the bumblebees that her father describes in his *Bumblebees*. By imagining her dead father, and herself, in such a "hibernaculum," she associates the subterranean chamber of her father's grave with hibernation and thus with rebirth rather than death. The imaginary reunification of her family takes place not in the home itself but in this dark tunnel of liminal space, in which domesticity is reduced to an uncomplicated tactile force, and pressure at the body's edge unifies physical comfort, familial affection, and artistic production.

Christina Britzolakis argues that for Plath the process of mythic self-reinvention operates textually. "The female Oedipal tragedy of the daughter-in-mourning is a retrospective bricolage of psychoanalytic, literary and biographical texts" (63). *Bumblebees* is one such text; almost every image in the first four lines of "Electra on the Azalea Path" can be traced directly to the book. Plath wants to recast her father's scientific work in a literary context, but she also yearns toward the suggestion of rebirth that it offers, one in which what seems like death is really hibernation and homecoming. In her journal entry describing the trip to the grave, she writes of her "temptation to dig him up" (*UJ* 473). In part, Plath is rendering her father into a text here, but the poem also suggests that he already exists for her as and in the scientific text he wrote, which describes burial without death. Moreover, Plath's awareness that her parents wrote the book together, as a young married couple, complicates Britzolakis's oedipal model. Reading *Bumblebees* would have reanimated her parents' relationship for her, even as the text portrays her father's reanimation of the bees. The description of the sleeping bee, tightly enclosed within its tunnel, is found between the pages of her father's book, tightly pressed between the "friendly fingered volumes" (*UJ* 20) on the bookshelves in her mother's home. This book, which her mother and father worked on together in the months immediately surrounding her birth, was a textual record of their collaboration and the family unity it implied. In her poetry and fiction, Plath attempts to worm her way into the book itself, and thus into that lost family. In the crevice beneath her mother's breezeway she re-creates the hibernaculum that her father describes in his book, thus physically lodging herself within a spatial environment that evokes a lost family wholeness while reinforcing the boundaries that same family threatens.

It seems unreasonable to suggest that Plath's interweaving of images from her father's work and her family's history into her own writing is not psychologically motivated. I would argue, however, that the psychological motives that Britzolakis and other critics identify in Plath's imaginative renderings of her family relationships and family home are also informed by a somatosensory impulse to identify a home space that can foster and protect her body's vulnerable edge. Her rendering of her relationship to her father, like patient B's to his mother, foregrounds spatially defined, deep pressure sensation. The queen bee's finger-width tunnel and the worm tunnel beneath the breezeway are at once psychologically resonant and neurologically palpable; both elements contribute to their artistic impact.

In her discussion of the comforting effect of pressure, Grandin describes a device in which sand is used to immobilize horses that refuse to be touched.

> Sand from an overhead hopper flowed down the stall walls and slowly filled up the stall so that the horse hardly felt it until he was buried up to his back. [. . .] He was alert and curious about his surrounding, and he acted like a normal horse in a stall, even though his body was now completely buried. (*Thinking* 86)

To be buried, Grandin suggests, is to be happy and comfortable. The gothic evocations of burial don't enter into Grandin's description; Grandin asks her reader to interpret the images she employs for their tactile qualities alone. Similarly, in Plath's poetry, burial suggests safe domestic enclosure as much as it indicates a preoccupation with death. I would argue that most critical analyses of Plath's work have overemphasized the psychological connotations of burial and underemphasized its somatosensory elements. Read in the context of tactile sensation, burial in Plath's writing has its comforting, reassuring side, just as it does for the horse Grandin describes. Plath's consistent use of burial imagery speaks less to the need to control the body's margin and more to the creation of a version of home in which that margin can be controlled.

Plath's soft-bodied bees and worms emerge from their safe tunnels into the absolute exposure of "the scorching rays of the sun" (*Bumblebees* 91). The inability to establish a firm sense of boundary often results in great anxiety about exposure to the surrounding world. Grandin compares this feeling of exposure among autistics to that of animals on the watch for predators. "Cattle have a very wide, panoramic visual field, because they are a prey species, ever wary and watchful for signs of danger. Similarly, some people with autism are like fearful animals in a world full of dangerous predators" (*Thinking* 168). Prince-Hughes, a primate anthropologist who has Asperger's syndrome, also argues that the sensory overloading typical of Autism Spectrum Disorders resembles animals' consciousness. She parallels her own sensory anxieties to the visual exposure gorillas are subjected to in a zoo enclosure, theorizing that the evolution of an upright carriage violates the bodily privacy natural to four-footed animals.

> One's naked belly and genitals are all uncovered and laid bare, as if standing had lifted a great warm cover made of the sacred space between body and ground. [. . .] This standing had often been too much for me to bear, and when it was, I would go and curl up somewhere, nursing the raw wound that my upright front had sustained in the million-year tearing away that my ancestors had undertaken. (121)

The animal's posture creates a natural "warm cover," a fleshly "sacred" enclosure that protects its physical vulnerability. The gorilla's body becomes a four-footed hiding place. Prince-Hughes, who had an earlier career as an exotic dancer, draws parallels between the glass-enclosed gorilla display and the dancing stage. Both "zoo animals and dancers [are] on display, exposed to hateful words and twisted judgments" (78). The club where she worked "had glass all around the stage. [. . .] Visitors dropped quarters into a meter to get a screen to go up, for about twenty seconds a quarter" (72). This structure, specifically designed to empower the viewer and disempower the dancer within, is the opposite of the squeeze machine, which isolates the body and enforces its boundary. The glass "walls" and constantly opening doors of the enclosure serve as pseudobarriers, encouraging rather than preventing access, a mechanical enactment of the sense of exposure Prince-Hughes already feels from Asperger's syndrome, in which the body's boundary is "never solid and always in danger of disappearing" (127). Prince-Hughes expresses the sensation of being visible to others as the dissolution of her body's edge; the shelters she constructs to hide in conceal "a melting point between my flesh and the ground" (127). Ultimately, she accepts the necessity of painful exposure to the world in order to help the gorillas she loves. "I would no longer allow the great permeability of my spirit to lead me to seek smaller and smaller shelters; I would let myself bleed out into the world and let it into me" (130). The phrase "bleed out" demonstrates her sense of raw vulnerability, and the medical connotations of the term suggest that to expose oneself to the world is not just to suffer but also to risk death. Linda, one of the women Davidson interviews, expresses her fear of a similarly catastrophic boundary loss.

> She clearly loses the ability to project a protective boundary around herself, and as a result, is both assaulted by external space, crumbling

inwardly under its pressure, and unable to prevent internal space from exploding outwards. Both sensations indicate a lack of containment, the crack that permits dispersion of self into its surroundings. (650)

This breaking open and bleeding out, resulting from the "permeability" of the self, is the constant fear that domestic space ought to soothe and contain. While public spaces like zoos or strip clubs engage in the power dynamics of exposure, the home should foster the tactile coherence that makes identity stable.

Too often, however, the home itself feels like an overcrowded panoptic space, especially for people whose personal boundary is already vulnerable. When Sylvia Plath and Ted Hughes move their young family to an idyllic country house, Court Green, in North Tawton, Devon, in 1961, her initial feelings of comfort and sustenance are gradually replaced by the fear of exposure and boundary violation. At first, there seems to be an idyllic balance between artistic productivity and domestic bliss in their Devon country house, like that of Otto and Aurelia Plath's apartment in Jamaica Plain. "[W]e have established a very pleasant rhythm here," she writes to her mother.

> Right after breakfast I go up to my study to work at the marvelous 6-foot natural wood table (which you helped finish Warren) while Ted carpenters or gardens in the back with Frieda along. He gives her lunch and puts her to bed about noon, and I come down and make our lunch and by the time I am through picking up the house and doing dishes, Frieda is up and out front with me, gardening, mending, or whatever, and Ted is in his study. (*LH* 429–30)

Creating and sustaining home, family, and artwork go hand in hand; the table she writes on associates her with her family of birth, her current family, her professional self, and nature. Like the rest of her house, moreover, her desk has plenty of space. "My whole spirit has expanded immensely—I don't have that crowded, harassed feeling I've had in all the small places I've lived in before" (428).

As time goes by, however, Plath's journals from this period begin to reveal anxiety about her personal, and especially her professional, space being violated. Although Court Green was a relatively large house, she could not seem to find a place to hide in it. "Mrs. H. materialized outside my study this morning: source of a great Fratch between Ted & me—my sense of surprise invasion. This is my only symbolic sanctum. [. . .] The sense that Mrs. H wanted to see how we lived in the back rooms" (*UJ*

651). Nurse D., who is employed to help with their second child so that Plath can have time to do her writing, always intrudes just when she has begun to work.

> Nothing Ted could say could stop her—she would forge up the stairs, he preceding desperate to warn me, and I would see her smiling white head over his shoulder at the study door. I would be in my pink fluffy bathrobe [. . .] and she would say "artist's outfit," go into the bedroom, find the bed unmade, and I would have hastily thrown a newspaper over the pink plastic pot of violently yellow urine I had not bothered to empty, on the principle that all housework wait till after noon. (644)

Plath's melodramatic rendering of Mrs. D.'s invasion is both comic and grueling because of its focus on the exact locations and sightlines of the figures involved. The opening up of her private sanctum of a study reveals it to be not the quietly tailored room of books and thoughts she imagines as a college student but a rumpled, squalid hovel, a failure as both domestic and intellectual space. Her semiclothed body and private bodily functions are laid bare. Mrs. D.'s sarcastic characterization of her bathrobe as an "artist's outfit" assaults Plath's sense of professional identity, dismisses her homemaking skills, and imposes on her body's margin all at the same time.

In "Eavesdropper" (*CP* 260), a poem written during this period, a nosy neighbor peers across into that same bedroom, keeping her under surveillance like "the big blue eye / That watches, like God, or the sky."

> Do not think I don't notice your curtain—
> Midnight, four o'clock,
> Lit (you are reading),
> Tarting with the drafts that pass,
> Little whore tongue,
> Chenille beckoner,
> Beckoning my words in (lines 28–34)

This persistent observation is like a skin affliction, a "Mole on my shoulder, / to be scratched absently, / To bleed, if it comes to that" (lines 4–5). Observation represents a sort of wounding, or flaying, for Plath, just as it does for Prince-Hughes. "We felt very new & shy," she writes to her mother about their first meeting with the village beekeepers, "I hugging my bare arms in the cool of the evening" (*UJ* 656). In "The Bee Meeting" (*CP* 112–12), her poem describing the event, the narrator dwells exten-

sively on the vulnerability of her body's edge. "In my sleeveless sum-
mery dress I have no protection / [. . .] I am as nude as a chicken neck"
(lines 3, 6). By contrast, her neighbors are "knights in visors." Throughout the poem, her difficulty fitting into the community is figured as a
desire to wear more clothing. Physiological fear of being stung by the
bees blends with her social fear of the community, and the poem ends
with emotional collapse and the terror of violent bodily violation.

> I am exhausted, I am exhausted—
> Pillar of white in a blackout of knives
> I am the magician's girl who does not flinch.
> The villagers are untying their disguises, they are shaking hands.
> Whose is that long white box in the grove, what have they accom-
> plished,
> > why am I cold. (lines 51–55)

The narrator feels in danger of being torn by knives and cut in two by the
magician's saw. Her alienation from the other beekeepers is apparent in
their relaxed ability to manage this boundary threat, realized in their protective clothing, while she must steel herself to do so. While the swarm
of bees poses part of the threat to her margin, she also identifies with the
queen bee, whose sanctum is being violated by "The villagers [who] open
the chambers, they are hunting the queen." The poem's last line suggests
that she feels the violation of the "long white box" as a personal violation, leaving her torn open and exposed, perhaps fatally. The image of the
"magician's girl" combines showmanship, enclosure (in the saw-divided
box), and the violent violation of that enclosure.

A similar elision of performance and bodily violation takes place in
"Lady Lazarus" (*CP* 244–47), which offers Plath's fullest portrayal of flaying through public exposure. The poem dwells on the tactile sensation
of being "unwrap[ped]." "Peel off the napkin / O my enemy. / Do I
terrify?— [. . .] / Soon, soon the flesh / The grave cave ate will be / At
home on me" (lines 10–12, 16–18). The title itself suggests the elision of
suicide and resurrection, but unlike the bumblebee poems, which attend
to the warm safety of the hibernaculum, this one focuses on the painful
emergence from the tomb, figured as tearing away of the body's margin:
"my skin / Bright as a Nazi lampshade" (lines 4–5). In a manuscript
of *The Bell Jar*, Plath explicitly compares Esther Greenwood to Lazarus.
"Lazarus would be cold and white as a pressed root after those four days
in the cave. What could the world be to him, risen. A senseless hell of
smiles, a furnace of sun consuming petal and leaf. [. . .] He would beg

to return to the cave and be left in peace" (qtd. in Peel 241). Lazarus never asked to be resurrected, and Plath figures his resurrection as a sort of brutal denuding, a violation of privacy recalling her father's breaking open of the bees' hibernacula. The exposure of the hibernating body to the public is a "big strip tease," in which Plath imagines stripping skin rather than clothes; as in Prince-Hughes's dance club, "There is a charge / For the eyeing of my scars" (lines 57–58). Lady Lazarus is on display in a spectacular environment which elides the strip club and the scientific laboratory, much like Prince-Hughes's elision between exotic dancing and going to the zoo. For both writers, being socially visible feels like flaying; visible accessibility becomes corporeal vulnerability. Ultimately, Plath comes to consider such painful exposure necessary to her work the same way Prince-Hughes does. Shortly after leaving her Devon home, she writes in her journal: "O, only left to myself, what a poet I shall flay myself into" (*UJ* 381).

While Plath's boundary anxieties emerge through and seem to be intensified by her professional life, Grandin has structured her career around the insights autism offers her. Having been able to successfully treat many of her anxieties about exposure through deep pressure therapy, Grandin has spent her career crusading for the use of this therapy among autistic young people. In her career in the meat-processing industry, she has applied the principles of immediate tactile pressure to livestock handling. The primary structure of the slaughterhouses Grandin designs is the "chute," a sort of squeeze machine in motion which allows pressure to be continually exerted on the animals even while they are moving. Rather than a floor conveyor belt, Grandin favors a straddling conveyor belt in which "[t]he animal rides the conveyor like a person riding a horse, supported under the belly and chest. Solid sides on each side of the conveyor prevent it from tilting off" (*Thinking* 179). By limiting visual sensation and intensifying pressure, Grandin is able to increase the speed at which the cows move, thus improving plant efficiency.

> I designed curved single-file alleys with solid sides. They help keep cattle calmer. The solid sides prevent the animals from being frightened by people and other moving objects outside the alley. A curved alley also works better than a straight one because the cattle are unable to see people up ahead, and each animal thinks he is going back where he came from. (173)

The meatpacking facility, Grandin suggests, should be an architectural complement to the cows' sensory needs, a building whose very shape enacts the physical sensations of its inhabitants. Grandin conceives the slaughterhouse not as a space in which cows are placed but as trajectories of motion through tightly enclosed chutes that the cows undertake voluntarily. The building's architecture should demonstrate the sort of dynamic bodily interactivity Juhani Pallasmaa argues for. "The experience of home is structured by distinct activities [. . .] not by visual elements. A building is encountered; it is approached, confronted, related to one's body, moved through, utilised as a condition for other things. Architecture initiates, directs and organises behaviour and movement" (63). The self-determination inherent in Pallasmaa's model seems almost impossibly ironic when applied to cows in an industrial slaughtering facility on their way to a sudden and violent death, yet Grandin's project of creating a comfortable experience for the livestock is based on this principle. Grandin takes an industrial device, the squeeze machine, into her home, domesticating it through using it on her own body. She then attempts to transpose the feelings of domestic comfort that it brings her back into the slaughtering process by designing new industrial devices designed to re-create those soothing tactile sensations. This represents the most extreme disjunction between an architectural structure and the apprehension of home space that one can imagine. To feel at home when one is about to be slaughtered is to be utterly blind to the purpose of the building around you, concentrated so fully on the comfort to be found at the body's edge that the body's existence ceases to matter. This transposition of domestic sensations to the killing floor seems at first glance abusive, even sadistic, as the tactile comfort it creates represents a form of deadly imprisonment. Similarly, the coercive overtones of the therapy used in Blairs et al.'s study made some of the hospital staff "ill at ease with the non-contingent 'tuck in' and 'positive' touch components" (219) even though "[i]t was emphasized to staff that the application of deep touch pressure was not a method of restraint and that B could end the session at anytime simply by sitting up or rolling over" (217). Because both Blairs et al. and Grandin focus their therapeutic interventions entirely on intense sensation at the body's edge, the psychological symbolism of the squeeze machine, or of enforced tucking in, cannot help taking on Kafkaesque or Orwellian resonances. Such an impression is misguided, they would argue, as it is based on reading bodily postures and tactile relations from afar, as symbols of power or psychological coercion, rather than attending to the actual somatosensory experience of the subject. In the same way that Plath's critics misread her burial imagery as pathological by neglecting its somatosensory elements, Grandin's readers might misinterpret the squeeze machine as a torture device. Seeing a teenage girl climb into a cattle chute looks terrifying, but Grandin's successful therapeutic endeavors are based on the fact that it feels good.

Grandin would describe this as the confusion of emotional empathy for sensory empathy. People who experience emotional empathy for the cows assume that the animals fear death and know they are going to die. Grandin argues that even at the point of slaughter, immediate physical apperceptions are far more important than emotional or philosophical responses. Rather than fearing death, it is "the little things that make them balk and refuse to move, such as seeing a small piece of chain hanging down from an alley fence" (167). When cattle do panic, Grandin points out, it is usually because they are prodded, painfully restrained, or made to fall; it has nothing to do with an awareness of mortality. When comforted by a properly designed space, however, they walk calmly toward death: "240 cattle per hour quietly walked up the ramp and voluntarily entered the double-rail conveyor system. It was as if they were going in to get milked" (180). The distinction between life and death ceases to be important, since it is anxiety and physical discomfort, rather than the killing blow, that make slaughtered cows unhappy. Her chute and conveyor systems thus represent a material embodiment of empathy, which she considers far more legitimate than any emotional identification with the cows' fate. The chute may be leading to a dairy barn, the livestock environment most redolent with connotations of domesticity and nurturance, or it may be leading to the killing floor, but the space itself serves as an orderly, calming, domestic space.

Unlike the stories of overcoming that Titchkosky critiques (188), Grandin's writing about her disability emphasizes the insight she gains from it. Her disability allows her a cognitive understanding of and a "sensory empathy" with the cows that the neurotypical population lacks. Grandin argues that her professional success as an advisor to the meatpacking industry is based on her ability to understand the hypersensitive sensory systems of animals as they move through the plant. "One of the reasons I am good at designing this equipment is that I can [. . .] put myself into a twelve-hundred-pound steer's body and feel the equipment" (*Thinking* 153). To solve a problem in an animal facility you need to "put yourself in their place—literally in their place. You have to go where the animal goes and do what the animal does" (*AT* 31). Grandin places greatest emphasis on replicating the postures of the animals' bodies in order to understand their bodily engagement with space. "I got down on my hands and knees and went through the chute the same way the pigs did. The managers probably thought I looked crazy, but that's the only way you can do it. You have to get to the same level as the animals" (33–34).

Grandin's early experience in the squeeze chute serves as the foundation for this approach. Her life-transforming communion with cows comes entirely through the replication of a particular physical posture and, most importantly, the tactile apprehension that posture allows. Her increasingly sophisticated manipulation of the squeeze machine's lever leads to more complex tactile sensations.

> To have feelings of gentleness, one must experience gentle bodily comfort. As my nervous system learned to tolerate the soothing pressure from my squeeze machine, I discovered that the comforting feeling made me a kinder and gentler person. [. . .] It is like a language of pressure, and I keep finding new variations with slightly different sensations. For me, this is the tactile equivalent of a complex emotion and this has helped me to understand complexity of feelings. (*Thinking* 84, 92)

Grandin elaborates her claims of "tactile equivalence" between pressure and emotion throughout her work. Just as the squeeze machine blends verbal and somatic perception in its "language of pressure," Grandin blends the emotional and physical significations of certain words. The "feeling" (emotion) of "gentleness" (empathetic kindness) is realized through the "feeling" (somatic apprehension) of "gentleness" (comforting touch). Grandin claims a progression from bodily sensation to complex emotion that would imply the superiority of the second: "Gentle touching teaches kindness" (85). Yet the ambiguity of her writing encourages the reader to treat emotion and sensation interchangeably. Grandin writes that the "feeling" the squeeze machine gives her "was one that I needed to cultivate toward other people" (84). Specifically, this feeling is "soothing, comforting contact" and "the relaxing feeling of being held" (85). She gives the specific example of learning to pet her cat more gently. "After I experienced the soothing feeling of being held, I was able to transfer that good feeling to the cat. As I became gentler, the cat began to stay with me, and this helped me understand the ideas of reciprocity and gentleness" (84). Grandin's use of the word "transfer" suggests that she is engaging in a psychic exchange, not just a somatic one. Communication through touch becomes essential to her understanding of the animals she works with.

> I always thought about cattle intellectually until I started touching them. [. . .] When I pressed my hand against the side of a steer, I could feel whether he was nervous, angry, or relaxed. [. . .] Sometimes

touching the cattle relaxed them, but it always brought me closer to the reality of their being. (85)

Her touch, like the squeeze machine touching her, can calm the cattle, but it also serves a communicating function; she feels their feelings. The somatosensory "reality" of the animals' emotional state is available only through tactile contact. While redesigning a restraint system for a kosher slaughterhouse, she memorizes the feel of the levers that control the animal's body. She describes the hydraulic system as being like a musical instrument; by accessing her haptic memory of the machine's controls, she can "allow the restrainer to become part of my body." "Through the machine I reached out and held the animal. [. . .] Body boundaries seemed to disappear, and I had no awareness of pushing the levers. The rear pusher gate and head yoke became an extension of my hands" (25). The hydraulic system allows her body to become the squeeze machine, calming the cow in a fully corporeal empathetic embrace.

Stuart Murray identifies autism as the latest example of a sentimental cultural equivalence between neurological difference and mystical knowledge, noting that the "notion of creativity within impairment, of insight from a space of purported damage, has a long history" (26). Yet Grandin herself embraces the mystification of her specialized awareness, portraying herself as a sort of sage or wise woman who knows the secrets of the brain and can speak to animals. At points, her discussions explicitly take on the frame of spiritual insights: she compares the Swift meatpacking plant to "Vatican City" (230) and names her signature engineering innovation—a cattle ramp system designed to calm the cows as they approach the killing floor—the "Stairway to Heaven." She marks the genesis of her personal faith as she reviews the construction of this device, which becomes the locus of her spiritual beliefs. "One night when the crew was working late, I stood on the nearly completed structure and looked into what would become the entrance to heaven for cattle. This made me more aware of how precious life is" (230). Holding the cow in the restraint system as it was slaughtered "felt like walking on water" (26). Her relation to the meatpacking industry makes the prophetic, or priestly, aspects of her work inevitable. In an article in *Judaism* magazine, Grandin advises kosher meat-processing plants on humanitarian slaughtering practices, referring to both the Torah and the Talmud to argue that a commonly used rear-leg restraint system "violates the spirit of [Mosaic] law" ("Humanitarian" 439). Her unique empathy for animal consciousness, combined with a spatial apprehension of the body's relation to built structures, leads her to a radically material version of spirituality. She writes in her diary, "I greatly matured after the construction of the Stairway to Heaven because it was REAL. It was not just a symbolic door" (*Thinking* 230).

Throughout this chapter, I have been implicitly arguing that the hypersensitivity experienced by people with Autism Spectrum Disorders is comparable to boundary anxieties inherent in domestic life. This parallel may seem overly metaphorical or a sloppy elision that evades clear neurological distinctions between autistic and neurotypical brains, but in describing the parallel, I am reiterating distinctions between intellectual and somatosensory processing that Grandin herself makes. Grandin proposes a fundamental distinction between thought processes, which cannot be translated from autistic to neurotypical populations, and tactile sensation, which, although differing in degree, represents a sort of universal language. Ann Jurecic argues that Grandin's writing invites the reader to experience her thinking even as "she offers examples that demonstrate they can never truly understand the difference of her mind. [. . .] Because Grandin thinks in pictures, her relationship to language must remain deeply alien to those who think linguistically—deeply alien[,] that is, to most of her readers" (12–13). On the other hand, Grandin is quick to assert the commonality between autistic and neurotypical somatic experience; not only do babies and deep-sea divers like the sort of pressure she experiences in the squeeze machine, but "deep pressure is a calming sensation for *just about everyone*" (emphasis mine). In a 1992 published experiment entitled "Calming Effects of Deep Touch Pressure in Patients with Autism Disorder, College Students and Animals," she purposely chooses nonautistic college students as her subjects in order to show that pressure sensations bridge the gap between autistic and nonautistic experience. If "just about everyone" can appreciate this somatosensory need for pressure and enclosure, then the alternative version of domestic experience which Grandin and Plath propose can also be appreciated by all of us.

Grandin and Plath both attempt to hone domesticity down to a private selection of tactile sensations. For Grandin, who does so therapeutically, the result is what most of us would consider an alarming elimination of all recognizable domestic structures. Grandin admits that her autism makes her care less about domestic niceties. The home of her friend Henry Spira, an animal welfare activist who is "probably slightly Asperger's," exemplifies interior design for people with Autism Spectrum Disorders. "He lived in a little rent-controlled apartment with his two cats and a bunch of pieces of cardboard boxes the cats had scratched up. He called them cat sculptures" (*Animals Make* 256–57). Neither aesthetic nor architectural order matters to Grandin as long as the home provides somatic control; as a result, she can feel at home even in a slaughterhouse.

By contrast, Plath attempts to balance her boundary anxieties and her need for privacy with her desire for close family contact and a traditional domestic life. The idealized cultural images of home life upon which Grandin places no value both enchanted and tortured Plath. Her continual attention to organizing and beautifying her living space seems like an attempt to apply visual, socially normative solutions to a tactile, somatosensory problem. After her divorce, she becomes desperate to find a living arrangement that will give her the privacy to work while caring for her two young children. When she discovers that W. B. Yeats's former apartment is available, she becomes obsessed with living "in the house of a famous poet, so my work should be blessed" (*LH* 478), and in her letters to her mother, she dwells endlessly on its precise location, the organization of its rooms, and the process of decorating it. "My bedroom has yellow and white wallpaper, straw mat, black floor borders and gold lampshade—bee colors— [. . .] I'd like to live in this flat forever" (492). Six weeks later she committed suicide.

The "peaceful imagined geography" to which autistics withdraw by going into cupboards, clothing racks, or squeeze machines allows them, Davidson argues, to reinforce their identities after encounters with a "tortuous" external world: "more positive emotions can emerge in the safe space of authors' own, separate territories [which represent a] sanctuary of sorts" (*In a World* 669). Grandin and Plath, in their focusing of domestic life inward toward such spaces, seek to create such a sanctuary, just as Jesus does when he exhorts his followers to go into their closets to pray. Jesus calls for a private communion with God, a relocation of sacred space into the tightest, most secret of domestic enclosures where tactile sensation would be most apparent. It is not enough to step into one's closet; one must also "shut thy door." Most closets and storerooms (the original Greek root used in Matthew 6:6 suggests a storeroom) are places we only lean on or step into briefly. By shutting the door, Jesus transforms utility space into lived space, the storeroom into the sanctuary. He thus enacts the reverse process from what takes place in the homes of the elderly or of hoarders; a place meant simply to house material becomes an emotionally charged and corporeally supportive environment. Like the "sacred space between body and ground" Prince-Hughes speaks of (121), the folding up of the body in the closet reestablishes its coherence. Spiritual communion in this secret place allows us to reemerge into the world renewed: "and thy Father which seeth in secret shall reward thee openly." To go into one's closet to pray, like the queen bee into her hibernaculum or Grandin into the squeeze machine, allows one to emerge spiritually and somatically reborn. While domestic anxiety is especially intense for people with Autism Spectrum Disorders, the pressures of the world, family, and home make all of us want to climb under the covers or into the closet on occasion. Perhaps in my childishly literal reading of Jesus's words, I had the right idea after all.

Chapter 7

The Leper's Studio

I wrote most of this book lying flat on my back. A few years ago I developed ischial bursitis, an inflammation of the pelvic bursa, which prevents me from sitting at a desk. This fairly comic affliction has not transformed my life, but it has changed my perception of how my body relates to the writing process. Formerly I thought of my work space in terms of surface and vantage point. My desktop, the drawing table of a former newspaper cartoonist, allowed me to fan books and papers out around the computer. I carefully chose where to place it so that I could have good over-the-shoulder natural light, glance out of the window when I looked up from the page, and occasionally run my eyes over certain much-loved prints on the wall. Now, rather than surface I focus on angles (of knees, waist, laptop screen) and reach (how closely do I need to place a pile of books?).

Being tied down like this has liberated me from the yearning I used to feel (and all my friends who write for a living still do) for the perfect study. I imagined it as a sort of garret deluxe, light-filled, book-lined, emptied of everything but intellectual energy, a space specifically designed for creativity (in opposition to domesticity) with a broad beautiful desk and a great view. Like Charles Dickens, who did much of his writing in a Swiss Chalet he had reconstructed next to his house, I wanted to be able to leave the laundry and backpacks and dishes behind and step into a purged and purified space, emptied of everything but the creative act.

In this chapter, I will focus on the embodied aspects of creative work in the home. While working does not represent the sort of crisis of embodiment I investigate in other chapters, our cultural assumption that our bodies require a separate, carefully constructed space in which to perform creative work seems to mark them as fragile or hypersensitive. The artist's body must be protected and fostered, removed to an empty, rarefied space that foregrounds visual experience and deemphasizes disorderly embodiment so that the artist is able to work effectively. I will focus on the work of Paul Gauguin and John Updike, both of whom suffered from a psoriatic skin disorder. Both Gauguin and Updike respond to the anxieties associated with their skin disorders through contradictory impulses to purify the home of all remnants or reminders of embodied existence—thereby rendering it an empty and chaste collection of planar surfaces—and to imagine the home as a body whose fragmented skin is itself a work of art. Like the writers discussed in the previous chapter, these works define domesticity in relation to the body's edge, but in this case, that edge is fragmentary and indefinable. Skin disorders that call into question the body's margin require us to establish a model of somatic identity and of domestic experience based less on boundary than on the creative interweaving of body and space.

> I will send you a photo of my studio as soon as I have taken one, showing the polychrome wooden panels, the statues among the flowers, etc. Just to sit here at the open door, smoking a cigarette and drinking a glass of absinth, is an unmixed pleasure which I have every day. [. . .] I want no other life, only this. (Thomson 252: Letter from Gauguin to Armand Seguin, January 1897)

Paul Gauguin thus enunciates his antibourgeois tropical idyll, in which the home as artist's studio is open to nature, stripped of middle-class trivialities, and teeming with sensual pleasures. Gauguin's self-made myth of a retreat to artistic primitivism resonates through the twentieth and twenty-first centuries, serving as a cultural counterpoint to middle-class domestic culture and providing an oft-invoked fantasy of creative escape from the home (Bortnick 4). Gauguin's life in Tahiti and the Marquesas was significantly less idyllic than that myth suggests; the artist was consistently impoverished, in despair over his career, and in terrible health. Nevertheless, Gauguin celebrated his alternative lifestyle in his letters, his writings, and, above all, his painting. While he enunciated his primitivist ideas in relation to sexuality, religion, and artistic self-expression, I would like to focus on how he enacts them through the aesthetic management and representation of domestic space. While Gauguin's Polynesian paintings tend to focus on vividly rendered human figures, they are often framed by or placed in relation to architectural structures. Gauguin experimented with the relationship between graphic art and architectural space throughout his career, and particularly in his final home on the Marquesas, the *Maison du Jouir*. This attention to architectural space suggests that rather than an antidomestic impulse, Gauguin was attempting to establish an alternate domestic aesthetic, focused less on interior comforts and more on identification between the body and the walls, ceilings, and exterior structures of the house. His artworks, both technically and thematically, suggest a preoccupation with parallels between architectural surfaces and the surface of the body. Gauguin's technical innovations, which were an aesthetic departure from the Impressionist use of color and pigment, involved making the surface of the canvas more apparent. I will argue that this artistic attention to bodily surface was informed by Gauguin's own compromised skin; the artist suffered from eczema throughout his life, complicated in his later years by syphilis, and the condition became increasingly severe during his years in Polynesia. The breezy, sensually pleasing domestic experience Gauguin describes, and the apprehension of boundary and identity it implies, were shadowed by the dysfunctions of his own bodily margins. The beautiful, unmarred skin of the figures in his Tahitian paintings bear artistic and political significance, as Alexandra Wettlaufer and Miriam Kahn have shown, but they also represent a paradisiacal image of bodily integrity painted by an artist whose own fragmenting skin was a constant preoccupation.

In opposition to Gauguin's image of the artist as absinthe-sipping primitivist, one might place John Updike, whose novels and stories celebrate, if somewhat ironically, suburban American domesticity. Updike meticulously represents late-twentieth- and early-twenty-first-century middle-class affection for the material comforts and conventional order of the home. While characters such as Harry Angstrom (a.k.a. Rabbit in *Rabbit Is Rich*) are at times haunted and disoriented by the vagaries of love and money, they seem to live out an affluent, enviable capitalist idyll, embodied in their well-kept homes, that contrasts starkly with Gauguin's antibourgeois vision. Yet, like Gauguin, Updike focuses on the meanings conveyed by surfaces in the home and the way personal identity adheres to the body's edge. Like Gauguin, moreover, Updike was a lifelong sufferer from a skin disorder, which he addresses in a chapter of his memoirs, "At War with My Skin," and his novel *The Centaur*, and which he describes in detail in his short story "From the Journal of a Leper."

> The form of the disease is as follows: spots, plaques, and avalanches of excess skin, manufactured by the dermis through some trifling but persistent error in its metabolic instructions, expand and slowly migrate

across the body like lichen on a tombstone. I am silvery, scaly. Puddles of flakes form wherever I rest my flesh. Each morning, I vacuum my bed. (181)

While promising to represent the "form" of the disease, Updike's narrator presents a sequence of images so multifarious and incompatible as to render his skin altogether formless. The description moves indiscriminately between color (spots, silvery), texture (plaques, scaly), and motion (avalanches, migrate). The mixing of metaphors, such as "[p]uddles of flakes," suggests the mixing of textures and social categories that his body surface involves. It exists in an imagistic realm that is gothic, replete with tombstones and avalanches, and humiliatingly pedestrian, as the final instance of vacuuming the bed drives home. Above all, Updike's representation foregrounds the painful preoccupation with materially grounding one's identity that the perceived failure of the body's edge creates. The home becomes littered with pieces of the homeowner; housework, or "cleaning up after oneself," literally amounts to cleaning up scattered fragments of one's body. As with accumulation or animal hoarding, the homeowner's own disorderly identity spreads throughout the home. Rather than a safe container that surrounds a safely contained body, the home threatens to become fragmentary and unbounded, littered with broken pieces of the self. Both Gauguin and Updike, I will argue, respond to the anxieties associated with their skin disorders through artworks that establish clear, idealized domestic and somatic boundaries while conversely creating an aesthetic philosophy in which full haptic engagement with one's artistic materials is necessary for authentic artistic creation. The alternative domesticity discussed in previous chapters involves removing the embodied experience of home from an architectural structure. Gauguin and Updike, on the other hand, propose a version of domestic experience in which architectural structure is primary, and the body is eliminated or is subsumed into the building and into the artistic process itself.

By the time Gauguin moved to Tahiti in 1891, he had already begun to distinguish himself technically from the Impressionists in several ways. Gauguin believed that the Impressionists had neglected drawing for brushwork, and he hoped to return to painting figures with clearly defined edges, in the tradition of Degas. He established these clear boundaries with "a painted dark blue outline underdrawing first, followed by paint layers built up slowly and thinly within the initial contours and final reinstatement of contours with dark blue" (Hale 183). This technique emphasized the bodily edges of his figures and made them more visually distinct. It is apparent in paintings such as *Tahitian Women Bath-*

ing (1891–92), *Two Tahitian Women* (1899), and *Where Do We Come From? What Are We? Where Are We Going?* (1897–98), in which central nude figures stand out from a darker ground, their skin seeming to glow with vitality. Gauguin painted these outlines so heavily that they sometimes soaked through to the back of the canvas; their clarity "enabled Gauguin literally to fill in the outlines and complete the painting with only minor changes" (Jirat-Wasiutynski and Newton 80). The warm bodily presence his paintings communicate derives from the clarity of the outlined forms and from Gauguin's approach to color, which he describes as having its own musical language (*Letters* 228). His application of color represents another technical innovation that distances Gauguin from the Impressionists; he "[tones] down important areas with muddy mixtures to offset his use of bright accents of pure color" (Jirat-Wasiutynski and Newton 131), thus intensifying and rarefying the skin tones of his central figures, making their bodies "remote from reality" (*Letters* 228). Color, Gauguin claims, should not be copied from nature, as it is "living matter, like the body of a living being" (Shackleford, "Return" 163). He perceived a particularly appealing color palette in the skin of Polynesians, which he describes as "a golden yellow" (Shackleford, "Splendor" 246) and which he celebrates in the title of his painting *And the Gold of Their Bodies* (he painted his studio windows "chrome yellow" during his stay in France between his trips to Tahiti [Prather and Stuckey 202]). Polynesian skin as Gauguin renders it is thus at once unreal and alive—perfect in both the richness of its tones and the distinctness of its unbroken boundaries. For Gauguin, whose legs were completely covered with bandages and "whose right leg was literally gnawed through by a horrible sore that was buzzing with green flies" (333), such spotless corporeality must have been particularly appealing.

This clarity of outline and surface is paralleled by the simplicity of architectural line and space in domestic paintings such as *Te Faaturuma* (*The Brooding Woman* 1891), *Te Rerioa* (*The Dream* 1897), and *Two Women* (1902). Except for a few pieces of fruit in *Te Faaturuma,* and a baby's cradle in *Te Rerioa,* the rooms are open spaces, devoid of domestic objects, like studios waiting for an easel. The rectilinear, peach-colored floor of *Te Faaturuma* fills most of the canvas, with geometrically regular walls, lintels, and moldings all intensifying the viewer's apprehension of the dwelling's emptiness. In all three paintings a single doorway opens in the back, through which we see a horseman (sometimes identified as the artist). The doorway opening parallels the viewer's perspective, so that we are looking through domestic space, our gaze uninterrupted by anything but the human figures. While clearly evocations of domestic life (food, the baby, the restful poses of the women), the paintings offer us domesticity at its least encumbered. Just as they offer us the skin as pure color and the body as pure form, the paintings represent the home as pure space.

Throughout his life, Gauguin was preoccupied with the spaces in which he worked and with the relationship between living space and studio space. Henri Mothere, the companion of his landlady in Le Pouldu, comments that the "only places where he created works of any worth were those where he had first set up his interior space according to his tastes" (Prather and Stuckey 112). Gauguin had a pattern of making living arrangements with other artists, most famously with Van Gogh in the yellow house in Arles, and then transforming their shared domestic space into a combination home and studio. He celebrates the full interpenetration of domestic studio and artistic space in a journal entry describing the production of Japanese Cloisonné vases. This artistic process represents the perfect blend of simple, sensual primitive culture and careful aesthetic practice. The family's house "is everything at once, a little factory, a sleeping-chamber, a refectory, etc.," and Gauguin emphasizes the smooth engagement of festive domestic life and artistic practice for a family "who are peasants for nine months of the year and artists for the three months of winter" (*Paul Gauguin's Intimate Journals* 63).

This equal interchange of studio and domestic space gradually shifts, however, as Gauguin began opening up his living space as much as possible and denuding it of domestic objects. Mothere describes how, in Le Pouldu, Gauguin and Meyer de Haan moved through a sequence of unacceptable studio spaces in homes and attics, finally settling on

> a little wooden shed that leaned against one end of their inn and had served, until that time, for storage and as a stable. Cleaned, floored, and with a window put in on the north side, it became the practical shelter where they gave in to their ardor for work without any worry of being interrupted or disturbed. Thus, the artistic solitude dreamed of by Gauguin first became a reality. Le Pouldu was the first of his "Tahitis," his "French Tahiti."(Prather and Stuckey 112, 121)

It seems rather strange to equate a cowshed with Tahiti unless, as Mothere implies, Gauguin's studio space had a symbolic significance for him, allowing an escape from bourgeois identity. Jean de Rotonchamp's description of Gauguin's home and studio in Paris in 1893, during his brief return to France, emphasizes the contrast between open studio space and marginalized living area.

To the left of the entrance was a small room containing a fireplace and a small, iron bed, which served as his bedroom. [. . .] [The studio was a] rather vast room, which was lit from the west through a lateral window that had been completely painted over with chrome yellow. [. . .] [T]he only furniture one saw other than the tools of profession, was a fairly good piano, which, moreover, the painter did not know how to play, and a heavily used sofa, in the purest Louis-Philippe style. (qtd. in Prather and Stuckey 202)

Gauguin crowds his living space into an antechamber and then constructs his studio as an empty space suffused with color. The few pieces of furniture serve as a parody of the domestic: a piano he cannot play; an elegant sofa worn and overused. While such arrangements of studio space are not unique to Gauguin, his impatient insistence upon organizing domestic space is a constant theme of his working career. Later in his life, he placed increasing emphasis on the openness of interior space, partly due to the influence of Polynesian architecture. He describes his home in the Marquesas as "[a] huge studio with a bed tucked away in one corner; everything to hand [. . .] raised two meters above the ground, for eating, doing carpentry, and cooking" (Shackleford, "Splendor" 244). While he still sleeps in his studio, the other domestic activities of cooking and eating have been moved outdoors. Gauguin empties, circumscribes, and illuminates domestic space, making it the architectural equivalent of the well-defined, warm-toned bodies in his paintings.

Gauguin's quest for such a purified domestic space seems to be a material enactment of what Gaston Bachelard, in his discussion of the relationship between domestic intimacy and the imagination, calls

the "hut dream," which is well-known to everyone who cherishes the legendary images of primitive houses. But in most hut dreams we hope to live elsewhere, far from the over-crowded house, far from city cares. We flee in thought in search of a real refuge. [. . .] The hut immediately becomes centralized solitude, for in the land of legend, there exists no adjoining hut. (31–32)

Bachelard argues that the hut dream is not a reaction against home life, but that we find "the root of the hut dream in the house itself" (31). Our ability to experience domestic intimacy is based on an imaginative hermitism existing at the very center of family life, allowing us to access an archetypal spatial experience. The hut represents "the essence of the verb 'to inhabit'" (32). Gauguin, who seems to have shared some of Bachelard's notions of a collective architectural unconsciousness, undertakes to bring the hut dream to life artistically.

In his story "Gesturing," Updike offers a similar aesthetic of domestic emptiness. Richard Maple, having just separated from his wife, goes in search of a new apartment.

> [H]e glanced to the window, saw the skyscraper, and knew this would do. The skyscraper, for years suspended in a famous state of incompletion, was a beautiful disaster, famous because it was a disaster (glass kept falling from it) and disastrous because it was beautiful: the architect had had a vision. He had dreamed of an invisible building, though immense; the glass was meant to reflect the sky and the old low brick skyline of Boston, and to melt into the sky. (567)

As in Gauguin's paintings, the reader's eye follows through the room and out the window, to experience the room as a frame for the landscape beyond. The landscape here is not a natural vista but a skyscraper, the John Hancock Tower, which serves as a mirror in which the empty space of the sky is rendered as pure color. Throughout the story (which Updike chose to include in his edited volume of the *Best American Short Stories of the Century*), we are given no details about the furniture or decorations of his apartment. It seems to consist almost entirely of a view of the sky reflected on "the blue skyscraper," which becomes "a companion of sorts, a single grand spectator. [. . .] [H]e felt it with him all the time" (569).

This emphasis on the reflective surfaces outside his window is matched by the purging of interior space. "Alone in his apartment, he discovered himself a neat and thrifty housekeeper. When a woman left, he could promptly set about restoring his bachelor order, emptying ashtrays which he describes as "a messy morgue" full of "long pale bodies" (568). Richard's desire to transcend the emotional complexities of his marriage and the vagaries of his aging body make him yearn for the simplicity of sanitized domestic space. He hopes for a life with the geometrical simplicity of the architectural surface that dominates his view, but he knows this can't be maintained. "It was an interim, a holiday. But an oddly clean and just one, rectilinear, dignified, though marred by gaps of sudden fear and disorientation" (570). The fragility of his emotional life is implicit in the Hancock Tower's flawed design, which causes the glass panels to flake off, like Updike's psoriatic skin, and litter the street below with glass. This parallel is made explicit in "From the Journal of a Leper," in which the same building appears; its "blue skin [. . .] shed windows as I shed scales" (182).

The Hancock Tower exemplifies a late-twentieth-century architectural aesthetic, which Pallasmaa argues "employs reflection, gradations of transparency, overlay and juxtaposition to create a sense of spatial thickness, as well as subtle and changing sensations of movement and light" (32). The skyscraper is rendered insubstantial, an "invisible building," through this use of reflection; it is a "blue skyscraper," not a silver one reflecting the blue sky.

> These products of instrumentalised technology conceal their processes
> of construction, appearing as ghostlike apparitions. The increasing
> use of reflective glass in architecture reinforces the dreamlike sense
> of unreality and alienation. The contradictory opaque transparency of
> these buildings reflects the gaze back unaffected and unmoved; we are
> unable to see or imagine life behind these walls. (31)

The transparency and overlay Pallasmaa describes are translated directly into Richard's emotional experience. "What a transparent wealth of previous lives overlay a city's present joy!" (Updike, "Gesturing" 570). Richard's environment of pure reflective panes allows him to move "like a water bug, like a skipping stone, upon the glassy tense surface of his new life" (570).

Richard's all-window domestic experience can also be understood as what Grant Hildebrand, in *Origins of Architectural Pleasure,* calls a surplus of "prospect." Hildebrand argues that humans need both the feeling of "refuge" provided by enclosed, nestlike spaces and the ability to survey the surrounding landscape from within this safe space (22). Homes emphasizing refuge tend to offer cozy, human-sized spaces, "protective retreats" (32), and comfortable surfaces that suggest physical intimacy and nurturance, whereas those emphasizing prospect offer expansive views of the surrounding landscape. Hildebrand argues for a balance between the two, as in Frank Lloyd Wright's Edwin Cheney house in Oak Park, Illinois.

> Few buildings have offered so consistently what I call a *nested hierarchy*
> of refuge and prospect. [. . .] [A]lcoves, deep eaves, broad expanses of
> window, and terraces and balconies suggest places of concealment and
> at the same time convey the availability of broad arcs of view over sur-
> rounding terrain. They tell us that the house in its entirety is likely to be

an effective refuge, and its interior is likely to offer unusually generous prospect. (33)

By contrast, Richard's apartment offers no alcoves or reclusive spaces, and prospect is such an overwhelming feature that it creates the dream-like sense of "immateriality and weightlessness" (32) that Pallasmaa describes. Indeed, it seems to verge on another of Hildebrand's archi-tectural categories, that of peril, in which "viewpoints are architectural precipices from which a fall would be fatal" (74). Buildings such as Mont-Saint-Michel are designed to create "thrilling elation" (74) through architecturally managed danger, thereby invoking the sublime. Richard's escape from his domestic entanglements within an empty reflective archi-tectural space represents an ascent into a sort of bachelor sublime, an ecstatic optical vertigo that replaces embodied intimacy with an optical embrace: "he had to go lean his vision against his inanimate, giant friend, dimming to mauve on one side, still cerulean on the other" (Updike, "Gesturing" 571).

Richard's hyperclean domesticity, like his attachment to the tower, is clearly related to his desire to banish embodied domesticity from living space and transcend time. Pallasmaa argues that such a transcendence of mortality is the implicit goal of recent architecture.

> All matter exists in the continuum of time; the patina of wear adds the enriching experience of time to the materials of construction. But the machine-made materials of today—scaleless sheets of glass, enameled metals and synthetic plastics—tend to present their unyielding surfaces to the eye without conveying their material essence or age. Buildings of this technological age usually deliberately aim at ageless perfection, and they do not incorporate the dimension of time, or the unavoidable and mentally significant processes of aging. This fear of the traces of wear and age is related to our fear of death. (31–32)

In "Gesturing," Richard discovers the words "With this ring I thee wed" carved into the glass of his window by a former owner, an etching that lends texture to the transparent surface and disrupts the purity of the reflections surrounding him. The scratches undercut the glass surface's "ageless perfection" and return Richard to a world in which windows, and marriages, become scarred and worn. The story ends with Richard's reintegration into the messy emotional and physical dynamics of his domestic life through his habitual bodily response to his wife's familiar physical gestures. He "knew that she would never stop gesturing within

him, never; though a decree come between them, even death, her gestures would endure, cut into glass" (Updike, "Gesturing" 575). Richard
feels his wife's hand movements as a tangible trace that, like the wedding
vow scrawled into the glass, returns him to an embodied, emotionally
engaged, way of living.

While there is a world of difference between the architectural designs
of the John Hancock Tower and of Gauguin's hut in Tahiti, both hold
out the possibility of a disembodied apprehension of architectural space.
Gauguin standing at his studio door sipping absinthe, like Richard standing at his window gazing at the skyscraper, is attempting to subsume
domestic experience into a fully visualized apprehension of sightline,
reflection, and pure color uninterrupted by bodies. Updike's story enunciates this ideal of male escape into sensually appealing domestic emptiness only to undercut it with an alternative aesthetic based on texture
and fragmentation. A similar dynamic is at work in Gauguin's paintings,
which idealize and purify the body's outline while at the same time vigorously asserting the tactile immediacy of the skin through the incorporation of texture into painted form.

Underdrawing was not the only way that Gauguin distinguished
himself from the Impressionists, particularly from his friend and companion Van Gogh. Where Van Gogh created texture in his paintings
through "impasto," the building up of thick layers of paint, Gauguin
chose to apply thin layers of paint, so that the texture of the canvas would
be apparent through the pigment. At times he would use no ground at
all "in order to fuse pigment and surface" (Jirat-Wasiutynski and Newton
80). While living with Van Gogh in Arles, Gauguin began painting on
jute, a coarse kind of canvas. He did so partly because jute was inexpen-
sive, but Vojtěch Jirat-Wasiutyński and H. Travers Newton Jr. suggest that
he "may also have been interested in its 'tooth' or texture; which gave it
the ability to hold paint well, since he applied a very thin ground" (119).
The thinness of the paint, combined with the coarseness of the fabric,
lends Gauguin's paintings a different sort of texture from Van Gogh's,
one that is inherent in the surface of the canvas rather than in the paint.

Revealing the canvas's texture has a variety of aesthetic effects.
Gauguin describes the resulting images as "vulgar" (Jirat-Wasiutyński
120), and he clearly means the roughness of the canvas to body forth his
"unpolished" (Thomson 259), primitivist style. It also renders it more
immediately corporeal to the viewer. Looking at a Gauguin painting, we
apprehend the way the light catches the "tooth" of the canvas, and we
recognize the painting's tangible qualities. Rather than the thick liquidity
of Van Gogh's surfaces, which delight us for the way they catch and toy

with reflected light, Gauguin's surfaces appeal to the fingertips. The visible apprehension of the canvas incites a tactile response, or at least the strong desire for one. We almost feel that we have touched the surface by looking at it, and since the surfaces we are looking at are skin surfaces, we almost feel that we have touched these warm, living bodies. By "fus[ing] pigment and surface," Gauguin elides visual and tactile perception. In his discussion of architectural tactility, Pallasmaa argues for the primacy of the sense of touch, even in visual art forms.

> All the senses, including vision, are extensions of the tactile sense; the senses are specialisations of skin tissue, and all sensory experiences are modes of touching and thus related to tactility. Our contact with the world takes place at the boundary line of the self through specialised parts of our enveloping membrane. (10–11)

Pallasmaa's argument is clearly more aesthetic than scientific, but it effectively enunciates the apprehension of the tangible through the visual that we see in Gauguin's painting. The body's edge, in Pallasmaa's rendering, seems to reach out into the visual field and stroke whatever we see.

In his discussion of painting in "Eye and Mind," Maurice Merleau-Ponty calls into question the Cartesian tendency to "set up before the mind a picture or a representation of the world" (162). Our bodies, he argues, as well as our apprehension of our own corporeality, are contiguous with the material world.

> Visible and mobile, my body is a thing among things; it is caught in the fabric of the world, and its cohesion is that of a thing. [. . .] Things are an annex or prolongation of itself; they are incrusted into its flesh, they are part of its definition; the world is made of the same stuff as the body. This way of turning things around, these antinomies, are different ways of saying that vision happens among, or is caught in, things. (163)

Merleau-Ponty suggests that vision and touch are always fused; the experience of perceiving another body, or a Gauguin painting, involves tactile enactment of vision. Our visual perception, being bodily, is interwoven with the rough fabric of the material world, to which it catches and coheres, so a distanced visual apprehension is impossible. Standing before a Gauguin painting, we are looking not at a picture "set up before the mind" but at a material, highly textured object "made of the same stuff as the body," and we respond with our bodies extended through our vision. As Mark Paterson points out, Merleau-Ponty also locates the painter's body within the artwork: "in painting on canvas the brush stroke is a mark, evidence of the manual touch of the painter" (Paterson 88). While painting his monumental work *Where Do We Come From? What Are We? Where Are We Going?*, Gauguin describes an entirely tactile process, almost as if he painted with his eyes closed. "No, it's all done without a model, feeling my way with the tip of a brush on a piece of sackcloth that is full of knots and rough patches; so it looks terribly unpolished" (Thomson 259). Our response to Gauguin's fusing of pigment and canvas is to recognize, in the roughness of the surface, our own rough, frangible surfaces; the world adheres to and becomes embedded in the flesh, and vice versa, like pigment fusing with canvas.

By invoking tactile sensation, Gauguin's technique also suggests the skin's frailty. Where Van Gogh's impasto, with its thick layers and swirls of paint, gives the canvas a solid, three-dimensional quality, Gauguin's canvases seem almost fragile, as though the paint might flake off at any moment. In fact, Gauguin recognized that this technique made the surface brittle and prone to flaking, and he wrote letters to Daniel de Monfreid giving instructions on how to repair the paintings after their long trip to France (Shackleford, "Return" 161–62). For all their fleshly presence, the figures in his paintings reveal, in the very texture of their skin, the rough, uneven materials of their creation and gesture, I would suggest, toward the rough surface of their creator's own skin. Gauguin's painted skin offers the viewer a paradox: it seems to be at once beautiful in its completeness and full of "knots and rough patches." As Merleau-Ponty notes, "It is by lending his body to the world that the artist changes the world into painting" (162). Pallasmaa offers a similar formulation of the body's involvement in artistic creation. "When working, both the artist and craftsman are directly engaged with their bodies and their existential experiences rather than focused on an external and objectified problem. [. . .] In creative work, a powerful identification and projection takes place; the entire bodily and mental constitution of the maker becomes the site of the work" (12). When that body is broken or crumbling, as Gauguin's was, this "identification and projection" results in an aesthetic in which fragmentation is inextricable from artistic creation.

Throughout his letters, Gauguin consistently elides his crumbling, debilitated body, his flaking paintings, and the physically exhausting, self-annihilating power of the artistic process. In a letter to Monfreid in which he complains that he has "not been able to hold a brush all month," he describes how his painting "erupts, brutally," how it "gush[es] forth like lava" (Thomson 258–59). His skin disease spreads "with fury over a very wide surface" (*Letters* 207), as his "big canvas has drained away all my energy" (Thomson 258). In a letter to Émile Bernard, he compares the aesthetic impulse to "a Nessus shirt which sticks to you and cannot be stripped off" (*Letters* 129). The stress of artistic creation impels him to thoughts of suicide, using the arsenic meant to treat his eczema, and he imagines his flesh being torn from his body; "I went to hide in the mountains, where my corpse would have been eaten up by ants" (Thomson 257). In March 1898, he writes, "I am rapidly breaking up, and I can see at no distant date the end for which I long so ardently" (*Letters* 213). Gauguin would live for another five years, but his experience of physically breaking apart, erupting, having his skin stripped off, demonstrates his apprehension of the artistic process as an embodied enactment of his skin disease, even as his paintings themselves celebrate the beauty of perfect, unblemished skin.

This attention to the skin's texture, and to texturing the surfaces of the home, would seem to contradict Gauguin's use of underdrawing and coloration, which led to visually coherent, flawless surfaces. To some degree, I believe, these two techniques demonstrate conflicting motives in regard to his own body; he wishes both to escape from his crumbling skin into a world of dermal perfection and to embrace it as fundamental to his creative process. But there is also a deeper coherence at work. Gauguin compares himself explicitly to God the creator in *Cahier pour Aline.* "It is said that God took a little clay in his hands and made every known thing. An artist, in turn (if he really wants to produce divine creative work), must not copy nature but take the natural elements and create a new element" (qtd. in Thomson 181). For art to be "divine" in its perfection, the artist must alter and perfect nature, making colors and forms impossibly pure, but he must do so through haptic engagement. In fact, the Bible does not portray God making "every known thing" from clay, only Adam; Gauguin, like Michelangelo, imagines a hands-on god, sculpting creation. And just as God handles clay, Gauguin is "feeling my way with the tip of a brush on a piece of sackcloth that is full of knots and rough patches." Gauguin's primitivism focuses on foregrounding the body—through color, outline, and texture—and also intensifying his own bodily engagement with the materials of his art.

In the Bible, Job, who also suffers from a psoriatic skin disorder, makes a similar claim for God's immediate, haptic engagement in the creative process. "Thine hands have made me and fashioned me together round about; yet thou dost destroy me. Remember, I beseech thee, that thou hast made me as the clay; and wilt thou bring me into dust again?" (Job

10:8–9). Job imagines God as a potter molding clay, and he chides him for being so quick to break his creation into fragments. Updike explicitly elides himself with Job in "At War with My Skin," comparing his skin condition to "one of those divinely imposed ordeals in the Bible" (46–47). He elaborates upon the imagery of pot making and breaking, skin surface and artistic surfaces, in "From the Journal of a Leper." The story portrays a professional potter whose artistic success derives from his reputation for perfection in the glaze and smoothness of his ceramics, even though his own bodily surface is ravaged by severe psoriasis. The circular motion of the potter's wheel makes completing boundaries his fundamental creative act—creation in terms of smoothness and enclosure. "Smoothness is the essence, the fingers must not be perturbed. The wheel turns. My hand vanishes up past the wrist into the orifice of whistling, whispering clay, confiding the slither of its womb-wall to me" (185). Creation must replicate the complete containment of the womb; the pot's surface serves as the artistic parallel to Didier Anzieu's "skin ego," supporting the potter's coherent self like a symbolic uterine wall. Updike's potter insists on such perfect uterine smoothness: "If the merest pimple of captured dust mote reveal itself to my caress, I smash the bowl. The vaguest wobble in the banding, and damnation and destruction ensue" (182). Updike's ironic evocation of divine power reveals the artist's intolerant perfectionism. Since the art form involves the manipulation of smooth surfaces, the potter's total haptic control over the clay allows him to compensate for his lack of control over his bodily surface.

The potter's aesthetic seems to presuppose the model of the "closed" or bounded body that has been critiqued by theorists including Lacan, Kristeva, and Bakhtin. In her discussion of the social semiotics of conjoined twins, Margrit Shildrick enunciates the assumptions of this discourse.

> Against an ideal of bodily closure that relies on the singular; the unified and the replicable, monstrosity, in the form of either excess, lack or displacement, offers a gross insult. [. .] The so-called normal and natural body, and particularly its smooth and closed up surface, is then an achievement, a model of the proper in which everything is in its place and the chaotic aspects of the natural are banished. ("You Are There" 162–63)

While theorists point to the failures of this "closed body" model to account for sexuality, disability, and socially aberrant physicality, it also fails to account for the thick, mobile corporeality of the skin itself. The epidermis, which continually produces and then sheds skin cells, is nothing like a wall or sheath. Keratinocytes, or skin cells, are produced at its lower layers; then they pile up, moving upward and outward, to die on the surface. This upward-and-outward motion of normal skin cells typically takes a month, but in skin diseases such as psoriasis, the natural processes of cell production are sped up, and the shedding of cells becomes visible. The upper layers of the epidermis flake off in scales or plaques, and the skin appears red and inflamed and bleeds easily. Even normal skin engages in this constant piling up and shedding, however, and thus it cannot be accurately described as either opened or closed; it continually radiates its own matter outward, not through orifices but through constant, minute movements that jumble any definitive boundary.

The striking character of the skin disorders experienced by Gauguin and Updike is not their breaching of a single smooth surface but their overabundant production of multiple, variously layered surfaces. The skin cells are not like human teeth, which, once knocked out, leave a clear gap, but shark teeth, which continually grow and replace one another in a haphazard barricade. More to the point, the skin surface is not like a perfectly glazed clay pot, and Updike's story shows how such an aesthetic of corporeal completeness can take a profound emotional toll. The potter loathes his own psoriatic body, which he thinks of as a faulty artwork: "I should have been smashed at birth" (Updike, "From the Journal" 182). He apprehends all the bodies around him as ceramic surfaces: "The waitress is glorious, her arms pure kaolin, her chiseled pout as she scribbles my order a masterpiece of Sevres *biscuit*" (183). After he undergoes ultraviolet light therapy to cure his condition, the potter loses his drive to compensate for his own imperfect surface by perfecting the surface of his pots, and he abandons both his artwork and his love life. He becomes preoccupied with visual reflection rather than haptic engagement, which Updike figures, once again, as the skyscraper. "Now I am aware of loving only the Hancock Tower, which has had its missing pane restored and is again perfect, unoccupied, changeably blue, taking upon itself the insubstantial shapes of clouds, their porcelain gauze, their adamant dreaming. I reflect that all art, all beauty, is reflection" (193). Pallasmaa argues that, because of its evasion of haptic experience, the "architectural mirror, that returns our gaze and doubles the world, is an enigmatic and frightening device" (31), and the ultimate fate of Updike's potter seems to bear this out. Ironically, his attempt to create a perfectly smooth surface to compensate for his own roughness had led him to a full tactile engagement with clay. Becoming "whole" physically, on the other hand, has led him away from tactility, toward an aesthetic model in which art is, in Merleau-Ponty's terms, "set up before the mind [as] a picture or a representation of the world" ("Eye" 162). Once he sees his bodily surface as beautiful and complete, like "T'ang ware," he becomes spiritually deadened: "I feel between myself and my epidermis a gap, a thin space where a wedge of spiritual dissociation could be set" (Updike, "From the Journal" 194). Ultimately, Updike suggests that the potter's aesthetic was always fundamentally flawed, as it celebrated an unreal, formal perfection while failing to account for the body's chaotic materiality.

Gauguin's painting, which glorifies the impossible beauty of the skin by revealing the knotty, roughly woven fabric underlying it, seeks to portray both the impermeable perfection and the inherent fragmentation of the body's surface. In *Two Tahitian Women* (1899), for example, the clarity of outline and contrasting colors between figure and ground (as well as allusions to the classical nude and Christian iconography) grant the two figures imagistic mass and stability. They seem statuesquely present, imposing in their embodied power. The visible texture of the canvas and the small flecks of missing paint, on the other hand, remind us of the artist's material process of creation, of Gauguin's physical engagement with the rough fabric. Their fragile surfaces suggest at once ancient or ruined works and the fragmentary nature of all human flesh.

Late in his career, Gauguin became preoccupied with portraying artworks as architectural features such as frescos and bas-reliefs, which were crumbling or in need of repair, thus revealing the materials of their creation. *Where Do We Come From? What Are We? Where Are We Going?* was first displayed "as an old fresco with the two top corners damaged to reveal the golden wall 'beneath' the painted surface" (Jirat-Wasiutynski and Newton 150). *Where Do We Come From?* as peeling fresco is at once a fully formulated artwork and a ruin that reveals the process of its creating. Moreover, since a fresco occupies the wall of a dwelling, it compacts this mercurial artistic creativity into the very surfaces between which domestic life is lived.

This interest in fresco and bas-relief is also apparent in Gauguin's paintings, and most obviously in the architectural carvings for his final home. In *Te Rerioa* (*The Dream*), the walls are covered by what might be frescoes and might be carvings of human, animal, and supernatural forms. Similar carvings appear in the base and headboards of the baby's cradle. The figures on the walls contribute to the eerie tone of the painting, and their strangeness is intensified by their *trompe l'oeil* quality. While somewhat three-dimensional, they seem in some spots to recede into the wall's surface, and in others to emerge from it. Significantly, they never interrupt the geometrical lines of the building or impose on its open space; they are fused with the structure of the room. In *Nevermore* (1897) a central nude figure lies dreaming, while the whole background of the painting is occupied by a wall, divided into rectangular panels decorated with vines and flowers (Shackleford, "Return" 157). As in the other interiors, a doorway opens upon the back wall, but the figures viewed through this doorway, and the bird in the window next to it, are so stylized as to seem almost mere decorations. Both the walls of the room and the openings from it present us with what amount to canvases, or carved panels. These enclosures are at once homes, studios, and structures that are actually made up of artworks. The surfaces of the house do not simply reflect but also become fully expressive, encrusted with art.

Gauguin had long been interested in architectural decoration. As he gradually emptied his living space of conventional domestic objects, he also increasingly transformed the walls and ceilings of the room into artworks. While living at the Inn of Marie Henry in Le Pouldu, Gauguin and Meyer de Haan decorated the dining room with murals on the walls and ceiling, purposefully placed original paintings and carvings, and decorative designs throughout. Victor Merlhes has shown how Gauguin was influenced in this project by the Egyptian wall paintings and Cambodian bas-reliefs he had seen at L'Exposition Universelle of 1889. While evoking primitive monumental art as well as Christian iconography, these works focus primarily on the two artists and their landlady, offering, according to Robert Welsh, "a striking richness of biographical data" including visual puns and private symbols (71). The Inn's decorative plan thus involved transforming domestic surfaces into artistic ones which nevertheless expressed the personal experience of the artist. It is not insignificant that the consistent theme of the artworks at the Inn was "Labor"; Gauguin's creative labor is expressed through fusing of art and walls, like the fusing of pigment and canvas.

Moreover, Gauguin frequently gestures toward his quest for the primitive in these works, including the wood carvings *The Caribbean Woman, Martinique Woman,* and his wood relief *Soyez Amoreuses,* which prefigure the wood panels that would decorate the *Maison du Jouir.* In these works, Welsh argues, "Gauguin presents himself and de Haan as outcasts or wanderers at the fringe of uncomprehending society [. . .] [l]ike the 'primitive' Breton people he admired" (71). The message of this sort of decoration is paradoxical: it points beyond the home toward an undomesticated existence while also reaffirming domestic structures as representations of the artist's identity. Artistic creativity is encrusted into the "skin" of the house, making it less stable as a conventional domestic space while also giving the walls greater aesthetic power and endurance. The *Maison du Jouir* represents the fullest realization of this transformation of domestic into artistic surface. As Gauguin moved from Tahiti to the Marquesas, his domestic space was emptied and simplified into the barest artist's studio, and ultimately an artwork, so that he was living in a building consisting of densely carved artistic surfaces. Sexuality rather than labor is the primary theme of these decorations. The panels *Soyez Amoreuses et Vous Serez Heureses* and *Soyez Mysterieuses,* as well as the left and right doorframe panels, demonstrate an intensification of tactile relative to visual perception. The bodies on these carvings do not emerge into three dimensions, as in bas-relief, but are flattened, only slightly higher than their background. The carvings are significantly less rounded than in *La Guerre et La Paix* (1901), for example, which was carved just the previous year. This is apparent when comparing the face at the center of *La Guerre et La Paix* and the face on the left door panel, or the hands and breasts of the figure on the right panel, with those of Adam and Eve in *La Guerre.* This flattening, along with the obvious chisel marks and simplified bodily features, suggests that Gauguin was trying to emphasize texture rather than form. While both vision and touch can efficiently apprehend the shape of objects, only touch can accurately perceive texture, because the hand, unlike the eye, can move the "high-acuity portion of its receptors" directly over an object (James 224). The sense of touch apprehends texture and form differently, using "two separate neural pathways, one specialized for material properties and the other for geometric properties of objects" (226). The apprehension of texture, such as the rough, fibrous surface of a tennis ball, is based on the perception of minute irregularities, or "microstructure." We perceive the round shape of the tennis ball through outline, or "macrostructure," which defines its geometric shape and size (Krueger 41–42). Susan J. Lederman and Roberta L. Klatzky argue that the two forms of apprehension are not only distinct but also tend to be mutually exclusive. "It is difficult both to enclose an object (for global shape, size) and to rub it (for texture) at the same time. [. . .] The texture or hardness of a surface is typically encoded haptically through restricted local exploration by use of lateral motion and pressure procedures, rather than edge following" (432). The carvings in *Maison du Jouir* offer a microstructural aesthetic. One could enclose portions of the bodies in *La Guerre et La Paix,* or earlier carvings such as *Caribbean Woman* and *Soyez Amoreuses,* which Gauguin carved in Brittany; the bodies emerge curvaceously from the wood. The panels for the *Maison,* by contrast, encourage us to focus on the shallow lip of wood at the body's edge, the roughness of the grain, and the jaggedness of the chisel marks; they inspire us to rub or brush our hands over their surface rather than to embrace or hold them. As with Gauguin's rejection of impasto for thin pigment, the artwork in these carvings is fused with its surface, which in this case is the architectural plane of the room.

Living between these walls and walking through the doorframe would inevitably involve actually touching these artworks, so that the surface of Gauguin's own body became part of their aesthetic operation. Unlike vision, haptic perception always compromises the body's edge. We perceive texture through "closely spaced discontinuities" (Krueger 41–42) that impact us somatically. "As you move your hand, your fingertips are grossly squashed inward and sideways. Your skin also deforms to follow, in part, the tiny irregularities on the surface of the object" (Lederman 132). To feel texture, our body's edge must become deformed, must take on the irregularity of the surface itself, disordering the perceived smoothness of our own surface. Lederman's phrase, "grossly squashed," suggests a sort of turmoil at the body's edge. In an experiment in which people ran their fingers over an aluminum grating, texture was perceived by "the depth to which the skin penetrates a groove" and the "volume [. . .] of the fingertip pressed into the groove" (137). The house ceases simply to be a frame for the body, a surface that parallels the closed skin, and becomes a textured surface that catches, deforms, and distorts the body brushing against it. The perception of texture amounts to getting caught in the fabric of the world, in Merleau-Ponty's terms. As Gauguin moved through the *Maison du Jouir,* his breaking skin must have brushed and broken against its walls, the materials of his body's surface, his domestic surface, and his artistic surface becoming indistinguishable from one another. Pallasmaa contends that a "wise architect works with his/her entire body and sense of self. While working on a building or an object, the architect is simultaneously engaged in a reverse perspective, his/her self-image or more precisely, existential experience" (12). In creating the *Maison du Jouir,* Gauguin was eliding the roles of visual artist and architect, creating a textural architecture based on microstructure rather than form.

Gauguin's retreat from bourgeois domesticity to the tropics is concomitant with an incorporation of his skin disease into his aesthetic. His initial attention to clear outline and open space develops into a tactile aesthetic in which vision and distance are transmuted into a texture. The *Maison du Jouir* embodies his attempt to fuse art, architecture, and his bodily experience in a surface that is at once fragile and rugged, wild and domestic, bespeaking both chaos and creation. For Updike, on the other hand, art allows him to protect himself from bodily fragmentation by becoming fully engaged with bourgeois society. He explicitly opposes artistic success and the psoriatic body in "At War with My Skin." "Because it came and went, I never settled in with my psoriasis, never adopted it as, inevitably, part of myself. It was temporary and in a way, illusionary, like my being poor, and obscure" (46). Updike's war with his skin is thus a class war, one he triumphantly wins. The ichorous monstrosity of his psoriatic body is firmly attached to his poverty-stricken childhood. Updike also makes a retreat to the tropics, but it is an upper-middle-class retreat, demonstrating his financial status while also alleviating the symptoms of his psoriasis. As he follows the sun that will temporarily cure his skin to a beachside Boston suburb, then to Martha's Vineyard, then to the Caribbean, he also climbs the socioeconomic ladder. Each choice to move to or vacation at a sunny, comfortable locale is driven by his hidden "leprosy." The contemporary leper colony turns out to be identical to the Caribbean luxury resort, and the redemption Job seeks is easily found on the beach in St. Thomas. To be "forgiven, by God: this notion, so commonly mouthed in shadowy churches, was for me a tactile actuality as I lay in my loathed hide under that high hard pellet" (68).

The "tactile actuality" of the skin's disintegration, which Gauguin incorporates into his artworks, becomes, for Updike, a secret that can be temporarily smoothed over with appealing fictions. Updike offers a therapeutic aesthetic, in which artistic power derives from the suppression or disguise of the crumbling body.

> [W]as not my sly strength, my insistent specialness, somehow linked to my psoriasis[?] [. . .] What was my creativity, my relentless need to produce, but a parody of my skin's embarrassing overproduction? Was not my thick literary skin, which shrugged off rejection slips and patronizing reviews by the sheaf, a superior version of my poor vulnerable own, and my shamelessness on the page a distraction from my real shame? I have never cared, in print, about niceness or modesty, but agonize over typos and factual errors—"spots" on the ideally unflecked text. Having so long carried a secret behind my clothes, I had no trouble with the duplicity that generates plots and surprises and symbolism and layers of meaning; dualism, indeed, such as existed between my skin and myself, appeared to me the very engine of the human. (75)

While granting that his psoriasis is the source of his creative drive, Updike considers his fiction a protective mechanism—a sort of verbal skin ego. His art allows him to hide or cover his broken skin behind the perfect spotless surface of the text and within various metaphorical constructions: a thick skin, sheaves of paper, layers of meaning. Artistic creativity represents a struggle with the body's vagaries, a struggle from which the heroic artist emerges triumphant. Updike reminds us that "the Italians call [psoriasis] *morbus fortiurum*—'the disease of the strong'" (75). More profoundly, Updike identifies his psoriasis with the fictional impulse, the fundamental creative act of his literary art. His fictional creations are themselves creators of false selves; his alienation from his own skin allows him to understand, and write about, the essential human act of disguise. The psoriatic body, by establishing a dualism between body and self, lays the imaginative foundation for the dualism of fictional reality.

In many of his novels and stories, Updike investigates how this dualism is enacted in the domestic spaces of successful middle-class Americans. In *Rabbit Is Rich*, Harry Angstrom visits his neighbor's house, the architectural structures and surfaces of which seem to body forth its owner's values no less than does the *Maison du Jouir*.

> Webb Murkett is handy about the house. [. . .] In every corner of the garrison colonial he and Cindy have shared for the seven years of their marriage there are hand-made refinements of rounded, stained, and varnished wood—shelves, cabinets, built-in lazy susans with as many compartments as a seashell—expressing the patience and homeloving-ness of the house's master. [. . .] Webb's previous marriages are represented in his great long sunken living room only by color photographs, in ensemble frames of unusual proportion that Webb himself has cut and grooved and cemented together of Lucite, of children too old to be his and Cindy's, caught in a moment of sunshine on the flagstone stoop of another suburban house. (282)

The Murkett house manifests its owners' devotion to family life and material comforts. Rather than clearing his living space, like Updike's other protagonist, Richard Maple, Webb builds shelves and cabinets—domestic objects designed to hold other domestic objects. The structural principle of the home is not emptiness but secrecy. Harry moves through the house, opening medicine cabinets and drawers, trying to discover his neighbors' vices and perversions. Webb's family history is idealized and made spectacular by his decorating his suburban homes with pictures of other, equally ideal ones. But these apparently revealing pictures are also false fronts; Webb excludes his former wives from these photographs through the careful sizing of his handmade frames: "though there are women beheaded or sliced to a splinter by the edge of a frame or another picture[,] [. . .] no face seems preserved of the vanished mistresses of all this fleeting family happiness" (282). The smooth Lucite surfaces of the pictures create fictions of domestic bliss through the violent excision of emotional difficulties. The many compartments of Webb's cabinets hold humiliating secrets, such as the sexually explicit pictures Harry finds in a drawer, that the house has been organized to keep—at least partially—hidden.

In fact the dirty Polaroids are not very well hidden in the drawer, and the wives are not fully cut out of the pictures; the home continually undercuts its own structures of domestic secrecy. By both hiding the truth and revealing his power to do so, Webb uses his home to demonstrate control over his own humiliating secrets. His art form, like Updike's, empowers him by constructing a disguise that is perpetually slipping. The house's shiny reflective surfaces are made up of layers that seem just about to flake off and peel away, like the window panels of the Hancock Tower. The novel, which uncovers parts of Harry's own secret past, suggests that Updike is as interested in unveiling his characters' secrets as he is in constructing them. Mary Ann O'Farrell argues that psoriasis has a particular association with self-consciousness because the facial ruddiness engendered by the disease seems to body forth embarrassment. Psoriatic writers manifest a "literary self-consciousness[,] [. . .] a self-loathing and humiliating mode" (140) that "expansively includes mortification in its sense of mastery" (134). By deploying the physical blush of psoriasis as literary humiliation, Updike the writer gains control over Updike the psoriatic body. His continual self-unveilings establish a coy, urbane distance between writer and reader and allow the body's vulnerability to be rendered invulnerable; "just as sophistication is a cure for embarrassment in Updike's functional logic, sophistication, by that same logic, is the cure for psoriasis" (138). Updike's memoir represents his attempt to reconcile artistic creativity and bodily dissolution by flagrantly exposing his many attempts to avoid such a reconciliation. "It pains me to write these pages. They are humiliating—'scab picking' to use a term sometimes leveled at modern autobiographical writers" (*Self-Consciousness* 48). Like the ceramicist in "From the Journal of a Leper," Updike largely sees his own art in response to, and thus in opposition to, his psoriasis. While his disease may have driven him to success, the two can never be fully reconciled. "To my body, which has no aesthetic criteria, psoriasis is normal, and its suppression abnormal" (*Self-Consciousness* 77). If the body is not an aesthetic entity, then art will always involve an escape from the body, and flight—from poverty, from public view, from one vacation destination to another—is one of the predominant images of "At War with My Skin."

Ultimately, Updike admits that his flight from embodiment through literary and social modes of success is doomed by the inescapability of physical life. While he celebrates the creative power that has allowed him to transcend his body, he ends by recognizing the inevitability of the body's dissolution. "I also foresee that when I weaken, when I am at last too ill for all these demanding and perilous palliatives, the psoriasis like a fire smoldering in damp peat will break out and spread triumphantly; in my dying I will become hideous, I will become what I am" (78). Updike's psoriasis becomes a manifestation of the unyieldingly fragmentary nature of physical life regardless of social status. Jay Prosser finds in Updike's anxiety-laden representations of his body the eruption of repressed oedipal desire for his mother, from whom he inherited psoriasis, as well as racial anxiety related to his mixed-race grandchildren (60–61). The tendency of the body, sexuality, and death to undercut an idyllic vision of middle-class life haunts his work. Yet throughout his fiction, Updike incorporates the chaotic aspects of creative power more thoroughly than he pretends to. Updike's preoccupation with the Hancock Tower does not simply emerge from obvious parallels with his psoriasis but suggests that, like Gauguin, he understands the body's relation to domestic space as one of parallel brokenness. Middle-class life, designed to cover rough mortal edges, inevitably fails to do so, and his stories and novels themselves represent this failure even as his writing life serves to alleviate his affliction. Updike foresees his final humiliation as "fire smoldering in damp peat" just as Gauguin describes his own artistic impulse as lava ready to gush forth; for Updike, art and humiliation are different layers of the same surface.

✢ ✢ ✢

Throughout this chapter I have argued that the embodied interweaving of the creative body, the artwork, and the architecture of the home serve as an example of tactile domesticity. Gauguin's desire for an antidomestic, disembodied studio space ultimately gives way to the layering of his home's walls with artworks as textured as his skin. The shiny reflective surfaces of late-twentieth-century America that Updike's characters idealize will always end up scratched and worn by their aging, crumbling bodies. In the process of writing this book, I have been constantly reminded that the life of the mind is inextricable from the body. Ischial bursitis, although relatively rare in the twentieth century, was common in pre-industrial times among weavers working in their homes. Sitting on the bottom bar of a frame loom, physically attached to fabric they were creating, caused the inflammation. It is ironic that this same injury has forced me to become more physically interwoven with the materials of my work. I am an academic writer, not a weaver or a painter, and I hardly feel the texture of my word-processed page the way Gauguin felt the canvas through his brush. Nevertheless, my physical limitations have forced me to think of my working body not as operating in a disembodied intellectual space, but at the specific points where my legs, hands, and skin meet couch, keyboard, and paper to become caught in the fabric of the world.

$\mathscr{P}$ostscript

Living and Dying at Home

> The reality of the building does not consist in roof and walls but in the space within to be lived in.
>
> —Lao Tse

Over the course of my argument for the significance of tactile experience in the home, two related theses have emerged. The first is that the homeowner's identity is deeply enmeshed in the habitual corporeal dynamics of the home. Attachment to the home is based on our physical engagement with it, and its spaces become interwoven with emotion and memory. This attachment can imperil the homeowner, as it does for the elderly, or intensify the pain of loss. Attempts to clear away the traces of identity, however, either by emptying them out, as in Gauguin's and Updike's domestic sublime, or by soiling and crowding them out, as with animal hoarders, tend to be risky and prone to failure.

The second argument is that domesticity can be collapsed to the body's edge; we can feel at home irrespective of the architectural space that surrounds us through sharing body image or bodily engagements with others, or simply through certain somatosensory comforts. Pet ownership and caregiving offer examples of bodily focused notions of domesticity in which architectural space collapses into intercorporeal space or ceases to exist entirely. In embodied grief, the sense of tangible loss is experienced at the body's edge and is reinforced by the body's motion through familiar domestic space. The body image forms in relation to both the bodies it has habitually touched and the spaces it has habitually moved through. For those with fragile boundaries resulting from neurological or psychological conditions, the only possible sensations of domestic comfort are those most immediately tactile ones.

Throughout this work I have attempted to demystify the physical behaviors through which memory and identity adhere to the spaces of the home. We unpack our selves onto the home's material spaces and structures, and we draw our sense of identity from the home which supports our habitual motions through it and interactions with our loved ones. This identification between the home and the self raises questions of design in relation to function: What functions—bodily, emotional, and material—are central to the home's purpose? How can we best design and maintain our homes so that they support our embodied selves through tactile interaction? I would like to address this question by examining the discourses of two cultural phenomena: the rise in home renovation and the rise in home hospice care. These two movements enunciate a cultural dispute about how the home defines and supports identity. In home renovation, domestic space is rendered almost infinitely plastic and transformational, a manifestation of taste, status, and ingenuity that disentangles identity from the limits of the body. In home hospice care, identity cannot be separated from the material structure and history of the home; familiar spaces, objects, and loved ones within it become increasingly contiguous with the self as death approaches. Martha Nussbaum claims that "human beings cannot bear to live with the constant awareness of mortality and of their frail animal bodies" (*Hiding* 17), and the discourse of home renovation seems to suggest that design can release us from such temporal and material burdens. Home hospice, which configures home space around bodily frailty, suggests, by contrast, that the home's most important function is to reconfirm and maintain identity as materially and historically located.

Over the past several decades, home renovation has followed the lead of new home design in emphasizing the opening up and emptying out of domestic space. This is best illustrated by the "great room" which Winifred Gallagher describes as "the latest development in a hundred-year-long experiment in which American culture has gradually shed traditional manners and mores to become more informal and open, while the home dropped walls and doors to the same end" (115). Like the great room, "open concept" kitchens, cathedral ceilings, and expansive "family" or "play" rooms, the names of which, like the spaces themselves, frequently blend together, allow extra space for flexible activity undefined by any one practical function. Increasing natural light is also a common feature of this architectural trend through the installation of larger windows, French doors, skylights, and sunrooms. In the renovation of smaller homes, measuring up to McMansion standards often means breaking down interior and exterior walls to increase light and space. New built-in storage shelves and cabinets are also a common accessory, allowing the open space to be as empty as possible. It is the arrival of a dumpster, rather than the arrival of a contractor's truck, that first signals to the neighbors that a renovation is under way. The elimination of accumulated disorder and the creation of open space are thus a form of purging: whatever memories or physical habits are contingent upon the home's former design or contents are relegated to the status of garbage.

Throughout this study I have discussed how tactile interchange between the spaces and surfaces of body and home inadvertently create one's domestic environment. The home comes to represent the self through the establishment of habitual bodily behaviors, such as smooth routines, by which we acclimate our bodily practice to the architectural forms, objects, and other bodies with which we live. The emptying of the home, which is framed by architects and real estate agents as the creation of "flexible" space, points to an implicit desire to render the body's impact on domestic experience as immaterial as possible. The great room is big enough that one never has to touch its walls or corners, or even the other family members with whom one shares it. David Owen notes that "[i]n newer houses, the family room is typically the size and shape of a church, and it is usually dominated by an enormous TV. (In some new houses, you get the feeling that the TV was bought first, and the house designed around it.)" (37) This focusing of the room toward electronic media contributes to its inhabitants' disembodiment, as though all domestic life in such a space were moving toward virtual existence. Juhani Pallasmaa notes that "[a]ll matter exists in the continuum of time; the patina of wear adds the enriching experience of time to the materials of construction," but much contemporary architecture employs artificial and durable materials that "deliberately aim at ageless perfection" (31–32). Architect Mark Mack puts it more simply: "The home is not meant to be stuck in history" (qtd. in Gallagher 117). Flexible design implies a model of identity based on a future self rather than the past; in home renovation, the best relation of body and domestic space is the one yet to be created. Rather than making a home ours by rubbing against and living within its surfaces, we make it ours at the moment of design, before our bodies have touched it.

In *House Thinking: A Room by Room Look at How We Live,* Gallagher argues that the home must "complement who you really are," that your home is "a personal expression" (64). This approach makes the homeowner's personality primary; basing home design on "who you really are" assumes a knowledge of oneself as well as the ability to construct a home that successfully represents that self. Gallagher offers many examples of homes that succeed at this sort of self-representation: a musician's home is structured around studio space; a shy scientific researcher's home emphasizes coziness and seclusion; an adventurous naturalist surrounds himself with antlers and unpainted wood. In *The Decoration of Houses,* her updating of Edith Wharton's 1898 home design manual, interior designer Alexandra Stoddard elaborates on Gallagher's claims. "Through the materials we use, through space, scale, proportion, and color, and through the furniture and objects we select to use as well as enjoy, we animate the things around us and bring greater depth and meaning to our everyday existence. When we succeed, our house becomes a real and seamless extension of who we are" (4). In Stoddard's and Gallagher's portrayals, the homeowner emerges as a heroic figure, capable of "animating" the dead world of the home, granting it psychological depth and philosophical meaning. She wields complete control over its space, furniture, and objects, which set no limitations on her. The phrase "a real and seamless extension" demonstrates the several contradictions underlying this form of disembodied domestic identity. The home becomes an "extension" of one's identity, but not of one's body, since it must be a "seamless" extension, lacking the awkwardness of physical engagement. The space is "real" in that it is full of furniture and objects, but the body within it seems unreal because unlimited.

Gallagher makes the elision between self-improvement and home improvement explicit in her discussion of environmental psychologist Connie Forrest's work with a woman undertaking a "big professional transition" and a home renovation at the same time.

> When the project began, she had rather drab hair and nondescript clothes. While her building's interior was being remodeled, she worked with Forrest not just on design issues but also on refining her vision of her inner self and her dreams of where she wanted to take her career. During the renovation of the exterior, the client lightened her mousey hair to her childhood blond and bought more colorful clothes. By the time the project was finished, the woman had altered her way of working, acquired a more vibrant, nature-oriented environment, and developed an exuberant personal style. (61)

The passage demonstrates the contradictions involved in trying to design a home around who we "really are." The home that Forrest designs corresponds directly to her client's personality and body, not as they are but as they fulfill her "dreams" of herself. Pallasmaa argues that the contemporary aesthetic of "ageless perfection" (32) traps us in "a dreamlike sense of unreality" (31), but Gallagher identifies the dream-self as the intended inhabitant of a renovated home. Forrest's client must work hard on "refining her inner vision of herself" so that this newly renovated personality can be expressed in the newly renovated home. Since by the time the home is finished she has become an entirely different person, it seems unclear how she can be confident that the home will continue to express her. By eliding flexibility in personality and domestic space, Gallagher contradicts her fundamental notion that the true self can be embodied in the home. We change our homes so that they will, we hope, correspond to the changes we have decided to make in ourselves.

In home hospice, however, the dominant dynamic is not transformation of the self and the home but the maintenance of the existing self through familiar sensory associations. The home hospice is of necessity "stuck in history"—the personal history of the homeowner—as Andrea Sankar explains in *Dying at Home: A Family Guide for Caregiving.* "Tending a terminally ill patient at home allows the caregiver to help preserve as much of the dying person's distinctive identity as possible. Being in the home keeps the dying person involved in a web of social interactions and relationships long after he or she is actively able to sustain these ties" (198). Sankar's emphasis on the "web" of social relations suggests that identity is to be found not in the dying body itself but in the spaces connecting it to other bodies and to objects and familiar domestic forms. The sustenance of identity is an interactive, intercorporeal process. The logic of home renovation involves the projection outward of identity onto the materials of the home; Gallagher and Stoddard suggest that we are most comfortable when we apprehend our interior lineaments reflected by exterior spaces. Sankar's model of domestic identity, by contrast, is located in the habitual engagement between our bodies and the home environment.

Maintenance, rather than flexibility, is the fundamental dynamic of the hospice home. David B. Resnik, a hospice volunteer, describes how his client Mr. Simpson refused to accept care for himself, insisting instead that Resnik undertake his customary chores.

> He was not able to lift anything heavy, but he was able to follow me around with his oxygen tank and show me what needed to be done. [. . .] Mr. Simpson and I cut and stacked firewood, put up the storm windows, cleaned up the yard, cleaned out the gutters, raked the

leaves, and fixed the roof on the house. We also planted a few tulips for his wife. (9)

Mr. Simpson's relationship to his home is one of maintenance and repair rather than renovation, of interaction rather than projection. The responsibilities the home has always placed upon him are, in part, what makes it familiar. His motion around the house to perform chores represents one of the "smooth routines" that, in Robert Rubenstein's terms, "stiffen consciousness of self and act in a sense ritually to reinforce or remind the person of who he or she was and still is" (82). Sankar points out that the routines associated with housework are instrumental in the goal of supporting a dying person's identity. "People derive security from the order of everyday life. Its sheer repetitiveness is reassuring. In situations such as this, normal everyday life stands in necessary contrast to the destruction being wrought to the fabric of that life" (51). The shuttling back and forth endemic to home maintenance creates the "fabric" of a life that most benefits hospice care recipients.

In contrast to the great room, in which open spaces gesture toward an unlimited future, maintaining the patient's life story often involves the dense packing of space with embodied history so that the hospice home may seem to resemble the hoarder's home. Lorie Verderame, a home hospice nurse, describes how she at first misinterpreted the crowded home of her client Ola. "This was absolutely *the* most cluttered space I have ever seen. There was a hodgepodge of furniture of every description, stacks of books (all classics), pieces of bric-a-brac, [. . .] and pieces of china, mostly chipped, on every shelf and horizontal surface, including the bathroom ledges and windowsills" (236). As she talks to Ola, however, she discovers that each object has its place and significance. Having spent her life as a cleaning lady, maintaining other peoples' homes, Ola had gradually collected second-hand "pretty things" from her employers, arranging them in her own home to remind her of her past. "She showed me a few of her favorite pieces: a Wedgewood plate, a Limoges teacup holding a soap pad at the stained kitchen sink" (236). While crowded and run-down, Ola's home succeeds as a museum to her past in large part because her skills as a cleaning woman have allowed her to maintain the self-representations she has assembled there. She explains that she left the South as an illiterate young woman with no possessions. "'Since then, just look at all I've gained,' she said, with a sweep of her arm to indicate her home." Ola's home is filled with her life story, to which she remains physically connected as that story comes to an end.

In home hospice, the inward spiral of environmental centralization is inevitable, and ultimately desirable, as the interactive "web of social interactions and relationships" gradually encircles the dying person's bed. The powerful corporeality of this web is apparent in Stan Clark's description of his wife, Alice's, death.

> When she died her two sisters and my three kids and I were all imme-
> diately there at the bedside, probably another ten people were there in
> the living room and dining room area. I started to say, "What are you
> doing?" to the nurse. The other nurse who was there then was moving
> the TV away—moving everything away so we could stand by the bed.
> She started telling my sister-in-law she had to be there by the bed and
> my sister-in-law said, "I don't want to be there." In the last few minutes
> of life Alice was still indicating the need for a bedpan because she had
> a sensation of losing her bowel control. And she had me hold onto her.
> (qtd. in Sankar 160)

The concentric rings of loved ones crowding around Alice's bed construct a literal web, expanding outward through the rooms of the home. Furniture must be rearranged to create space for such densely packed caregiving, creating the antithesis of the family "great room." Rather than emptying space so that family members can be "in the same place at the same time, but no longer necessarily dong the same thing" (Gallagher 116), every space is filled with a unified mass of bodies that become contiguous with the dying person's body.

Home hospice assumes that the function of the home is to sustain and support the embodied self, to hold us like a loved one. The promise of home renovation, by contrast, seems to be that home design can transcend embodiment and personal history. My argument throughout this book suggests that this promise can never be fulfilled—nor should we want it to be. Every space ultimately becomes marked and organized by bodily experience. Even in great rooms the empty space gets filled with the objects our bodies leave, use, or carry. While a skillful designer can try to predict and enable family interaction, domestic spaces often get used in quirky, unexpected ways; the vast family room lies empty while people huddle together on a couch in the tiny study. Our family members and pets rub against and move around us, enacting their love and establishing the stories of our lives through particular postures and motions in particular rooms. These embodied affiliations weave through any space, no matter how grand, like the web surrounding Alice Clark's bed.

At the center of this web, husband and wife embrace, and the domestic space around and contiguous with them resonates with their familiar touch. But this web of tactile affection has its dark and painful threads. Even in the home, among family members, such corporeal co-extension involves the sort of physical and psychic perils Rebecca Brown and Nesta Rovina describe encountering as home health care workers. One of Alice's sisters is too afraid, or too repulsed, to come close to her. Stan fears that, at this moment of emotional bonding, Alice may lose control of her bowels, thus embarrassing and disgusting the assembled family. The risks to those who make up her web of relations may even outlive Alice. Once she is gone, the comforting touch Stan shares with his wife may remain with him, unsettling and distressing him, as painful as a phantom limb. The tactility of our home lives grants us vividly embodied tenderness, but it carries with it a significant price.

❖ ❖ ❖

Throughout this work I have tried to point out both the rewards and the consequences of tactile intimacy in the home. Placing our memories within domestic spaces and objects materially supports our sense of personal history, but it can also render our bodies more vulnerable. Finding domestic comfort in our particular physical relations to beloved pets can redeem homelessness, but it can also destroy the home we have. While almost nothing can be more satisfying or meaningful than using our own bodies to love and care for other bodies, we cannot do so without losing some of our freedom, or health, or self in the process.

The temptation to label tactile experience as pathological or self-destructive emerges, in part, from its inevitable association with physical pain and mortality. But just as tactile apprehension may foreground human weakness, it also offers a profound and enduring means of emotional support. Defining domesticity as a set of bodily operations, of intimate and dynamic engagements with resonant and familiar material forms, allows us to feel at home even when we no longer can be. As I have suggested in my discussion of caregiving, of animal companionship, and of embodied grief, the corporeal blending of body image itself often serves to define a space as home, regardless of its architectural location. My friend's mother is coming to live with her for hospice care. To do so, she must abandon her habitual motions through her kitchen and bedroom, her bodily memory of every doorknob and light switch, the pressure of her hand against the doorjamb and molding and counter edge and stove handle. She will move into her daughter's new home, one she has only rarely visited, and, truth be told, never much liked. The bodily self-affirmation of routine postures and customary haptic sensations are lost to her with the loss of her tidy Midwestern bungalow. By moving to her daughter's home, however, she is embracing a new sort of tangible comfort and familiarity in her children's and grandchildren's arms and hands. Their bodies, moving around and against her, caring for her, create, in this unfamiliar place, a recurrent embodied intimacy that replaces the sustaining tangibility of her former home. A grandchild, or a cat, will sit on her lap or her bed; her daughter's hair, as she leans across to adjust the sheets, will brush her face. The space of home will become for her the space created around her failing body by the bodies of those she loves and will not need to be located within any particular set of walls. In leaving the house she has lived in all her life, she will be, in every way that matters, coming home to die.

This is not to suggest that the home as an architectural space does not leave its material imprint upon us. As I have argued in my discussion of memory and domestic mess, of animal hoarding, and of Sylvia Plath's aesthetics, the houses we live in shape and determine our bodily relations to the world. The last time I walked past my childhood home, the new owners had undertaken a major renovation, adding a great room and nearly doubling the original size of the house. Were I to step into it now, I would not automatically know which way to turn, where the living room used to be, where my old bedroom could be found. The walls have been either painted or knocked down; the scratches left by my father's wheelchair on the wood floor have been sanded away, and the last of the cat hair has long since been vacuumed up. The tangible traces of my childhood have thus been purged, except perhaps from a few hidden corners—a hand mark on a closet wall; a nick on a molding; a smooth spot on a banister.

There is one secret stash of my material past left, however. Shortly before my father passed away, he received a government assistance grant to improve his home's insulation, and he had several feet of fiberglass foam blown into the attic. As he proudly announced this to me, I didn't have the heart to tell him that all of my middle and high school notebooks and cherished souvenirs, and all of my childhood stuffed animals, were carefully stored there. As I walk by the house, I think of those blue bunnies and worn tan bears floating in foam, like insects in amber. I can still remember, in my fingertips, their soft pilled coats and smooth plastic eyes, just as I remember in my muscles the acrobatic moves needed to avoid cats and wheelchairs and piles of books as I moved through the living room. I remember the saggy springs and worn maroon mohair of the chair; the lift and pull it took to close the sliding bathroom door;

the rough frame board I needed to grasp to pull myself up into the attic. Gaston Bachelard writes that our childhood memories of home operate both as dreams and as bodily sensations.

> To inhabit oneirically the house we were born in means more than to inhabit it in memory; it means living in this house that is gone, the way we used to dream in it. [. . .] At times, a few steps have engraved in our memories a slight difference of level that existed in our childhood home. A certain room was not only a door, but a door plus three steps. (16, 26)

The home I grew up in had its precise number of steps and doors, corners and closets, that are engraved upon my body even as they shape my dreams. The touch of my childhood home now exists only in my body's memory, but it still exists, preserved, like my old teddy bears, in a solid continuum of tactile sensation, right against my skin.

Works cited

Abraham, Nicolas and Maria Torok. *The Shell and the Kernel: Renewals of Psychoanalysis.* Ed. Nicholas Rand. Chicago: University of Chicago Press, 1994.

Acampora, Ralph. "Oikos and Domus: On Constructive Co-Habitation with Other Creatures." *Philosophy and Geography* 7.2 (2004): 219–35.

Allen, John. *Homelessness in American Literature: Romanticism, Realism, and Testimony.* New York: Routledge, 2004.

Anzieu, Didier. *The Skin Ego.* Trans. Chris Turner. New Haven: Yale University Press, 1989.

Archer, John. *The Nature of Grief: The Evolution and Psychology of Reactions to Loss.* New York: Routledge, 1999.

Arluke, Arnold. *Just a Dog: Understanding Animal Cruelty and Ourselves.* Philadelphia: Temple University Press, 2006.

Bachelard, Gaston. *The Poetics of Space.* Trans. Maria Jolas. Boston: Beacon Press, 1994.

Bakhtin, Mikhail M. *Rabelais and His World.* Trans. Helene Iswolsky. Bloomington: Indiana University Press, 1984.

Barker, Pat. *Union Street & Blow Your House Down.* New York: Picador, 1982.

Baudrillard, Jean. *The Systems of Objects.* 1968. Trans. James Benedict. New York: Verso, 1996.

The Beales of Grey Gardens. Dir. Albert Maysles and David Maysles. Criterion Collection. Image Entertainment, 2006.

Belk, Russel W. "Attachment to Possessions." *Place Attachment.* Ed. Irwin Altman and Setha M. Law. New York: Plenum, 1992. 37–55.

Benthien, Claudia. *Skin: On the Cultural Border between Self and the World.* Trans. Thomas Dunlap. New York: Columbia University Press, 2002.

Bernstein, Susan. *Housing Problems: Writing and Architecture in Goethe, Walpole, Freud and Heidegger.* Stanford: Stanford University Press, 2008.

Blairs, Sharon, Susan Slater, and Dougal J. Hare. "The Clinical Application of Deep Touch Pressure with a Man with Autism Presenting with Severe Anxiety and

Challenging Behavior." *British Journal of Learning Disabilities* 35.4 (2007): 214–20.

Blakemore, Sarah-Jayne, Teresa Tavassoli, Susana Calo, Richard M. Thomas, Caroline Catmur, Uta Frith, and Patrick Haggard. "Tactile Sensitivity in Asperger Syndrome." *Brain and Cognition* 61.1 (2006): 5–13.

Bloomer, Kent. *The Nature of Ornament: Rhythm and Metamorphosis in Architecture.* New York: Norton, 2000.

Bloomer, Kent and Charles W. Moore. *Body, Memory, and Architecture.* New Haven: Yale University Press 1977.

Blundell, Mary Whitlock. *Helping Friends and Harming Enemies: A Study in Sophocles and Greek Ethics.* New York: Cambridge University Press, 1989.

Bordo, Susan. *Unbearable Weight: Feminism, Western Culture, and the Body.* Berkeley: University of California Press, 1993.

Bortnick, Jenny. "The Polynesian Perverse: Gauguin's Tahiti as Sexual Fantasy." Unpublished essay, 2009.

Bowlby, John. *Attachment and Loss.* Vol. 3. New York: Basic Books, 1980.

Britzolakis, Christina. *Sylvia Plath and the Theatre of Mourning.* Oxford: Clarendon, 1999.

Brown, Rebecca. *The Gifts of the Body.* New York: HarperCollins, 1994.

Burdick, E. Miller. "The Feminist Discourse of Sylvia Plath's *The Bell Jar.*" *College English* 49 (1987): 872–85.

Chapman, C. Richard. "Pain, Perception and Illusion." *The Psychology of Pain.* Ed. Richard A Sternbach. New York: Raven Press, 1986.

Charon, Rita. *Narrative Medicine: Honoring the Stories of Illness.* New York: Oxford University Press, 2006.

Charon, Rita and Maura Spiegel. "Editor's Preface." *Literature and Medicine* 20 (2001): vii–x.

Cheever, Susan. *Home Before Dark.* Boston: Houghton Mifflin, 1984.

———. "Little Dog, Big Heart." *Woman's Best Friend: Women Writers on the Dogs in Their Lives.* Ed. Megan McMorris. Everyville, CA: Seal Press, 2006. 27–34.

Chichester, David. "The American Touch: Tactile Imagery in American Religion and Politics." *The Book of Touch.* Ed. Constance Classen. Oxford: Berg, 2005. 49–69.

Classen, Constance. "Fingerprints: Writing about Touch." *The Book of Touch.* Ed. Constance Classen. Oxford: Berg, 2005. 1–12.

Courcey, Kevin. "Further Notes on Therapeutic Touch." *Quackwatch.* http://www.quackwatch.org/01QuackeryRelatedTopics/tt2.html.

Das, Santanu. "The Dying Kiss: Intimacy and Gender in the Trenches of the First World War." *The Book of Touch.* Ed. Constance Classen. Oxford: Berg, 2005. 188–97.

Davidson, Joyce. "A Phenomenology of Fear: Merleau-Ponty and Agoraphobic Life-Worlds." *Sociology of Health & Illness* 22 (2000): 640–60.

———. "'In a World of her Own . . .': Re-Presenting Alienation and Emotion in the Lives and Writings of Women with Autism." *Gender, Place and Culture: A Journal of Feminist Geography* 14.6 (2007): 659–77.

Davis, Lennard J. *Enforcing Normalcy: Disability, Deafness, and the Body.* London:

Verso, 1995.

de Certeau, Michel. *The Practice of Everyday Life.* Trans. Steven F. Randall. Berkeley: University of California Press, 1984.

Dembicki, Diane and Jennifer Anderson. "Pet Ownership May Be a Factor in the Improved Health of the Elderly." *Journal of Nutrition for the Elderly* 15 (1996): 15–31.

Derrida, Jacques. "The Animal That Therefore I Am (More to Follow)." Trans. David Wills. *Critical Inquiry* 28 (2002): 369–418.

———. "By Force of Mourning." Trans. Pascale-Anne Brault and Michael Naas. *Critical Inquiry* 22.2 (1996): 171–92.

Dickens, Charles. *Bleak House.* 1853. New York: Penguin Classics, 1987.

Doty, Mark. *Heaven's Coast: A Memoir.* New York: HarperCollins, 1996.

Douglas, Mary. *Leviticus as Literature.* New York: Oxford University Press, 1999.

Doyle, Arthur Conan. *Sherlock Holmes: The Major Stories with Contemporary Critical Essays.* Ed. John A Hodgson. Boston: Bedford/St. Martin's, 1994.

Eighner, Lars. "Lizbeth." *Living with the Animals.* Ed. Gary Indiana. Winchester, MA: Faber and Faber, 1995.

———. *Travels with Lizbeth.* New York: St. Martin's, 1993.

"Federal Definition of Homlessness." *Homes and Communities.* 31 Mar. 2009. United States Department of Housing and Urban Development. 20 May 2009. http://www.hud.gov/homeless/definition.cfm.

Fox, Rebekah. "Animal Behaviors, Post-Human Lives: Everyday Negotiations of the Animal Human Divide in Pet-Keeping." *Social and Cultural Geography* 7.4 (2006): 525–37.

Frank, Arthur W. *The Renewal of Generosity: Illness, Medicine, and How to Live.* Chicago: University of Chicago Press, 2004.

———. *The Wounded Storyteller: Body, Illness and Ethics.* Chicago: University of Chicago Press, 1995.

Freud, Sigmund. "Mourning and Melancholia." *The Standard Edition of the Complete Psychological Works of Sigmund Freud.* Trans. James Strachey. Vol. XIV. London: Hogarth, 1957.

Gallagher, Winifred. *House Thinking: A Room by Room Look at How We Live.* New York: Harper, 2006.

Garrity, Thomas F., Lorann Stollones, Martin B. Marx, and Timothy P. Johnson. "Pet Ownership and Attachment as Supportive Factors in the Health of the Elderly." *Anthrozoos* 3.1 (1989): 35–44.

Gass, Thomas Edward. *Nobody's Home: Candid Reflections of a Nursing Home Aide.* Ithaca: Cornell University Press, 2004.

Gauguin, Paul. *Letters to His Wife and Friends.* Ed. Maurice Malingue. Trans. Henry J. Stenning. Boston: MFA Publications, 2003.

———. *Paul Gauguin's Intimate Journals.* Trans. Van Wyck Brooks. New York: Liveright, 1949.

Gilman, Sander. *The Jew's Body.* New York: Routledge, 1991.

Gollub, Peter. "Four Hoarding Questions." E-mail interview. 9 July 2007.

Grandin, Temple. *Animals Make Us Human: Creating the Best Life for Animals.* Boston: Houghton Mifflin Harcourt, 2009.

———. *Animals in Translation: Using the Mysteries of Autism to Decode Animal Behavior.* Orlando: Harcourt, 2006.

———. "Calming Effects of Deep Touch Pressure in Patients with Autistic Disorder, College Students and Animals." *Journal of Childhood and Adolescent Psychopharmacology* 2 (1992): 63–72.

———. "Humanitarian Aspects of Shehitah in the United States." *Judaism* 39.4 (1990): 436–47.

———. *Thinking in Pictures, Expanded Edition: My Life with Autism.* New York: Vintage, 2006.

Grey Gardens. Dir. Albert Maysles, David Maysles, Ellen Hovde, and Muffie Meyer. 1975. DVD. Criterion Collection. Janus Films, 2001.

Grosz, Elizabeth. *Volatile Bodies: Toward a Corporeal Feminism.* Bloomington: Indiana University Press, 1994.

Hale, Charlotte. "Gauguin's Paintings in the Metropolitan Museum of Art: Recent Revelations through Technical Examination." *The Lure of the Exotic: Gauguin in New York Collections.* Ed. Colta Ives, Susan Alyson Stein, and Charlotte Hale. New Haven: Yale University Press 2002. 175–95.

Hall, Donald. *Without.* Boston: Houghton Mifflin, 1998.

Haraway, Donna. *The Companion Species Manifesto: Dogs, People, and Significant Otherness.* Chicago: Prickly Paradigm Press, 2003.

———. "Encounters with Companion Species: Entangling Dogs, Baboons, Philosophers, and Biologists." *Configurations* 14 (2006): 97–114.

Harvey, Elizabeth D. "The Touching Organ: Allegory, Anatomy and the Renaissance Skin Envelope." *Sensible Flesh: On Touch in Early Modern Culture.* Ed. Elizabeth D. Harvey. Philadelphia: University of Pennsylvania Press, 2003. 81–102.

Heaney, Seamus. *The Cure at Troy: A Version of Sophocles'* Philoctetes. New York: Farrar, Straus and Giroux, 1991.

Hernandez, Nelson. "301 Cats—184 of Them Dead—Found in Md. Home." *Washington Post.* 21 Dec. 2005. B03.

Hildebrand, Grant. *Origins of Architectural Pleasure.* Berkeley: University of California Press, 1999.

The Hoarding of Animals Research Consortium (HARC). "What Is the Definition of Animal Hoarding." 2004. http://www.tufts.edu/vet/cfa/hoarding/.

The Holy Bible. King James Version. Oxford: Oxford University Press, 1999.

Howard, J. Keir. *Disease and Healing in the New Testament: An Analysis and Interpretation.* Lanham, MD: University Press of America, 2001.

Howes, David. *Empire of the Senses: The Sensual Culture Reader.* Oxford: Berg, 2005.

Irigaray, Luce. *Elemental Passions.* New York: Routledge, 1992.

James, Thomas W., Sunah Kim, and Jerry S. Fisher. "The Neural Basis of Haptic Object Processing." *Canadian Journal of Experimental Psychology* 61.3 (2007): 219–29.

Jay, Martin. *Downcast Eyes: The Denigration of Vision in Twentieth-Century French Thought.* Berkeley: University of California Press, 1993.

Jirat-Wasiutyński, Vojtěch and H. Travers Newton, Jr. *Technique and Meaning in the Paintings of Paul Gauguin.* Cambridge: Cambridge University Press, 2000.

Josipovici, Gabriel. *Touch: An Exploration.* New Haven: Yale University Press, 1996.

Jurecic, Ann. "Mindblindness: Autism, Writing, and the Problem of Empathy." *Literature and Medicine* 25.1 (2006): 1–23.

Kahn, Miriam. "Tahiti: The Ripples of a Myth on the Shores of the Imagination." *History & Anthropology* 14.4 (2003): 307–26.

Katz, Joel. "Individual Differences in the Consciousness of Phantom Limbs." *Individual Differences in Conscious Experience.* Ed. Robert G. Kunzendorf and Benjamin Wallace. Philadelphia: John Benjamins, 2000.

———. "The Reality of Phantom Limbs." *Motivation and Emotion* 17 (1993): 147–78.

Klein, Julie Thompson. *Crossing Boundaries: Knowledge, Disciplinarities, and Interdisciplinarities.* Charlottesville: University Press of Virginia, 1996.

———. *Humanities, Culture, and Interdisciplinarity: The Changing American Academy.* Albany: State University of New York Press, 2005.

———. *Interdisciplinarity: History, Theory, & Practice.* Detroit: Wayne State University Press, 1990.

Klein, Melanie. *Love, Guilt and Reparation and Other Works 1921–1945.* New York: Free Press, 1975.

Kleinman, Arthur. *The Illness Narratives: Suffering, Healing, and the Human Condition.* New York: Basic Books, 1988.

Krieger, Delores. *Accepting Your Power to Heal: The Personal Practice of Therapeutic Touch.* Santa Fe: Bear & Company, 1993.

Kristeva, Julia. *Powers of Horror: An Essay on Abjection.* New York: Columbia University Press, 1982.

Krueger, Lester E. "Tactual Perception in Historical Perspective: David Katz's World of Touch." *Tactual Perception: A Sourcebook.* Ed. William Schiff and Emerson Foulke. Cambridge: Cambridge University Press, 1982. 1–54.

Kruger, Katherine A. and James A. Serpell. "Animal-Assisted Interventions in Mental Health: Definitions and Theoretical Foundations." *Handbook on Animal-Assisted Therapy: Theoretical Foundations and Guidelines for Practice.* 2nd Edition. Ed. A. H. Fine. New York: Academic Press, 2006. 21–38.

Kyle, Ken. *Contextualizing Homelessness: Critical Theory, Homelessness and Federal Policy Addressing the Homeless.* New York: Routledge, 2005.

Lawson, Wendy. *Life behind Glass: A Personal Account of Autism Spectrum Disorder.* London: Jessica Kingsley Publishers, 2000.

Lawton, M. Powell. *Environment and Aging.* Albany: Center for the Study of Aging, 1986.

Lederman, Susan J. "The Perception of Texture by Touch." *Tactual Perception: A Sourcebook.* Ed. William Schiff and Emerson Foulke. Cambridge: Cambridge University Press, 1982. 130–67.

Lederman, Susan J. and Roberta L. Klatzky. "Haptic Classification of Common Objects: Knowledge-Driven Exploration." *Cognitive Psychology* 22 (1990): 421–59.

Lessing, Doris. "An Old Woman and Her Cat." *Stories.* New York: Knopf, 1978.

———. [Jane Somers, pseudo.] *The Diary of a Good Neighbour.* New York: Knopf, 1983.

Marks, Laura U. *The Skin of the Film: Intercultural Cinema, Embodiment and the Senses.* Durham: Duke University Press, 2000.

May, William F. *The Physicians Covenant: Images of the Healer in Medical Ethics.* Louisville, KY: Westminster, 2000.

McColgan, Gillian and Irene Schofield. "The Importance of Companion Animal Relationships in the Lives of Older People." *Nursing Older People* 19.1 (2007): 21–23.

McKeon, Michael. *The Secret History of Domesticity: Public, Private, and the Division of Knowledge.* Baltimore: Johns Hopkins University Press, 2006.

McRuer, Robert. *Crip Theory: Cultural Signs of Queerness and Disability.* New York: New York University Press, 2006.

Melzack, Ronald. "Phantom Limbs, the Self and the Brain (The D.O. Hebb Memorial Lecture)." *Canadian Psychology* 30 (1989): 1–16.

Merleau-Ponty, Maurice. "Eye and Mind." Trans. Carleton Dallery. *The Primacy of Perception.* Ed. James M. Edie. Evanston: Northwestern University Press, 1964.

———. *Phenomenology of Perception.* Trans. Colin Smith. London: Routledge & Kegan Paul, 1962.

Merlhes, Victor. "Gauguin and the Inn of Marie Henry at Pouldu." *Gauguin's Nirvana: Painters at Le Pouldu 1889–1890.* Ed. Eric M. Zafran. New Haven: Yale University Press, 2001.

Michalko, Rod. *The Two-in-One: Walking with Smokie, Walking with Blindness.* Philadelphia: Temple University Press, 1999.

Miller, William Ian. *The Anatomy of Disgust.* Cambridge: Harvard University Press, 1997.

Mitchell, David T. and Sharon L Snyder. *Narrative Prosthesis: Disability and the Dependencies of Discourse.* Ann Arbor: University of Michigan Press, 2000.

Murray, Stuart. "Autism and the Contemporary Sentimental: Fiction and the Narrative Fascination of the Present." *Literature and Medicine* 25.1 (2006): 24–45.

"Novel Therapeutic Deep-Pressure Vest for Reducing Anxiety in Children." *Brown University Child & Adolescent Psychopharmacology Update* 10 (2008): 8.

Nussbaum, Martha C. *Hiding from Humanity: Disgust, Shame, and the Law.* New York: Princeton University Press, 2006.

———. *Upheavals of Thought: The Intelligence of the Emotions.* Cambridge: Cambridge University Press, 2001.

O'Farrell, Mary Ann. "Self-Consciousness and the Psoriatic Personality: Considering Updike and Potter." *Literature and Medicine* 20.2 (2001): 133–50.

Owen, David. *Around the House: Reflections on Life under a Roof.* New York: Villard, 1998.

Paillard, Jacques. "Body Schema and Body Image: A Double Dissociation in Deafferented Patients." *Motor Control: Today and Tomorrow.* Ed. G. N. Gantchev, S. Mori, and J. Massion. Bulgaria: Akademicno Izdatelstvo, 1999.

Pallasmaa, Juhani. *The Eyes of the Skin: Architecture and the Senses.* Chichester, England: John Wiley, 2005.

Parslow, Ruth A., Anthony F. Jorm, Helen Christensen, Bryan Rodgers, and Patricia Jacomb. "Pet Ownership and Health in Older Adults: Findings from a Survey of 2,551 Community-Based Australians Aged 60–64." *Gerontology* 51.1 (2005): 40–47.

Pastalan, Leon A. and Janice E. Barnes. "Personal Rituals: Identity, Attachment to Place, and Community Solidarity." *Aging, Autonomy, and Architecture: Advances in Assisted Living.* Ed. Benyamin Schwarz and Ruth Brent. Baltimore: Johns Hopkins University Press, 1999. 81–89.

Paterson, Mark. *The Senses of Touch: Haptics, Affects and Technologies.* Oxford, England: Berg, 2007.

Patronek, Gary J. "The Problem of Animal Hoarding." *Municipal Lawyer* (May/June 2001): 6–9, 19. The Hoarding of Animals Research Consortium. 2004. http://www.tufts.edu/vet/cfa/hoarding/pubs/municipalawyer.pdf.

Peel, Robin. *Writing Back: Sylvia Plath and Cold War Politics.* Madison, NJ: Farleigh Dickinson University Press, 2002.

Phelan, Peggy. *Mourning Sex: Performing Public Memories.* New York: Routledge, 1997.

Plath, Otto Emil. *Bumblebees and Their Ways.* New York: Macmillan, 1934.

Plath, Sylvia. *The Bell Jar.* New York: Knopf, 1998.

———. *The Collected Poems.* Ed. Ted Hughes. New York: Harper, 1981.

———. *Johnny Panic and the Bible of Dreams: Short Stories, Prose, and Diary Excerpts.* New York: Harper, 1979.

———. *Letters Home.* Ed. Aurelia Schober Plath. New York: Harper, 1975.

———. *The Unabridged Journals of Sylvia Plath 1950–1962.* Ed. Karen V. Kukil. New York: Random House, 2000.

Prather, Marla and Charles F. Stuckey, eds. *Gauguin: A Retrospective.* New York: Macmillan, 1987.

Prince-Hughes, Dawn. *Songs of the Gorilla Nation: My Journey through Autism.* New York: Harmony, 2004.

Prosser, Jay. "Skin Memories." *Thinking through the Skin.* Ed. Sara Ahmed and Jackie Stacey. New York: London, 2001. 52–68.

Pym, Barbara. *Quartet in Autumn.* London: Macmillan, 1977.

Quantrill, Malcolm. *Environmental Memory: Man and Architecture in the Landscape of Ideas.* New York: Schocken Books, 1987.

Quintilian. *Institutio Oratoria.* Trans. H. E. Butler. Vol. IV. 1922. Cambridge, MA: Harvard University Press, 1961.

Ramachandran, V. S. and Sandra Blakeslee. *Phantoms in the Brain.* New York: Quill, 1998.

Raymond, Jon. "Train Choir." *Livability.* New York: Bloomsbury, 2009.

Resnik, David B. *Dying Declarations: Notes from a Hospice Volunteer.* New York: Haworth, 2005.

Rew, Lynn. "Friends and Pets as Companions: Strategies for Coping with Loneliness among Homeless Youth." *Journal of Child & Adolescent Psychiatric Nursing*

13.3 (2000): 125–33.

Rickels, Laurence A. *Aberrations of Mourning: Writing on German Crypts.* Detroit: Wayne State University Press, 1998.

Robinson, Marilynne. *Housekeeping.* 1980. New York: Farrar, Strauss and Giroux, 1987.

Rosner, Victoria. *Modernism and the Architecture of Private Life.* New York: Columbia University Press, 2005.

Rovina, Nesta. *Tree Barking: A Memoir.* Berkeley: BayTree Books, 2008.

Rowles, Graham D. "Aging in Rural Environments." *Elderly People and the Environment.* Ed. I. Altman, M. P. Lawton, and J. F. Wohlwill. New York: Plenum, 1984. 129–57.

Rubinstein, Robert L. "Stories Told: In-Depth Interviewing and the Structure of Its Insights." *Qualitative Gerontology.* Ed. Shulamit Reinharz and Graham D. Rowles. New York: Springer, 1988. 128–46.

———, Janet C. Kilbride, and Sharon Nagy. *Elders Living Alone: Frailty and the Perception of Choice.* Hawthorne, NY: Aldine de Gruyter, 1992.

——— and Patricia Parmalee. "Attachment to Place and the Representation of the Life Course by the Elderly." *Place Attachment.* Ed. Irwin Altmanand and Setha M. Law. New York: Plenum, 1992. 134–63.

Sankar, Andrea. *Dying at Home: A Family Guide for Caregiving.* Baltimore: Johns Hopkins University Press, 1999.

Schilder, Paul. *Das Körperschema.* Berlin: Julius Springer, 1923.

Seamon, David. *A Geography of the Lifeworld: Movement, Rest, and Encounter.* New York: St. Martin's, 1979.

Shackleford, George T. M. "The Return to Paradise: Tahiti, 1895–1897." *Gauguin Tahiti.* Ed. George T. M. Shackleford and Clair Freches Thory. Boston: MFA Publications, 2004. 145–65.

———. "Splendor and Misery: Gauguin in the Marquesas Islands." *Gauguin Tahiti.* Ed. George T. M. Shackleford and Clair Freches Thory. Boston: MFA Publications, 2004. 243–259.

Shenk, Dena, Kazumi Kuwahara, and Diane Zablotsky. "Older Women's Attachments to Their Home and Possessions." *Journal of Aging Studies* 18 (2004): 157–69.

Shildrick, Margrit. *Embodying the Monster: Encounters with the Vulnerable Self.* London: Sage, 2002.

———. "'You Are There, like My Skin': Reconfiguring Relational Economies." *Thinking through the Skin.* Ed. Sara Ahmed and Jackie Stacey. New York: Routledge, 2001. 160–74.

Somers, Jane. *The Diary of a Good Neighbour.* New York: Knopf, 1983.

Sophocles. *The Women of Trachis.* Trans. Michael Jameson. *The Complete Greek Tragedies: Sophocles II.* Ed. David Grene and Richmond Lattimore. Chicago: University of Chicago Press, 1957.

———. *Philoctetes.* Trans. David Grene. *The Complete Greek Tragedies: Sophocles II.* Ed. David Grene and Richmond Lattimore. Chicago: University of Chicago

Press, 1957.

Spark, Muriel. *Memento Mori.* 1959. New York: Avon, 1990.

Steinbeck, John. *Travels with Charley: In Search of America.* New York: Viking, 1962.

Steketee, Gail, Randy O. Frost, and Hyo-Jin Kim. "Hoarding by Elderly People." *Health & Social Work* 26.3 (2001): 176–84.

Stewart, Susan. *On Longing.* Baltimore: Johns Hopkins University Press, 1984.

Stoddard, Alexandra. *The Decoration of Houses.* New York: William Morrow, 1997.

Tanner, Laura E. *Lost Bodies: Inhabiting the Borders of Life and Death.* Ithaca: Cornell University Press, 2006.

Taylor, Heidi, Pauline Williams, and David Gray. "Homelessness and Dog Ownership: An Investigation into Animal Empathy, Attachment, Crime, Drug Use, Health and Public Opinion." *Anthrozoos* 17.4 (2004): 353–68.

Tennyson, Alfred Lord. *Tennyson's Poetry.* Ed. Robert W. Hill, Jr. New York: W. W. Norton, 1971.

Thompson, Rosemarie Garland. *Extraordinary Bodies: Figuring Physical Disability in American Culture and Literature.* New York: Columbia University Press, 1997.

Thomson, Belinda, ed. *Gauguin by Himself.* Boston: Little, Brown and Co., 1993.

Titchkosky, Tanya. *Reading and Writing Disability Differently: The Textured Life of Embodiment.* Toronto: University of Toronto Press, 2007.

Turner, Joan G., Ann J. Clark, Dorothy K. Gauthier, and Monica Williams. "The Effect of Therapeutic Touch on Pain and Anxiety in Burn Patients." *Journal of Advanced Nursing* 28.1 (1998): 10–20.

Updike, John. *The Centaur.* New York: Ballantine, 1996.

———. "From the Journal of a Leper." *Problems and Other Stories.* New York: Knopf, 1979.

———. "Gesturing." *The Best American Short Stories of the Century.* Ed. John Updike and Katrina Kenison. Boston: Houghton Mifflin, 1999. 565–80.

———. *Rabbit Is Rich.* New York: Fawcett, 1982.

———. "At War with My Skin." *Self-Consciousness: Memoirs.* New York: Knopf, 1989.

Van Sant, Gus. "Kelly Reichardt." *The Bomb: A Quarterly Arts and Culture Magazine* (Fall 2008). 14 May 2009. http://www.bombsite.com/issues/105/articles/3182.

Verderame, Lorie. "I'll Never Forget . . . Dignity." *Journal of Hospice and Palliative Nursing* 7.4 (2005): 236–37.

Weil, Kari. "Killing Them Softly: Animal Death, Linguistic Disability, and the Struggle for Ethics." *Configurations* 14.1 (2006): 87–96.

Weinstein, Norman. "Artful Writing." *Chronicle of Higher Education* 54 (2008): B21.

Weiss, Gail. *Body Images: Embodiment as Intercorporeality.* New York: Routledge, 1999.

Welsh, Robert. "Gauguin and the Inn of Marie Henry at Pouldu." *Gauguin's Nirvana: Painters at Le Pouldu 1889–1890.* Ed. Eric M. Zafran. New Haven: Yale University Press, 2001. 61–71.

Wendy and Lucy. Dir. Kelly Reichardt. Oscilloscope, 2009.

Wettlaufer, Alexandra K. "She Is Me: Tristan, Gauguin and the Dialectics of Colonial Identity." *Romanic Review* 98 (2007): 23–50.

Wills, David. *Prosthesis.* Stanford University Press, 1995.

Wittman, Richard. "Architecture, Space, and Abstraction in the Eighteenth-Century French Public Sphere." *Representations* 102 (2008): 1–26.

Wolff, Geoffrey. "Suburban Suffering." Rev. *Cheever: A Life. The New York Times Book Review.* 15 Mar. 2009. 1.

Woodward, Kathleen. "Freud and Barthes: Theorizing Mourning, Sustaining Grief." *Discourse* 13 (1990–91): 93–110.

———. "Grief-Work in Contemporary American Cultural Criticism." *Discourse* 15 (1992–93): 94–112.

Woolf, Virginia. *To the Lighthouse.* New York: Harcourt, Brace, Jovanovich, 1989.

*I*ndex